INVESTIGATING ONLINE HERITAGE CRIME

Investigating Online Heritage Crime

New Directions, New Technologies, Emerging Markets

Edited by

Damien Huffer and Evie Handby

berghahn
NEW YORK • OXFORD
www.berghahnbooks.com

First published in 2026 by
Berghahn Books
www.berghahnbooks.com

Library of Congress Cataloging-in-Publication Data

A C.I.P. cataloging record is available from the Library of Congress
Library of Congress Cataloging in Publication Control Number: 2025038603

British Library Cataloguing in Publication Data

A catalogue record for this book is available from the British Library

EU GPSR Authorized Representative

LOGOS EUROPE, 9 rue Nicolas Poussin, 17000, LA ROCHELLE, France
Email: Contact@logoseurope.eu

ISBN 978-1-83695-305-0 hardback
ISBN 978-1-83695-306-7 epub
ISBN 978-1-83695-307-4 web pdf

https://doi.org/10.3167/9781836953050

Contents

Illustrations

Figures

Tables

Acknowledgments

Dr. Handby
I would like to thank my wonderful coeditor and friend Dr. Damien Huffer for his dedication to making this book a reality and for giving me the opportunity to be a part of it. It has been a pleasure to work with you.

Given that my chapter in this volume is based on my PhD research, I would also like to thank my former supervisors Professor Malcolm Choat and Dr. Chris Muller for their guidance. I am also grateful to Dr. Zac Roberts for his constant encouragement and support.

Dr. Huffer
I would like to thank my wonderful coeditor and friend Dr. Evie Handby for sticking by the project through thick and thin over its duration. Now we know just how much blood, sweat, and tears are involved in putting together an edited volume. Working with you has made it so much easier.

I would also like to thank my parents and family for their unflagging support in this new book endeavor and in all things, including inspiration for the cover art. I also thank Professor Shawn Graham for his initial suggestion that a volume around this topic is needed, and that we could do it. Last, but certainly not least, I am grateful for the unflinching support of my in-laws and Dr. Nathan Charlton; my second family.

Damien and Evie would both like to express our sincere thanks to Caryn Berg, Emma Wallace, and Amanda Horn for their invaluable assistance at the beginning and throughout this endeavor. We also express our sincere gratitude to all our chapter authors for sharing our vision and trusting us to bring your hard work to fruition. Fighting back against heritage crime is a huge task, so we are glad you're with us in the fight.

Introduction

Damien Huffer

The purpose of this volume is to bring together new research highlighting how the trafficking of cultural heritage and human ancestral remains operates on smaller or "lesser-known" English- and non-English-language social media and e-commerce platforms. It was born out of two main realizations. Firstly, heritage crime of all types remains relatively understudied and the fight against it under-resourced compared to other categories of illicit online trafficking, such as wildlife, drugs, and CSAM (Child Sexual Assault Material). Secondly, as academic research concerning heritage crime grows and frontline law enforcement agencies increase their understanding of the depth and breadth of cultural heritage trafficking in the digital age, it is becoming apparent that online trafficking (of all categories) occurs within an online "ecosystem" of interconnected platforms. Research and reporting repeatedly demonstrates that poor internal regulation and the "legal liability shield" against even criminal user content that the US Communications Decency Act § 230 provides to all US-headquartered platforms has allowed a wide variety of crime to flourish (e.g., Allison and Martin 2024; Carvalho et al. 2023; Elkhazeen et al. 2022; Harrington et al. 2023; Hodgson 2024).

Most media attention paid to online cultural heritage trafficking has focused on the proliferation of public and business pages and private or secret groups on Meta platforms, especially Facebook and Instagram (e.g., Pester 2022; Huffer and Graham 2023; Tahir and Tabhika 2024), even despite antiquities, historic artefacts, and human remains all being against platform terms of service (Arraf 2020). However, the role of e-commerce platforms, live auctions, brick-and-mortar stores' websites, etc., as places where heritage trafficking occurs has been known for at least two decades (Lidington 2002; Chappell and Huffer 2014). Researchers and law enforcement alike, while monitoring Meta platforms, are also noticing that cross-platform sales and advertising are becoming relatively commonplace in the trafficking of items and people alike (e.g., Nam et al. 2023; Sebagh 2021). This includes not only the same sales post showing up in multiple locations on Facebook and on the original poster's Instagram, eBay, or Etsy accounts, when they have them. Furthermore, dealers can use Facebook pages or groups, YouTube, TikTok, or similar short- and long-form video platforms merely to advertise their collection, linking to sales on other platforms or directing viewers to the websites of brick-and-mortar stores or live auctions.

As the social media and e-commerce landscape worldwide continues to face calls (or actual legislative pressure) to be externally regulated and held liable for criminal or harmful content, response has usually involved ignoring the problem, adding new features, promising changes to the algorithm, incorporating new initiatives to use AI to detect harmful content, or enabling the rise of off-shoot platforms such as Instagram's Threads. By these means, the interconnected "ecosystem" by which all black- and gray-market trafficking occurs becomes increasingly complex. At the current juncture, we know that the online movement of cultural property is much bigger than any one e-commerce platform and increasingly reliant on the unregulated spaces within social media. However, a comprehensive understanding of how trafficking networks form and disband, their offline geographic extent (i.e., which borders and jurisdictions must be crossed to get items purchased online from seller to buyer), and how high-profile dealers reach and influence new customers will be incomplete until sufficient attention is paid to a much wider range of online spaces.

Like, Subscribe, Bid, Retweet, and Upvote: Understanding the Entire "Ecosystem"

The interconnected "ecosystem" of platforms on which trafficking in cultural heritage occurs today includes eBay, Etsy, YouTube, TikTok, Snapchat, still active first-generation platforms such as Tumblr, a wide range of smaller or region/language-specific e-commerce platforms, online auction sites or aggregators such as Catawiki, Invaluable and Live Auctions, and, to a lesser extent, Twitter/X. On Meta platforms, prices for suspect or illicit goods are required or voluntarily provided within the text of sales posts, or written on the images themselves, negotiated in the comments, or indicated via number and object emojis. Final negotiations usually take place via direct messaging (now end-to-end encrypted). On most e-commerce platforms, however, the original asking price or ever-increasing bids are publicly visible on the listing itself, sometimes requiring one to create an account first. Expressions of interest or price enquiries within the comments sections on short- or long-form videos can also lead to final negotiations on social media platforms, WhatsApp or similar messaging apps, email, or offline.

Illicit trafficking research that focuses on specific platforms outside of Facebook and Instagram is expanding, but some topics and platforms have seen more attention than others, and most research continues to target English-language platforms. Twitter/X has seen some attention for the proliferation of drug or wildlife content, but very little concrete research into heritage crime (e.g., Dundler 2019; Clarke et al. 2019; Katsuki, Mackey, and Cuomo 2015; Xu et al. 2019). YouTube has received somewhat more attention for permitting and recommending questionable content that arguably encourages trafficking or cruel behavior (e.g., El Bizri et al. 2015; Harrington, Macdonald, and D'Cruze 2019; Jyoti 2024; Moloney et al. 2021; Gondhali et al. 2024), bolstered by a general user-led push toward professional content and the use of "response" videos to amplify or contradict the content of other creators (Kim 2012; Lewis, Marwick, Partin 2021).

The content on TikTok and Snapchat, being newer image and short-form video platforms, is also relatively uncharted territory where heritage is concerned, but Graham, Huffer and Simons (2022) examined aspects of the human remains trade vis-à-vis one specific dealer. Most trafficking-related research or investigative reporting to date has focused on drug or weapon content (Levine 2022; Love 2023; Walsh 2024; Whelan, Noller, and Ward 2023). Heritage crime on Reddit is also just beginning to be examined, but it is known anecdotally (Leeson 2024). Trafficking of any kind outside of the English-language internet, as well as country-specific e-commerce platforms and more secretive platforms such as VKontakt or Telegram, is also beginning to be investigated (Huffer et al. 2022; Xu et al. 2020; Toomes et al. 2023). Most multiplatform illicit trafficking research or investigative reporting has also not involved heritage crime (e.g., Hall, Koenraadt, and Antonopolous 2017; Haupt et al. 2024; Losey et al. 2022; Malik 2023; Pytka, Moore, Heenan 2023; Salter and Hanson 2021), but it does provide precedent for why no category of online crime can be fully understood through research on one or a very few platforms only.

The Online Antiquities Trade's Origins—What Led to Today's Situation?

To understand what makes today's online heritage crime (i.e., the global trade in antiquities, human remains, Indigenous material culture, historical artifacts, etc.) unique, and how and why it is now a multiplatform "ecosystem," it is important to look to the past. By "the past" we mean the mid-1990s, when today's e-commerce giants—eBay (as AuctionWeb) by Pierre Omidyar (Rothman 2015), and Amazon (as an online bookseller service called Cadabra) by Jeff Bezos (Hopkins, 2023)—were founded. Stepping even further back into the murky early internet days, it is arguable that e-commerce as a concept began in 1979, when Michael Aldrich demonstrated that televisions could be connected to nascent computers for commerce purposes (Aldrich 2011).

As e-commerce began in both theory and practice, the late 1990s and early 2000s saw the possibility for instantaneous online gratification and both B2C (business-to-consumer) and C2C (consumer-to-consumer) commerce expand, especially with the launch of services like PayPal in 1998. This was albeit not without (ongoing) controversy and initial conflict with preexisting services such as eBay (Jackson 2004). Various other related platforms serving English- and non-English-speaking markets, such as Alibaba, Etsy, Marktplaats.nl, Weibo, Taobao, and others, all launched before 2010.

Thus, licit and illicit e-commerce already had numerous platforms on which it could be conducted before social media or long- or short-form video platforms entered the picture. It was already becoming a global phenomenon before these other platforms not initially designed for e-commerce nevertheless became "weaponizable" by those who realized that algorithms were ideal for expanding one's customer base. One of the first articles to recognize in writing that the internet and e-commerce would open a vast new frontier in the antiquities trade was Lidington (2002). As readers of this volume will come to see in the forthcoming chapters, this prediction has proven correct. While eBay and other e-commerce platforms grew in market share and user base from the mid-1990s onward, and the categories of cultural heritage available increased immensely, illicit trade of certain categories of item were exposed and faced generally effective bans (Kim 2012; Vergano 2016). Halling and Seidemann (this volume) present a detailed analysis of what human remains trafficking on eBay looked like before the ban. However, the trade in many other categories of antiquities continued apace and continues to this day.

Social media's rise was becoming exponential by the mid-2000s, with platforms such as MySpace and Tumblr demonstrating that peer-to-peer networking was popular and that communities of practice could be formed around common interests or subcultures with less anonymity and more multimedia content than chat forums allowed (Robards 2012; Angwin 2009; Bronstein 2020). YouTube was launched in 2005 at the start of the "Web 2.0" era, and it quickly supplanted earlier video-sharing platforms (Novak 2020). It was these earliest forms of social media that first attracted public and law-enforcement attention to the reality that organized crime of various types had taken root there (e.g., Womer and Bunker 2011; Stedman 2007; Schulz 2016). As Hardy (this volume, but see also, e.g., Hardy 2020, 2021) has made clear in his ongoing research, online forums and chat rooms, arguably the earliest means to form social networks online, continue to play a role in global heritage trafficking today.

The chapters in this volume provide snapshot case studies of what the current landscape across several platforms and several topics looks like, each rooted in the recent historical context of their particular topic. The thread of new research embedded in its socio-temporal setting that we weave through this volume paves the way for Graham's conclusion, in which he discusses the possible future of online markets for heritage in the era of increased AI and neural network infiltration into our lives (and subsequent debate around its ethics and public responses to it).

Why Understanding Online Trafficking on "Lesser-Known" Platforms Matters

With the overview given above regarding what the online trafficking landscape currently looks like, its origins and development, and some similarities and differences between how specific categories of platform operate, this section further contextualizes the research presented in this volume by laying out our argument for why understanding these relatively understudied topics or locations of online heritage crime is so important. Especially at this juncture, when the global internet and the various uses of social media are more in flux and are being more actively critiqued than ever before.

Fundamentally, as other platforms continue to take market share from Meta (Kemp 2024) and Meta platforms and others face increased scrutiny, the question of whether other platforms will fill the void that buyers and sellers need to shape and maintain their online "personas" as trusted sellers or adherents to the ethical and cultural "norms" that guide specific trafficking communities (e.g., Dundler 2021, 2019; Kamleitner et al. 2019), remains poorly understood. It is a question that all concerned with counteracting cultural heritage (and all) online trafficking must begin to resolve now. Doing so will prove vital to policy and regulatory efforts against the "weaponization" of the internet overall, as well as provide data and information to the governing bodies of newer platforms (e.g., Bluesky, Mastodon) and payment apps that wish to actively prevent their platform or service from being exploitable for trafficking.

Understanding the interconnected online trafficking "ecosystem" on and beyond Meta platforms also matters because research is showing that, aside from the proliferation of CSAM, most categories of black- and gray-market commerce, including cultural heritage, do not need the dark web to change hands (e.g., Paul 2018; Stringham et al. 2023; Graham and Huffer 2023). There is also an open-ended question regarding how readily traffickers can "ad launder" money via posts or videos on numerous platforms to show off what they have or could provide if contacted obtaining ad revenue in the process (e.g., Papadogiannakis et al. 2024; Handby 2023). Research from marketing and e-commerce in general suggests that the number of positive online reviews given to sellers and the format of the reviews influences perceptions of trust and value that potential new customers have in sellers (e.g., Hamby, Daniloski, and Brinberg 2015).

The power of positive or negative reviews to affect both licit and illicit commerce is directly related to the proliferation of individual or organized "fake review" campaigns across the internet and various approaches taken to identify and counteract their proliferation (e.g., Sahut, Laroche, and Braune 2024; Shukla and Goh 2024). There is also the risk that content promoting pseudoarchaeology or "dark tourism," originally posted on YouTube, TikTok, or similar platforms, goes "viral" and inspires looting or vandalism (Basaraba 2024; Feagans 2019). Underpinning it all is the reality that, as collectors and dealers in cultural heritage continue to realize that Meta platforms are monitored by law enforcement and civilian researchers, other forums will be sought out as sellers consistently weigh risk vs. reward of using e-commerce or social media to conduct business.

Chapters in This Volume

This volume brings together both established experts and upcoming scholars to discuss, for the first time, research, and case studies of broad-spectrum heritage crime on several of the abovementioned "lesser-known" platforms. While certain chapters also focus on eBay or Meta platforms, the work within is unique and included due to either the category of heritage crime investigated or evidence for cross-platform sales demonstrative of the interconnectivity of the online cultural heritage trafficking "ecosystem."

Handby (chapter 1) explores how YouTube is used to buy and sell supposedly "ancient" manuscripts. The chapter takes a qualitative approach to examine how the manuscripts are advertised, the language used to describe them, the kinds of information their sellers reveal about themselves, and whether any patterns of interaction emerge in the comment sections of the videos that feature these so-called "ancient" manuscripts. The chapter, partially based on Handby's doctoral research, investigates the presence of a particular subsection of the black market in antiquities on YouTube, an American video-sharing platform with over 2.5 billion monthly active users. The market for authentic or forged antiquities sold or advertised via YouTube has not yet been the subject of investigation and, therefore, remains a potentially underestimated factor in the persistence of the online trade and transfer of illicit or gray-market historical artefacts and the potential for platforms to also be vectors of false advertising and fraud.

Farrar (chapter 2) presents some of the only research to date examining heritage crime on Reddit. Examining the content of posts and comment threads within subreddits focused on arrowheads, metal detecting, and other such antiquities-collecting interests, the author considers two issues. Firstly, who are the users engaging in these activities, what are their motivations, and how do they reflect on their ideological position within the American political landscape? Secondly, with Reddit being a global platform, though more so within the English-speaking world, how are American views on legality and ethics of cultural heritage collection exported through the promotion of these activities?

Halling and Seidemann (chapter 3) present a new analysis of the nature and demographic profile of human remains circulating on eBay over multiple years after the alleged 2016 ban, delving into questions of "who" the trafficked dead likely represent, bioanthropologically speaking. Hardy (chapter 4) presents new research on an "old-school," but still prolific, category of platform utilized by traffickers—

online forums. He takes research in a different direction by examining how looters, dealers, and collectors of antiquities exploit these specialist online forums, where interactions are organized around the subjects of discussion rather than the participants in the discussion. Hardy discusses the depth and breadth of these platforms as repositories of intelligence on aspects of trafficking networks not necessarily shared on more surface-web platforms. The content of these forum archival records is discussed within the context of the social and legal precarity that allows them to thrive.

Liu (chapter 5) examines the state of online cybercrime and heritage crime in China, both via state-owned social media such as Douyin and Weibo, as well as online auction houses—both poorly understood digital markets where heritage crime is concerned. Liu takes a "criminogenic thing" approach to an examination of the role of the objects or artworks themselves as facilitators of online crime. This analysis is contextualized through a reform-oriented analysis of the loopholes in current Chinese art market legislation, and how best Chinese civil society can respond. Finally, Rattenbury and Tynan (chapter 6) and Breda (chapter 7) together continue to expand global knowledge of today's online human remains trade, both via forums not previously explored or only seen anecdotally, such as UK auction houses and their legal and ethical context (chapter 6), or how platforms themselves (in this case Facebook) shape the networks of kinship, friendship, and trust that form between buyers and sellers to create a microcosm of "oddities culture" within the broader social media "ecosystem" (chapter 7). Collectively, these final chapters (along with chapter 3) push forward what researchers, law enforcement, descendant communities, and the public can understand about "who" is collected and why.

It is our intent that this volume will provide everyone with a vested interest in online heritage crime with a more detailed understanding of how antiquities and human remains trafficking works outside of (but often connected to) the most well-known platforms. Putting focus on other platforms still understudied as sites of cultural heritage trafficking also allows us to step back and query the legislative and regulatory failings that have allowed not just Meta but all platforms to operate as a figurative "Wild West." Indeed, tech companies' business decisions over the past decade have facilitated the creation of one of the world's largest digital black markets for trafficked artifacts.

Civilian researchers, NGOs, activists, law enforcement agencies, policy experts, and sometimes platform representatives themselves have a continuing need to appreciate the full extent of online heritage crime across the e-commerce and social media "ecosystem," and the overarching policy and regulatory landscape most platforms operate within. Increased knowledge of the interconnectivity of platforms is especially important in cases where a platform (such as eBay or Etsy) has attempted to algorithmically ban certain items, and enforce these bans, only to find that buyers and sellers are finding ways to circumvent them using linked sales on other platforms. As platforms continue to rise and fall in popularity, legislative scrutiny slowly advances in many jurisdictions, and new platform "species" are introduced to the "ecosystem," this volume is a valuable snapshot of where things stand now.

Dr. Damien Huffer is a research fellow with the Wildlife Crime Research Hub, School of Biological Sciences, University of Adelaide, as well as an honorary research associate with the School of Social Science, University of Queensland, and the Department of History, Carleton University. He is a cofounder of the Alliance to Counter Crime Online (https://www.counteringcrime.org; @CounteringCrime on Bluesky), as well as the Museum of Looted Antiquities project (https://mola.omeka.net/; @museumofloot). His research interests include heritage crime, the illicit wildlife trade, forensic anthropology, cybercriminology, digital humanities method and ethics, the online human remains trade, and "Big Tech" regulation and policy.

REFERENCES

Allison, Charmayne, and Xavier Martin. 2024. "Police Concerned about Rise in Tiktok 'Crimfluencers' in Alice Springs and Youth Crime Curfew Continues." ABC. Retrieved May 2024 from https://www.abc.net.au/ news/2024-04-03/alice-springs-nt-youth-curfew-social-media-impact-tiktok/103657084.

Aldrich, Michael. 2011. "Online Shopping in the 1980s." *Annals of the History of Computing* 33(4): 57–61.

Angwin, Julia. 2009. *Stealing MySpace. The Battle to Control the Most Popular Website in America.* New York: Random House.

Arraf, Jane. 2020. "Facebook Has Moved to Ban Sales of Looted Antiquities. Will It Make a Difference?" NPR. Retrieved May 2024 from https://www.npr.org/2020/07/31/896180883/facebook-has-moved-to-ban-sales-of-looted-antiquities-will-it-make-a-difference.

Basaraba, Nicola. 2024. "The Rise of Paranormal Investigations as Virtual Dark Tourism on YouTube." *Journal of Heritage Tourism* 19(2): 287–309. https://doi.org/10.1080/1743873X.2023.2268746.

Bronstein, Carolyn. 2020. "Pornography, Trans Visibility, and the Demise of Tumblr." *Transgender Studies Quarterly* 7(2): 240–54.

Carvalho, Antônio F., Igor Oliveira B. de Morais, and Thamyrys B. Souza. 2023. "Profiting from Cruelty: Digital Content Creators Abuse Animals Worldwide to Incur Profit." *Biological Conservation* 287: 110321. https://doi.org/10.1016/j.biocon.2023.110321.

Clarke, Tara A., Kim E. Reuter, Marni LaFleur, and Melissa S. Schaefer. 2019. "A Viral Video and Pet Lemurs on Twitter." *PLOS One* 14(1): e0208577. https://doi.org/10.1371/journal.pone.0208577.

Dundler, Lauren. 2021. "#Antiquitiesdealers; The Construction and Use of 'Dealer Persona' in the Internet Market for Antiquities." In *Crime and Art: Sociological and Criminological Perspectives of Crimes in the Art World*, ed. Naomi Oosterman and Donna Yates, 45–61. New York: Springer.

Dundler, Lauren. 2019. "'Still Covered in Sand. Looked Very Old'—Legal Obligations in the Internet Market for Antiquities." *Heritage* 2(3): 2311–26. https://doi.org/10.3390/heritage2030142.

El Bizri, Hani R., Thaís Q. Morcatty, Jéssica J. S. Lima, and João Valsecchi. 2015. "The Thrill of the Chase: Uncovering Illegal Sport Hunting in Brazil through YouTube™ Posts." *Ecology and Society* 20(3): 30. http://dx.doi.org/10.5751/ES-07882-200330.

Elkhazeen, Abu, Chris Poulos, Xin Zhang, John Cavanaugh, and Matthew Cain. 2022. "A TikTok™ 'Benadryl Challenge' Death—A Case Report and Review of the Literature." *Journal of Forensic Science* 68(1): 339–342. https://doi.org/10.1111/1556-4029.15149.

Feagans, Carl. 2019. "When Pseudoarchaeology Causes Harm." Retrieved May 2024 from https://ahotcupofjoe.net/2019/01/when-pseudoarchaeology-causes-harm/.

Gondhali, Ulhas, Antonia Merzon, Thanaphon Nunphong, Tzu-Ying Lo, Yu-Hsuan Liu, and Gohar A. Petrossian. 2024. "Crime Script Analysis of the Illegal Sales of Spiny-Tailed Lizards on YouTube." *Crime Science* 13(8). https://doi.org/10.1186/s40163-024-00206-w.

Graham, Shawn, and Damien Huffer. 2023. "The Antiquities Trade and Digital Networks: Or, the Supercharging Effect of Social Media on the Rise of the Amateur Antiquities Trader." In *The Oxford Handbook of Archaeological Network Research*, edited by Tom Brughmans, Barbara J. Mills, Jessica Munson, and Matthew A. Peeples, 528–42. Oxford: Oxford University Press.

Graham, Shawn, Damien Huffer, and Jaime Simons. 2022. "When TikTok Discovered the Human Remains Trade: A Case Study." *Open Archaeology* 8(1): 196–219. https://doi.org/10.1515/opar-2022-0235.

Hall, Alexandra, Rosa Koenraadt, and Georgios A. Antonopoulos. 2017. "Illicit Pharmaceutical Networks in Europe: Organising the Illicit Medicine Market in the United Kingdom and the Netherlands." *Trends in Organized Crime* 20: 296–315.

Hamby, Anne, Kim Daniloski, and David Brinberg. 2015. "How Consumer Reviews Persuade through Narratives." *Journal of Business Research* 68(6): 1242–50.

Handby, Eveline. 2023. "Trafficking Fake 'Ancient' Torahs in Turkey: A Media Analysis." *Public Archaeology* 2023(1): 1–20. https://doi.org/10.1080/14655187.2023.2218729.

Hardy, Samuel Andrew. 2020. "'You Just Have to Wear It': Trafficking of Metal-Detected Antiquities from South-East Asia." In *Policing Transnational Crime: Law Enforcement of Criminal Flows*, edited by Saskia Hufnagel and Anton Moiseienko, 63–95. New York: Routledge.

Hardy, Samuel Andrew. 2021. "It is Not Against the Law, If No-One Can See You: Online Social Organisation of Artefact-Hunting in Former Yugoslavia." *Journal of Computer Applications in Archaeology* 4(1): 169–87.

Harrington, Lauren, David Macdonald, and Neil D'Cruze. 2019. "Popularity of Pet Otters on YouTube: Evidence of an Emerging Trade Threat." *Nature Conservation* 36: 17–45. https://doi.org/10.3897/ natureconservation.36.33842.

Harrington, Lauren A., Angie Elwin, Suzi Paterson, and Neil D'Cruze. 2023. "The Viewer Doesn't Always Seem to Care—Response to Fake Animal Rescues on YouTube and Implications for Social Media Self-Policing Policies." *People and Nature* 5(1): 103–18. https://doi.org/10.1002/pan3.10416.

Haupt, Michael Robert, Raphael Cuomo, Manying Cui, and Tim K. Mackey. 2024. "Is This Safe?: Examining Safety Assessments of Illicit Drug Purchasing on Social Media Using Conjoint Analysis." *Substance Use & Misuse* (2024): 1–13. https://doi.org/10.1080/10826084.2024.2310507.

Hodgson, Elli. 2024. "Exposed: The Sick World of TikTok Animal Abusers Using Catapults to Kill Wildlife in Kent." Retrieved May 2024 from https://www.kentonline.co.uk/kent/news/exposed-the-sick-world-of-tiktok-animal-abusers-306137/.

Hopkins, Colby. 2023. "The History of Amazon and Its Rise to Success." Retrieved March 2025 from https://sites.lsa.umich.edu/mje/2023/05/01/the-history-of-amazon-and-its-rise-to-success/.

Huffer, Damien, and Duncan Chappell. 2014. "The Mainly Nameless and Faceless Dead: An Exploratory Study of the Illicit Traffic in Archaeological and Ethnographic Human Remains." *Crime, Law & Social Change* 62: 1311–153. https://doi.org/10.1007/s10611-014-9528-4.

Huffer, Damien, and Shawn Graham. 2023. *These Were People Once: The Online Trade in Human Remains and Why It Matters*. New York: Berghahn Books.

Huffer, Damien, Jamie Simons, Tom Brughmans, and Shawn Graham. 2022. "'Alleen voor studiedoeleinden' (For Study Purposes Only): The Human Remains Trade on Marktplaats.nl." *Anthropologica et Praehistorica* 131.2020 (2022): 177–93.

Jackson, Eric M. 2004. *The PayPal Wars: Battles with eBay, the Media, the Mafia, and the Rest of Planet Earth*. Los Angeles: World Ahead Press.

Jyoti, Archana. 2024. "YouTube Happy Hunting Ground for Wildlife Traffickers." Retrieved May 2024 from https://www.dailypioneer.com/2024/pioneer-exclusive/youtube-happy-hunting-ground-for-wildlife-traffickers.html.

Kamleitner, Bernadette, Carina Thürridl, and Brett A. S. Martin. 2019. "A Cinderella Story: How Past Identity Salience Boosts Demand for Repurposed Products." *Journal of Marketing* 83(6): 76–92. https://doi.org/10.1177/0022242919872156.

Katsuki, Takeo, Tim K. Mackey, and Raphael Cuomo. 2015. "Establishing a Link between Prescription Drug Abuse and Illicit Online Pharmacies: Analysis of Twitter Data." *Journal of Medical Internet Research* 17(12): e280. https://doi.org/10.2196/jmir.5144.

Kemp, Simon. 2024. "Digital 2024: Global Overview Report." Retrieved May 2024 from https://datareportal.com/reports/digital-2024-global-overview-report#:~:text=5 percent 20billion percent20social percent20media percent20user,at percent20the percent20start percent20of percent202024.

Kim, Erin. 2012. "Etsy Blocks Sales of Drugs and Human Remains." Retrieved March 2025 from https://money.cnn.com/2012/08/10/technology/etsy-bans-drugs/index.html.

Kim, Jin. 2012. "The Institutionalization of YouTube: From User-Generated Content to Professionally Generated Content." *Media, Culture & Society* 34(1): 53–67. https://doi.org/10.1177/01634437114 27199.

Leeson, Madison. 2024. "Reddit and the Illicit Antiquities Trade; Trends in the Online Trafficking and Authentication of Cultural Heritage." Retrieved May 2024 from https://www.meer.com/en/79881-reddit-and-the-illicit-antiquities-trade.

Lewis, Rebecca, Alice E. Marwick, William Clyde Partin. 2021. "'We Dissect Stupidity and Respond to It': Response Videos and Networked Harassment on YouTube." *American Behavioral Scientist* 65(5): 735–56. https://doi.org/10.1177/0002764221989781.

Levine, Alexandra S. 2022. "These TikTok Accounts Are Hiding Child Sexual Abuse Material in Plain Sight." Retrieved May 2024 from https://www.forbes.com/sites/alexandralevine/2022/11/11/tiktok-private-csam-child-sexual-abuse-material/?sh=2e2386a63ad9.

Lidington, Helen. 2002. "The Role of the Internet in Removing the 'Shackles of the Saleroom': Anytime, Anyplace, Anything, Anywhere." *Public Archaeology* 2(2): 67–84. https://doi.org/10.1179/pua.2002.2.2 .67.

Losey, John E., C. Chen, A. E. Davis, J. F. Deitsch, J. G. Gertin, J. A. Gorneau, E. M. Hallock, J. P. Jordán, Z. J. Kim, E. G. Kubinski, N. R. Laurenz, S. B. Li, E. K. Mullen, A. O'Brien, L. I. Richardson, S. Vincent, S. Y. Wang, E. L. Yarhouse, A. Scgydlowsky, and P. D. Curtis. 2022. "Insects and Spiders on the Web: Monitoring and Mitigating Online Exploitation of Species and Services." *Global Ecology and Conservation* 36: e02098. https://doi.org/10.1016/j.gecco. 2022.e02098.

Love, Julia. 2023. "How SnapChat and TikTok Became Recruiting Tools for Cartel-Backed Smugglers." Retrieved May 2024 from https://www.bloomberg.com/news/features/2023-11-15/mexican-cartels-exploit-snapchat-whatsapp-for-human-smuggling.

Malik, Abdul Moiz. 2023. "The 'Game' of Human Trafficking on Social Networks." Retrieved May 2024 from https://www.dawn.com/news/1763746.

Moloney, Georgia K., Jonathan Tuke, Eleonora Dal Grande, Torben Nielsen, and Anne-Lise Chaber. 2021. "Is YouTube Promoting the Exotic Pet Trade? Analysis of the Global Public Perception of Popular YouTube Videos Featuring Threatened Exotic Animals." *PLOS One* 16(4): e0235451. https://doi.org/ 10.1371/journal.pone.0235451.

Nam, Kyungae, Shin, Bae Hochul, Kim Byunghyun, and Eun Young. 2023. "Survival of Illegal Fentanyl Sales in the Twittersphere and Tumblr Sphere: A Cross-Sectional Forensics Approach." *Drug Targets and Therapeutics* 2(1): 62–69. https://doi.org/10.58502/DTT.23.0006.

Novak, Matt. 2020. "Here's What People Thought of YouTube When It First Launched in the Mid-2000s." Retrieved March 2025 from https://paleofuture.com/blog/2020/2/14/heres-what-people-thought-of-youtube-when-it-first-launched-in-the-mid-2000s#:~:text=There percent20were percent20actually percent20a percent20 number,the percent20scene percent20when percent20YouTube percent20arrived.

Papadogiannakis, Emmanouil, Panagiotis Papadopoulos, Evangelos P. Markatos, and Nicolas Kourtellis. 2024. "Ad Laundering: How Websites Deceive Advertisers into Rendering Ads Next to Illicit Content." *Companion Proceedings of the ACM on Web Conference 2024*, 782–85.

Paul, Katie A. 2018. "Ancient Artifacts vs. Digital Artifacts: New Tools for Unmasking the Sale of Illicit Antiquities on the Dark Web." *Arts* 7(2): 12. https://doi.org/10.3390/arts7020012.

Pester, Patrick. 2022. "Desecrated Human Skulls Are Being Sold on Social Media in UK's Unregulated Bone Trade." Retrieved May 2024 from https://www.livescience.com/human-skulls-desecrated-uk-human-remains-trade.

Pytka, Jennifer M., Alec B. M. Moore, and Adel Heenan. 2023. "Internet Trade of a Previously Unknown Wildlife Product from a Critically Endangered Marine Fish." *Conservation Science and Practice* 5(3): e12896.

Robards, Brady. 2012. "Leaving MySpace, Joining Facebook: 'Growing Up' on Social Network Sites." *Journal of Media & Cultural Studies* 26(3): 385–98. https://doi.org/10.1080/10304312.2012.665836.

Rothman, Lily. 2025. "The Small-Scale Story behind eBay's Big Bucks." Retrieved March 2025 from https://time.com/4013672/ebay-founded-story/.

Sahut, Jean Michael, Michel Laroche, Eric Braune. 2024. "Antecedents and Consequences of Fake Reviews in a Marketing Approach: An Overview and Synthesis." *Journal of Business Research* 174: 114572. https://doi.org/10.1016/j.jbusres.2024.114572.

Salter, Michael, and Elly Hanson. 2021. "'I Need You All to Understand How Pervasive This Issue Is': User Efforts to Regulate Child Sexual Offending on Social Media." In *The Emerald*

International Handbook of Technology-Facilitated Violence and Abuse, edited by Jane Bailey, Asher Flynn, and Nicola Henry, 729–48. Bingley, UK: Emerald Publishing Limited.

Schulz, Cara. 2016. "New Orleans Witch Faces Charges for Stealing Human Bones." Retrieved March 2025 from https://wildhunt.org/2016/09/new-orleans-witch-faces-charges-for-stealing-human-bones.html.

Sebagh, Lonie. 2021. "Policing Illegal Drug and Wildlife Trades—The Role of the Police, Legal Online Platforms, Private Organisations and Individuals, and Cybercriminal Traders." PhD thesis, University of Oxford.

Shukla, Aishwarya Deep, and Jie Mien Goh. 2024. "Fighting Fake Reviews: Authenticated Anonymous Reviews Using Identity Verification." *Business Horizons* 67(1): 71–81.

Stedman, Elizabeth P. 2007. "Myspace, but Whose Responsibility? Liability of Social-Networking Websites When Offline Sexual Assault of Minors Follows Online Interaction." *Villanova Sports & Entertainment Law Journal* 14(2007): 363.

Stringham, Oliver C., Jacob Maher, Charlotte R. Lassaline, Lisa Wood, Stephanie Moncayo, Adam Toomes, Sarah Heinrich, Freyja Watters, Charlotte Drake, Sebastian Chekunov, Katherine G. W. Hill, David Decary-Hetu, Lewis Mitchell, Joshua V. Ross, and Phillip Cassey. 2023. "The Dark Web Trades Wildlife, but Mostly for Use as Drugs." *People and Nature* 5(3): 999–1009. https://doi.org/10.1002/pan3.10469.

Tahir, Tariq, and Kamal Tabikha. 2024. "Facebook Trade in Fake Relics Fuels Middle East Looting." Retrieved May 2024 from https://www.thenationalnews.com/news/mena/2024/04/26/facebook-trade-in-fake-relics-fuels-middle-east-looting/.

Toomes, Adam, Stephanie Moncayo, Oliver C. Stringham, Charlotte Lassaline, Lisa Wood, Mariah Millington, Charlotte Drake, Charlotte Jense, Ashley Allen, Katherine G. W. Hill, Pablo García-Díaz, Lewis Mitchell, and Phillip Cassey. 2023. "A Snapshot of Online Wildlife Trade: Australian E-Commerce Trade of Native and Non-native Pets." *Biological Conservation* 282: 110040. https://doi.org/ 10.1016/ j.biocon.2023.110040.

Vergano, Dan. 2016. "eBay Just Nixxed Its Human Skull Market." Retrieved March 2025 from https://www.buzzfeednews.com/article/danvergano/skull-sales.

Walsh, Paul. 2024. "Man Whose Snapchat Group Sold Illegal 'Switches' and Ghost Guns in Minnesota Gets Two Years." Retrieved May 2024 from https://www.startribune.com/man-whose-snapchat-group-sold-illegal-switches-and-ghost-guns-in-minnesota-gets-two-years/600361084/.

Whelan, Jai, Geoffrey E. Noller, and Ryan D. Ward. 2023. "Rolling through Tiktok: An Analysis of 3,4-Methylenedioxymethamphetamine-Related Content." *Drug and Alcohol Review* 43(1): 36–44. https://doi.org/10.1111/dar.13640.

Womer, Sarah and Bunker, Robert J. 2011. "Sureños Gangs and Mexican Cartel Use of Social Networking Sites." In *Narcos over the Border. Gangs, Cartels and Mercenaries*, edited by Robert J. Bunker, 81–94. New York: Routledge.

'Xu, Qing, Jiawei Li, Mingxiang Cai, and Tim K. Mackey. 2019. "Use of Machine Learning to Detect Wildlife Product Promotion and Sales on Twitter." *Frontiers in Big Data* (2019): 28. https://doi.org/10.3389/fdata.2019.00028.

Xu, Qing, Mingxiang Cai, and Tim K. Mackey. 2020. "The Illegal Wildlife Digital Market: An Analysis of Chinese Wildlife Marketing and Sale on Facebook." *Environmental Conservation* 47(3): 206–12. https://doi.org/10.1017/S0376892920000235.

CHAPTER 1

How to Sell an Ancient Manuscript on YouTube
Investigating a Hidden Corner of the Internet Market in Antiquities

Evie Handby

Introduction

Researchers have been increasingly interested in understanding how social media is used to facilitate the exchange, sale, and purchase of likely stolen or illegally excavated antiquities across the Middle East and North Africa (Al-Azm and Paul 2018, 2019; Votey 2021; Hashemi and Waddell 2022; Tahir and Tabikha 2024; see also Huffer and Chappell 2014; Huffer et al. 2019; Huffer and Graham 2017, 2023). Whereas recent research and investigative efforts into the presence of black markets in antiquities on social media have largely focused on Meta-owned Facebook and Instagram, which have remained two of the world's most popular social networking services for over a decade, published evidence of similar activity on other, non-Meta social media platforms is scarce. This chapter, which is partially based on the findings of my doctoral project, investigates the presence of a particular subsection of the black market in antiquities on YouTube, an American video-sharing platform with over 2.5 billion monthly active users (Statista 2024). Although the Google-owned platform was previously recognized in 2017 as an emerging venue for the trade in illicit antiquities (Brodie 2017: 5–6), it has not yet become the subject of any investigation, and for that reason, it remains a potentially underestimated contributor to the persistence of the online trade and transfer of historical artifacts of questionable origin and/or authenticity.

This chapter takes as its case study a largely unexplored corner of the social media market in illicit antiquities: the buying and selling of fakes. It focuses on the trade in supposedly ancient Jewish books and examines how constructions of value, authenticity, and expertise are shaped in and through buyer/seller interactions in the comment sections of YouTube videos featuring these fakes and through the content and metadata of the videos themselves. In doing so, this chapter reveals the various ways these ancient books, which are portrayed and widely perceived as genuine on the platform, are marketed and sold on YouTube and how the company itself facilitates the formation of dealer communities that congregate around these objects.

Though the harms of fake antiquities flooding the online market are becoming increasingly recognized (most recently Tahir and Tabikha 2024), there is still a tendency among researchers to view forgeries as warranting less immediate urgency or concern than (authentic) stolen or likely looted artifacts. To the susceptible or uninformed consumer, however, the boundaries between real and fake are blurred in most online contexts. By prioritizing a largely unexplored corner of the trade in illicit antiquities on social media, this chapter contributes to a growing body of research into black markets in antiquities on non-Meta platforms and opens up new possibilities for future cross-platform comparative research into the existence and impact of fake antiquities in other social media markets.

(Fake) Ancient Jewish Books

Though marketed as "very old" (قديم جدا) or "ancient" by sellers on YouTube, the objects that form the focus of this chapter have been variously described by experts and online commentators as childish and obviously modern fakes destined for the tourist market. They are routinely ridiculed and dismissed as crude fakes that resemble something a student would do for a class assignment, "unlikely to fool anyone with knowledge of Hebrew or Jewish history" (Schiffman and Magness quoted in Lever 2023). These supposedly ancient books, which have surfaced predominately in Turkey over the last decade (see Handby 2023), are typically made of a dark brown or beige leather and embellished with an assortment of popular yet highly anachronistic Jewish, Christian, and sometimes even satanic or Illuminati-related symbols. The supposedly ancient Jewish books in particular are filled with sections of handwritten Hebrew text in metallic gold ink; however, the text is almost always complete gibberish. For further reference, images of the books, which are regularly seized from smugglers by Turkish law enforcement and exhibited in the country's press as historical artifacts, can easily be found by Google Image searching *tarihi eser kitap ele geçirildi!* (historical book seized).

Data and Method

This chapter forms part of my doctoral research on the modern production and trade of fake antiquities in parts of the Middle East and North Africa. As part of this broader project, I investigated how a particular group of fakes—ancient Jewish books—were advertised and sold on YouTube and how constructions of value, authenticity, and expertise were shaped in and through interactions between buyers and sellers in the comment sections of videos featuring the fakes and through the content and metadata of the videos themselves. In my doctoral research on YouTube, I was as equally concerned with how buyers and sellers were using the platform to conduct business and how the platform itself facilitates and indirectly promotes dealer activity through monetization and policy gaps. It is these concerns about how buyers and sellers of the supposedly ancient books use YouTube to conduct business and the false constructions of value and authenticity they uphold and promote that form the focus of this chapter.

Preliminary observations of the YouTube market revealed that pocket communities of ancient Jewish book dealers typically gather in the comments sections of *other* videos featuring ancient (typically Jewish) books. To locate further videos and the communities they harbor, then, I conducted a series of manual searches on YouTube using a selection of relevant Arabic words and phrases. Manual searches produced approximately ninety-five videos of the ancient books, of which 78 percent had received comments. The remaining 22 percent of videos had either received no comments at the time of data collection or the comments section had been disabled by the video's uploader—these videos were included in my doctoral research but did not form the focus of the analysis. All three videos were uploaded to YouTube in 2018.

This chapter draws from qualitative methods to examine the contents and comments sections of the three most commented-on videos (hereafter Videos 1, 2 and 3) included in the dataset, which together have accumulated approximately seventeen hundred comments since being uploaded (by separate users) throughout 2018. All three videos feature one or more supposedly ancient or old book described by their respective uploaders in Arabic as a "very old antique Jewish book" or an "ancient Jewish book." Though none were explicitly listed as for sale, two of the three uploaders included their contact number in the video's description box (inviting viewers to communicate), and the other included a link to their personal Facebook page—all of which are enough to suggest that the books featured in the videos were probably for sale at one point in time.

While this chapter examines a relatively large sample of comments across three YouTube videos, it should be said that the average ancient book video typically receives less than fifty comments. Videos with more than one hundred comments are uncommon. It is difficult to ascertain why some videos generate more user traffic (likes, views, or comments) than others, especially given the popular public uncertainty about how the YouTube algorithm actually works (MacDonald 2023). In the case of Videos 1, 2 and 3, it is likely that their relative popularity is a direct result of cross-posting. In other words, the videos' uploaders or viewers shared the video to more than one online location or platform, thereby generating more traffic than usual.

Ethical Consideration

YouTube presents unique ethical challenges for the dissemination of data, especially where illicit activity is concerned. Despite the open accessibility of the platform, working with such publicly available information for research purposes is complicated. In 2005, the year YouTube was founded, Jan Colvin and Jane Lanigan argued that it was necessary to remove "any references to the identity of [an] individual, Web site, or group; location, and time of post" to minimize a potential loss of confidentiality (2005: 36). It goes without saying, however, that the digital landscape has evolved considerably over the last two decades and, as a result, internet and social media research practices have evolved along with it (Markham and Buchanan 2015: 606, 610). Navigating the ethical questions and concerns surrounding the collection, use, and dissemination of publicly available information for research purposes has become increasingly complicated, and the task of protecting individual user privacy continues to grow more complex. On YouTube, for example, including the title of a video in the published research would likely be enough to trace it back to its source. Here, removing any references to the identity of its uploader is not enough to protect a potential loss of confidentiality, especially if the user is unaware that any data associated with them is being used for research purposes (which they may not have otherwise consented to). In some cases, for example, researchers of drug markets on Facebook and Instagram have avoided publishing screenshots altogether, instead creating lookalike copies of the actual dealer profiles they encountered (Demant et al. 2019: 54).

This chapter does not feature any screenshots, video titles, or references to the identities of the YouTube users discussed below. While every effort has been made to avoid any potential loss of confidentiality in this article, I acknowledge, however, that the risk of identification can never fully be nullified. As Harry Evans, Steve Ginnis, and Jamie Bartlett put it, "There can be no guarantee of full anonymity within social media research" (2015: 4). Even if the author field or username is removed, it would still be possible to search for the content online; moreover, "it is unlikely that 'masking' content can fully guarantee that the author cannot be identified" (2015: 4).

Policy Problems: Banning Historical Artifact Sales on Social Media

Several years ago, Facebook (now Meta) introduced a new policy to its Community Standards that prohibited "the exchange, sale or purchase of all historical artifacts on Facebook or Instagram" (Swann 2020). According to the platform's existing Coordinating Harm and Promoting Crime policy, content promoting the sale of historical artifacts was only removed "when it is clear that such items have been looted." In the June update, however, the definition of a historical artifact was expanded to include "rare items of significant historical, cultural, or scientific value," meaning that "selling products of archaeological discoveries, human remains and mummified body parts, ancient scrolls and manuscripts" was now prohibited.

Although the news of the June 2020 update was generally well received, the effectiveness of the policy and Facebook's commitment to enforcing it were called into question. Amr al-Azm, cofounder of the ATHAR Project, remarked that Facebook's reliance on user reports and automated systems to identify content that violates the new standard was "simply not enough" and that the company should instead "invest in teams of experts to identify and remove networks rather than playing whack-a-mole with individual posts" (Swann 2020). It was elsewhere pointed out that Facebook already had a policy banning the sale of human remains on the platform and that the inclusion of human remains and mummified body parts in the new policy made it clear that the preexisting policy was insufficiently, if at all, enforced. Despite some initial success, the long-term effectiveness of the policy in combating the trafficking of historical artifacts on the platform still remains to be seen. Today, the policy (summarized as prohibiting "content that attempts to buy, sell, trade, donate or gift, or asks for, historical artefacts") is tucked away in a corner of Facebook's Transparency Center among other Restricted Goods and Services (Meta 2024).

Unlike Facebook and Instagram, where users are required to log in to an existing account to access the platforms' content or create a new one entirely, content uploaded to YouTube is accessible to its visitors regardless of whether they have an account or not (with the exception of age-restricted content). In fact, one of the main reasons why YouTube has managed to maintain its dominant position in the industry is precisely because of how accessible it is (Mohsin 2023). Unlike Facebook and Instagram, content that attempts to buy, sell, trade, donate, or gift, historical artifacts, or asks for such artifacts, is not prohibited on YouTube. In its policies regarding Illegal or Regulated Goods or Services, users are told that facilitating the sale of illegal or regulated goods by posting links, email addresses, phone numbers, or other means of contacting a seller directly is not allowed (Google 2024a). According to the current policy, this applies to "videos, video descriptions, comments, live streams, and any other YouTube product or feature" and includes content that aims to directly sell, link to, or facilitate access to "alcohol, bank account passwords, stolen credit cards, or other financial information, counterfeit documents or currency, controlled narcotics and other drugs, explosives, organs, endangered species or parts of endangered species, firearms and certain firearms explosives, nicotine products, online gambling casinos, pharmaceuticals without a prescription, sex or escort services, unlicensed medical services, and human smuggling" (Google 2024a). Although users are reminded that this is not an exhaustive list, nowhere on YouTube is it explicitly stated that the buying, selling, or trading historical artifacts is in violation of the platform's Community Guidelines or policies.

Given that YouTube's reporting tool directly reflects its existing policies and Guidelines, viewers would struggle to report content that attempts to buy, sell, or trade historical artifacts of questionable origin and/or authenticity even if they wanted to. Violative comments, on the other hand, must be flagged in a separate reporting tool and can only be reported as "unwanted commercial content, pornography or sexually explicit material, child abuse, hate speech or graphic violence, and harassment and bullying" (Google 2024b). It might be possible to report comments left by users attempting to buy, sell, or trade historical artifacts by selecting "unwanted commercial content," but even then, YouTube warns its users that the tool is to be used with extreme caution. If misused, a user may be banned from the platform altogether.

The introduction of a policy that prohibits the exchange, sale, or purchase of historical artifacts on Facebook in June 2020 came as a response to the widely publicized findings of the ATHAR Project's report on black markets in antiquities preceded by years of public activism. Like Facebook, YouTube has a long and problematic history of cracking down on questionable, illicit, or downright illegal content only in response to adverse press coverage, public outcry, threats of legislation, or advertiser backlash. In the absence of public awareness and platform oversight, then, it is within this context that dealer communities have formed and flourished on YouTube over the last half decade.

How to Sell an Ancient Manuscript on YouTube

Supposedly ancient books are sold on YouTube in one of two ways. First, a user will upload a video featuring one or more ancient books and indicate explicitly or implicitly its availability in the video's title or description (usually using the words *for sale* or by inviting interested buyers to communicate with them via a phone number or link to a personal Facebook page). Second, a user will leave a comment on an existing ancient book video advertising their own old or ancient books ("I have a book *just like this*, 800-years-old, pure gold," or "I have a Jewish book written in Hebrew for sale. It's small, twenty pages and made of leather [+phone number redacted]"). In the following section, I draw from qualitative methods to examine three popular videos of supposedly ancient Jewish books and the contents of their comment sections. The first video (Video 1) has been viewed around 80,000 times and received nearly 900 comments. The second (Video 2) has been viewed nearly 40,000 times and received nearly 500 comments, while the third (Video 3) has received nearly 60,000 views and 450 comments (all as of May 2024).

As a space where buyers and sellers can conduct business openly and without fear of consequence, the YouTube comments section offers unique insight into the perspective of people actively or previously involved in a particular subsection of the online trade in illicit antiquities, and reveals how low-level trading communities form, flourish, and wane over time. In this research, ninety-five videos featuring very old or ancient books were located, of which five were uploaded between 2012 and 2016, sixty between 2017 and 2020, and thirty between 2021 and 2023. Of these, 78 percent had received comments: thirty-four videos had received less than ten comments, thirty-one had received anywhere between ten and one hundred comments, and only eight had accumulated over one hundred comments (up to nine hundred). Naturally, however, these figures represent what existed on the platform at the time of data collection and cannot account for old or ancient book videos that had previously been taken down or made private. The following discussion is informed by nearly two thousand user comments that were posted beneath the three videos uploaded throughout 2018 by three separate users.

Video 1

Uploaded in 2018, Video 1 is the most popular ancient Jewish book video identified in this research, currently with around seventy-eight thousand views and just under one thousand comments. Despite being uploaded over five years before this research, the video is still attracting comments from other Arabic speakers expressing their opinion on the contents of the video or attempting to sell their own supposedly ancient books. While the book is not explicitly listed as for sale in the video, its title, or its description, the uploader's choice of username (which signals an involvement in the antiquities trade) and the inclusion of a link in the video's description directing viewers interested in communicating with them to their (now defunct) Facebook page both suggest that the supposedly very old book was probably once available for purchase.

Video 1 is typical of its genre in the sense that it follows the same pattern as most other ancient Jewish book videos, which are typically filmed vertically on a smartphone in a dimly lit room; the books are usually only illuminated by the phone's flashlight or a bright overhead light. The quality of the videos is consistently very low. The supposedly ancient books will be laid out on a table, a scene the viewer looks down on from above. With the exception of a pair of hands flipping through its pages, the books are the only objects ever shown on camera. In the videos identified in this research at least, no other artifacts or contraband were featured in the videos—apart from one seller who used two packets of cigarettes for scale. There is rarely anyone talking while the books are being filmed, though sometimes the sound of a busy street, children's cartoons, or people talking among themselves can be heard in the near distance. The videos usually only include one or two people: either one person will hold the recording device while the other slowly flips through the book, exhibiting the contents of each page to the viewer/potential buyer, or one person will hold the camera in one hand and flip through the book's pages using the other.

Video 1 features an old standard-sized book and small vertical scroll both made from the same type of dark brown leather. Here, one person films as another (hereafter H1) slowly flips through the old book's pages. H1 begins by unfastening the leather scroll attached to the book, moves it off camera, and then starts to flip through the book's pages, which are variously decorated with an assortment of animals, religious figures, and symbols interspersed with sections of handwritten text in an unidentified language. The letters, which were handwritten in metallic gold ink, vaguely resemble those of the Samaritan alphabet, which one user points out in the comments section: ". . . the writing is the ancient Hebrew used by the Samaritan Jews in Palestine" (all comments included in this chapter were translated from Arabic by the author and paraphrased where possible).

After flipping through the book's pages, pausing for about three to five seconds on each, H1 returns to the scroll placed aside at the beginning of the video and unravels it to reveal more of the same metallic gold handwriting and a large illustration of an Orthodox priest or bishop. After exhibiting its front and back to the viewer, H1 rerolls the scroll and fastens it back onto the side of the very old book. The video ends.

Despite being uploaded over five years before this research, Video 1 has still managed to generate a relatively regular stream of comments from other Arabic-speaking viewers expressing an interest in the contents of the video, sharing their opinion (whether positive or negative), or attempting to sell their own very old/ancient books. Comments, then, can loosely be divided into three categories: (1) Interest, (2) Opinion, or (3) Trade-Related. In Videos 1–3, and most other old/ancient book videos with more than ten to twenty comments, Trade-Related comments are by far the most common and, as the extract of comments from Video 1 below demonstrate, typically follow the same pattern.

Sample 1: Typical Trade-Related Comments

I have eighteen Jewish and Hebrew artifacts

I have books and manuscripts in Syria [+phone number redacted]

I have two Jewish books for sale, one silver and the other leather

I have old Hebrew books for sale

I have an old Christian book for sale [+phone number redacted]

Call me, I have a very old book

I have an old book with sixteen pages that I want to sell.

I have two Jewish books for sale, one silver and the other leather

As the extract above demonstrates, Trade-Related comments usually include basic information about the supposed age, language, material, and availability of the books. Users attempting to sell the books will also occasionally reveal how many they have in their possession ("I have eighteen Jewish and Hebrew artifacts," "I have a very old book"), which can range anywhere from one to twenty—though it is difficult to know how many a user could be referring to when they claim to have an unspecified amount of "old Hebrew books" for sale). Noticeably, only two of the comments above included a phone number; in fact, commenters on Video 1 rarely posted their phone numbers unprompted. Most sellers willingly offer up information about the books but, unsurprisingly, reveal very little about themselves, how to contact them, or where in the world they or the books are located. As explored further below, sellers can be divided into two groups based on the extent of the information they share—Tier 1 and Tier 2. Tier 1 sellers provide minimal information about the books and remain vague about how to contact them and where they or the books are located. Likely due to the vagueness of their original comments, Tier 1 sellers are more likely to generate replies from interested buyers, whereas Tier 2 sellers, on the other hand, are those whose comments convey a stronger sense of urgency or seriousness in wanting to conduct business and whose comments attract fewer replies. These sellers provide enough information up front so that no further communication via the YouTube comments section is (or should be) necessary. Perhaps the most illustrative example of a Tier 2 seller in the comments section of Video 1 is, "I'm an Iraqi from [city] and I'm looking for a direct buyer. I have a Jewish book and I don't deal with intermediaries. Contact me only via [instant messaging app] at [@username]."

In Video 1, most users who posted Trade-Related comments rarely acknowledged or expressed an interest in the content of the video or its uploader. As the above samples of comments demonstrate, the majority of ancient book sellers instead use the comments section for the sole purpose of attempting to sell their own books ("I have books and manuscripts in Syria [+phone number]") or to establish contact with other dealers ("Are there any Jewish antiquities dealers here who can contact me?"). There were, however, a small collection of Trade-Related commenters beneath Video 1 who expressed a clear interest in the contents of the video and/or communicating with its uploader:

Sample 2: Attempts to Establish Contact

What's your number?

My brother, I want to buy this. Is it available??

How much?

I want to buy this for whatever price

How much is it? I'll buy it

To be clear, none of the comments left by users attempting to establish contact ever received a (public) response from Video 1's uploader and, even further, many of these comments were posted *years* after it was uploaded. At least in the case of Video 1, users who expressed a clear interest in communicating or conducting business with the uploader were left in the dark. In fact, it appears the channel owner (User 1) has not been active on the platform for quite some time (Video 1 was the first and only video uploaded to the channel by this user). Over the years, however, other traders have begun to take advantage of User 1's absence by intercepting the comments left by prospective buyers (like those in Sample 1 above) in the hopes of profiting from their apparent interest in very old and ancient Jewish books. In one instance, one commenter (OP1) attempted to elicit a response from User 1 by expressing an interest in buying the book and asking how much it was ("How much is it? I'll buy it"). With no reply from User 1, another user chimed in with their own offer for OP1: "I have a friend who has books written in gold who wants to sell them." In an older exchange, another user (OP2), left a comment asking for User 1's phone number ("What's your number?"). Again, receiving no response, other users quickly cut in to advertise their own books: "I have old Jewish books" replied one user; "What country are you in?" asked another. "Morocco," the previous user replied. A new user then entered the thread with another offer: "I have a book that's over 1,800 years old"; however, the exchange ended there (Dialogue 1, below).

Dialogue 1: Exchange between Commenters

OP2: What's your number?

R1: I have old Jewish books

R2: @R1 What country are you in?

R1: @R2 Morocco

R3: @R2 I have a book that's over 1,800 years old

Though Trade-Related comments dominate the comments section of Video 1, what remains are a small collection of (1) Interest and (2) Opinion comments from viewers sharing their verdict on the books' authenticity or warning the uploader to be cautious of them ("Burn it brother, these are impure Jewish magic books"). Among these, accusations of forgery appear in varying levels of detail but are generally kept brief (Sample 3).

Sample 3: Accusations of Forgery in Video 1

Forged hahah

If it's from the city of Fes, it's a fake.

This is forged

Forged

This was forged in the Syrian village of [name]

This is a book made by the [Syrian city name] mafia

It's obvious the book isn't old, it looks too deliberate. Plus its pages have clearly been recently cut

> It's clear this isn't genuine. Here's my number. [Call me] I'll prove to you that it's forged [+phone number redacted]

Though accusations of forgery are present (on a small scale) in Video 1's comments section, they do not appear to have deterred other prospective buyers. Most of the comments exposing the very old antique Jewish books' inauthenticity were posted several years ago, and many more Trade-Related comments have been posted since.

Over the years, Video 1 has continued to generate a steady stream of traffic from like-minded sellers looking to sell similarly very old, antique or ancient Jewish or Christian books. As the extracts above demonstrate, the average commenter beneath Video 1 showed little to no real interest in the video's content or its uploader—instead using the comments section as a means to market their own ancient books either by posting an original comment or intercepting an existing comment or thread. Over time, then, Video 1 has become a beacon for like-minded sellers that signals the video and its comments section as a forum to buy, sell, or trade similar ancient books. The concept of a 'beacon video' in the context of the online antiquities trade is explored further in the following sections.

Video 2

Video 2 was uploaded to YouTube in early 2018 by a user whose choice of username again signals their involvement in the antiquities trade. Observing a similar strategy among Facebook traffickers, the ATHAR Project noted how users "sometimes create fake profiles or modify their genuine personal profiles in order to signal their profession as a looter or smuggler" (Paul and Al-Azm 2019: 8), which, through a heightened facade of professionalism, likely helps drive potential buyers to their profile or channel. The video, which features three supposedly ancient Jewish books from a Middle Eastern country (as described by the uploader) has been viewed nearly forty thousand times and received nearly five hundred comments. The old books are not explicitly listed as for sale by the uploader anywhere in the video's title, description, or the video itself; however, by providing their phone number in the video description, the user (whose username is already enough to indicate the books are/were for sale), implies that the books are/were available.

Video 2 follows a similar pattern to Video 1. The viewer is shown three small leather books laid out on a table, which are illuminated by the phone's flashlight. The person recording stands in front of the books while another person (P1), standing behind the table, begins to pick up the largest of the three books. Unfastening its clasps, P1, who is wearing white latex(?) gloves, opens the large leather book to reveal an assortment of cryptic illustrations in metallic red, silver, and gold ink on each of its pages. One page features a demon-like figure with bright red eyes;

there is nothing discernibly 'Jewish' about the large leather book. After showing the viewer each of the book's pages, P1 sets it aside and moves on to the two smaller leather books shown earlier and repeats the same process. Unlike the larger leather book, Jewish symbols like the Star of David and menorah are seen throughout both the smaller books' pages alongside sections of gibberish Hebrew text hand-written in metallic gold ink. P1 stacks the two smaller books on top of the larger book and the video ends abruptly.

Like Video 1, the comments section of Video 2 is full of Trade-Related comments left by other dealers with their own very old or ancient Jewish books and manuscripts to sell. In terms of Opinions and Interest, however, Video 2 is much more diverse. Alongside accusations of forgery are comments about the larger leather book and the "Jewish black magic" it supposedly contains ("satanic from the get-go . . ."), requests for expert or valuation advice ("I have five books, can someone evaluate them for me?") and references to the quality of the video itself ("We can't even see the pages half the time because the lighting is so bad").

Ranging from general to specific in the level of information shared by sellers, Trade-Related posts are present throughout the comments section. Unlike Video 1, Tier 2 sellers (who typically provide much more information about the books, their contact information, and their geographic location) appear in greater number. As the extract of comments below demonstrates, here users begin to include authenticating devices into their comments to enhance the books' value ("I have two recently excavated Jewish books") and attempt to one-up or compete with the video's uploader ("I have Jewish books much better than these").

Sample 4: Trade-Related Comments beneath Video 1

I have old Jewish manuscripts for sale

I have an old Jewish book in Turkey. Contact me [+phone number redacted]

I have a large, old Jewish book that I want to sell if anyone is interested. I'm from Morocco. Contact me on WhatsApp [+phone number redacted]

I have Jewish books for sale in [city] that have stars of David on them, much better than these for sale. Contact me

I have an old, authentic Hebrew book with drawings and a manuscript with inscriptions [+phone number redacted]

I have statues, bracelets and gold coins for sale. Serious people only

I have a Christian book for sale. Contact me on WhatsApp [+phone number redacted]

For a forgery to be convincing, wrote Anthony Grafton, it needs to come with a believable backstory associated with it; "a mysterious yet impressive origin story that explained how the forger had come across a previously unknown "stunning novelty" (Grafton 1990: 57–58). Though ancient book sellers on YouTube do not construct mysterious yet impressive stories about the books' origins, there are a handful of sellers in the comments section of Video 2 who attempt to heighten the perceived authenticity of the books by drawing attention to their provenance and value. One user claimed, for example, that "I have two Jewish books that were recently excavated if anyone is interested." Another made sure to mention that their old book was genuine ("اصلي") ("I have an old, authentic Hebrew book with drawings and a manuscript encased in a cylindrical tin"), which in the context of old/ancient book videos is surprisingly uncommon. Explored further below, authenticating devices are more commonly employed in the videos themselves and the ways the books are physically exhibited to the viewer. In Video 2, for example, the act of wearing white (albeit latex) gloves signals the handler's desire to emulate museum collection and care-handling practices which have historically involved the use of white cotton gloves—what P1 evidently perceives to be a distinctly professional way of handling the supposedly ancient books (on the contested use of cotton gloves in object handling, see Baker and Silverman 2005; Sampson 2023).

Comments from viewers unconvinced by the handler's attempt to enhance the perceived value or authenticity of the books ("Forged," "all fake," "These are sooo fake . . . bad ones at that") and those who express concern over the "demon-like" drawings shown on the pages of the larger leather book form the focus of most Interest- and Opinion-related comments. As the extract below demonstrates, though there is nothing obviously Jewish about the larger leather book, its association with the smaller Hebrew books is enough to incite viewers' fears about Jewish black magic and satanic worship.

Sample 5: Comments about Jewish Black Magic/Satanism

Satanic from the get-go . . .

Apparently, this book has secrets about black magic . . . No wonder they're so "successful"

These demon drawings are freaky

Please, don't open the books. They contain very dangerous Jewish black magic . . .

A book of the Satanic-worshiping masonic jews

The books are bound in human leather

[Replying to above] Human leather?! I hope not but anything these Satanists do wouldn't surprise me . . .

Suspicions about a deeper connection between the ancient Jewish books and satanic worship are not unique to the comments section of Video 2, either. Other supposedly very old or ancient Jewish books emblazoned with satanic symbols have surfaced in recent years that have similarly incited conspiratorial thinking among certain antisemitic Christian groups. In 2019, for example, police in northwest

Turkey seized a pair of supposedly two-thousand-year-old Torah scrolls similarly decorated with an assortment of overtly satanic and Illuminati symbols. Among the antisemitic conspiracists who latched onto the news of the so-called satanic Torahs was Christians for Truth, an independent news site run by a collective of anonymous (and self-styled) nondenominational Christians, who compared the news of the Torahs to the discovery of secret internal documents belonging to the Illuminati two hundred years earlier. The occult, they claimed, "has always been an integral part of Judaism—with satanic elements born out of the mystery religious cults of ancient Babylon which have nothing to do with the Old Testament or Christianity except as deceptive window dressing to fool the public into tolerating our so-called 'spiritual elders' the Jews, along with their satanic-kabbalistic plans for world domination" (Christians for Truth 2019). For some readers of the Christians for Truth collective, the Torahs were yet further proof—"like we really needed any more—of the jewish connection to satan" (Christians for Truth 2019). It is beyond the scope of this chapter to fully explore the extent of the conspiracy-thinking that surrounds fake ancient Jewish books online; however, the undercurrent of suspicion, fear, or distrust the books promote, especially in unchecked online spaces such as these, should not be understated.

Similar to Video 1, a common strategy used by sellers in Video 2 was to intercept potential sales between two other users and offer up their own old/ancient books instead. In the exchange below, one user (OP2) posted an original comment saying that they have a friend in Syria (where the books in the video were also supposedly found) with a Jewish book for sale. The comment attracts the attention of a potential buyer who asks for more information, to which OP2 responds with their Snapchat username and Instagram handle to communicate further. Another user, RB, joins the thread to ask where in Syria OP2 is from. Receiving no reply, RC cuts in with an offer of their own. As the thread below reveals, neither RB nor RC exchanges contact information, and the exchange eventually fizzles out after a new user, RD, joins the thread.

Dialogue 2. Attempts to Intercept Prospective Sales

OP2: I have a friend in Syria with a Jewish book for sale

RA: Where are you? What's your number?

OP2: [@ RA] Message me on Snapchat [+username]

OP2: [@ RA] or on Instagram [+username]

RB: Where in Syria are you?

RC: [@ RB] I have [some] in Syria if you want

RB: [@ RC]: Where in Syria?

RC [@ RB] Give me your number so we can chat.

RB [@ RC]: I don't give my number to anyone, [. . .] if you want to talk to me, come to [northern Syrian city] so you can see what I have. Where are you?

RC: [@ RB] [northwestern Syrian city]
RD: I have a Hebrew Jewish book in Egypt

Like Video 1, the comments section of Video 2 has amassed a community of users looking to buy, sell and trade very old or ancient Jewish books. Despite being uploaded over five years ago, Video 2's comments section similarly harbors a collective of buyers and sellers who show very little interest in the content of the video itself. Though the comments section of Video 2 harbors a much more diverse set of views and opinions on the books themselves and the beliefs, suspicions, or fears they feed into, the same strategy of intercepting prospective sales employed by sellers in Video 1 also form an important part of user interactions in the comments section of Video 2. Both videos were filmed in a similar environment and follow a similar pattern; however, through the use of white gloves in particular, the individual handling the ancient books reveals a much stronger need to attract buyers through a performance of authenticity or appeal to expertise.

Video 3

Video 3 features what its uploader describes as a very old antique Jewish book. Since being uploaded in 2018, it has amassed nearly 30,000 views and around 450 comments—the most recent of which were left in 2023. Like Videos 1 and 2, the channel owner's username also points toward an involvement in the antiquities trade. The channel owner has not uploaded any videos since Video 3 (or any before it), suggesting the channel was created for the sole purpose of selling the book.

Video 3 features a small, dark brown, leather-bound book with a large gold menorah on its front cover and a Star of David on its back. The book itself is encased in a wooden chest similarly decorated with a large gold menorah, which has been placed on top of a table (or the floor?) and illuminated by a phone's flashlight. At the beginning of the video, the person filming (MH), shows the viewer all sides of the wooden chest before opening it to reveal a small antique Jewish book. MH takes the book out of the chest and begins to flip through its pages, each decorated with an assortment of elaborately drawn animals, Jewish symbols (Star of David and menorah) and sections of Hebrew text handwritten in metallic gold ink. The book, which is about the size of MH's palm, is small enough that he fumbles and drops it a few times in the process of flipping through its pages. After showing the viewer its front and back cover, MH places the small book back inside the wooden chest and the video abruptly ends.

The comments section of Video 3 is almost entirely made up of Trade-Related comments from users with old/ancient Jewish or Hebrew books to sell; with few exceptions, Interest- or Opinion-related comments are virtually nonexistent. Video 3 has slowly collected a small community of dealers, a combination of Tier 1 and 2 sellers, since being uploaded in 2018. As the extract below demonstrates, Trade-Related comments follow a similar pattern to those in Videos 1 and 2. Here, sellers include varying degrees of information about themselves and their preferred method of contact ("Talk to me on WhatsApp if you're interested"), or the books' content or physical features ("I have a book with Jewish symbols"). In terms of how many books the sellers actually have, most are as vague ("I have many old Jewish books") as they are specific ("I have nine books").

Sample 6: Trade-Related Comments beneath Video 3

I have two Jewish books for sale, one is silver and the other is made of leather

I have old Hebrew books for sale

I have a Hebrew book written in gold

I have many old Jewish books

I have a book. It's more than 3,000 years old

I have books and manuscripts in Syria

I have a very old Jewish book. Talk to me on WhatsApp if you're interested [+phone number redacted]

I have Jewish manuscripts and an old antique book [+phone number redacted]

I have nine books [+phone number redacted]

I have a book with Jewish symbols that I found in an old house in [city], Turkey. It's 150,000 dollars. If you want to communicate, leave your number and I'll contact you.

I have a book with the same symbol on the case if anyone is interested

I have an old Jewish book. Message me on WhatsApp [+phone number redacted]

I have old Jewish books

I have a Hebrew Jewish book in Egypt

The comments beneath Video 3 offer unique insight into ancient book sellers' advertising strategies (if we can call it that) and how they operate on the platform more broadly. For a start, the users who left the first and last comments in the above extract ("I have two Jewish books for sale, one is silver and the other made of leather" and "I have a Hebrew Jewish book in Egypt") posted the same comments beneath Videos 1 and 2 around the same time. By posting the same comment on two separate videos of very old or ancient Jewish books, it becomes clear that their advertising strategy is not entirely random. Instead, the users behind these comments have either actively sought out videos of similar old/ancient books in which to advertise their own books *or* have clicked on any old/ancient book videos pushed forward by the algorithm. Either way, the intention behind posting the same comment multiple times across separate videos reveals a marked desire to advertise as widely as possible.

Users expressing a direct interest in the contents of the video and communicating with its uploader form a small but important percentage of Trade-Related comments beneath Video 3. The sample of comments below, most of which were posted several years before this research, highlights the small level of interest among viewers in the 'very old antique Jewish book' shown in the video and the types of interactions these kinds of comments generate.

> **Sample 7: Interest in the Video and Its Uploader**
>
> How much is the book?
>
> Can we contact you?
>
> How much is it?
>
> What's your number?
>
> Hi . . . I want to buy this. Please reply to me if you see this.

As discussed earlier, a common strategy among sellers is to intercept a prospective transaction between two other users by offering up another, potentially rarer or more valuable, Jewish book. Unlike Videos 1 and 2, the same strategy exists among the Trade-Related comments in Video 3 but on a much smaller scale. Video 3 is the only video on the uploader's channel (hereafter Dealer 1), suggesting Dealer 1 created the channel with the express purpose of selling the book. By leaving their phone number in the video's description box, it is reasonable to assume that Dealer 1 expected anyone interested to connect with them via WhatsApp rather than going to the effort of communicating with interested buyers in the comments section. As was the case in Videos 1 and 2, other dealers exploit the uploader's apparent absence by attempting to divert interested buyers' attention away from the video (with varying degrees of success) (Sample 8).

> **Sample 8: Exchange between Sellers**
>
> OP3: Hi . . . I want to buy this. Please reply to me if you see this.
>
> TA: I have an old Jewish manuscript that's more than 950 years old

Among the hundreds of Trade-Related comments beneath Video 3 is a small handful of Opinion/Interest comments drawing attention to the fact that the book is a forgery. Rather than dismissing the book as inauthentic in a few short words, commenters beneath Video 3 offered lengthier explanations as to why they thought the book was fake: "Nice, but fake. One of its pages has the emblem of the modern state of Israel on it . . . Good try but you wasted your gold paint there."

Regardless of whether the 'very old antique Jewish books' featured in Video 3 were ever sold; it is clear by the contents of its comments section that the video has become home to a small-scale virtual marketplace for old/ancient books in which like-minded sellers attract prospective buyers by claiming to possess similar artifacts to those shown in the video. Like Videos 1 and 2, Video 3 operates as a beacon for other old/ancient book sellers, and even sellers of other types of historical artifacts. In fact, alongside the hundreds of Trade-Related ancient book comments were users attempting to sell (presumably old or ancient) statues ("I am from Syria and I have three statues and a cross for sale"), "a silver-gilt scepter" and other artifacts from the Ottoman period.

Conclusion

There is a tendency to view the presence of fakes on the online market as warranting less immediate concern than stolen or likely looted artifacts. After all, the idea that antiquities forgery is only a problem for those gullible enough to "[throw] away their money without looking closely enough at their purchase" is one that was held by scholars for centuries (Thompson 2018: 417). Today, a consequence of this pervasive belief is an uncertainty about what the problem with antiquities forgery actually is, what dangers the presence of these objects on the market pose and to whom. In an article for the National on black markets in Middle Eastern antiquities on Facebook, Maamoun Abdulkarim, former director general for Antiquities and Museums in Syria, aptly warned that "the phenomenon of selling items on Facebook, despite them being fake, is dangerous. . . . It sends a signal to people that they can make money by faking objects, especially in countries that suffer from problems of war, lack of security, and widespread poverty due to poor economic conditions" (Tahir and Tabikha 2024). Not only that, but to the susceptible or uninformed consumer, the boundaries between real and fake are blurred in most online contexts. In the unchecked online spaces explored in this chapter, pocket communities of antiquities dealers flourish not only in the absence of any platform or regulatory oversight but in and through an ecosystem that upholds and promotes (whether consciously or not) a facade of authenticity.

This chapter set out to explore how buyers and sellers of (fake) ancient Jewish books use the popular video-sharing platform YouTube to conduct business and how the platform itself facilitates the formation of these trading communities. Through an analysis of three popular YouTube videos featuring supposedly ancient Jewish books, this chapter has uncovered the various strategies employed by users to sell ancient books, identify potential buyers, and even poach a competitor's potential buyer. What underlies each marketplace examined above, then, is a distinct sense of competition between sellers that manifests in the ways they attempt to one-up or antagonize one another ("I have Jewish books for sale that have stars of David on them, much better than *these*") or through attempts to poach another seller's prospective customer.

Though YouTube is an unlikely venue for the sale of antiquities, this chapter reveals that the platform has harbored pocket communities of ancient book dealers for the last half decade at least. Each of the videos discussed in this chapter has, over time, received a steady influx of comments from buyers and sellers of supposedly ancient books and other historical artifacts who flock to particular videos in the hopes of securing a buyer or connecting with existing networks of dealers. By magnifying a smaller and largely overlooked corner of the online trade in illicit antiquities, this chapter opens up possibilities for future cross-platform comparative research into the strategies used by dealers of fake antiquities in other online contexts and the various visual or textual authenticating devices they use to enhance the perceived value of the artifacts on offer.

Dr Evie Handby recently completed her PhD in the discipline of history and archaeology at Macquarie University, Sydney. Guided by theories of nonhuman agency, her PhD research examined the modern production and proliferation of fake antiquities in Turkey and surrounding regions. Her broader research interests center around forgery, the illicit antiquities trade, social media, and media history.

REFERENCES

Al-Azm, Amr, and Katie Paul. A. 2018. "How Facebook Made It Easier Than Ever to Traffic Middle Eastern Antiquities." *World Politics Review.*

Al-Azm, Amr, and Katie Paul. 2019. "Facebook's Black Market in Antiquities: Trafficking, Terrorism, and War Crimes." Antiquities Trafficking and Heritage Anthropology Research (ATHAR) Project.

Baker, Cathleen A., and Randy Silverman. 2005. "Misconceptions about White Gloves." *International Preservation News* 37: 4–9.

Brodie, Neil. 2017. "How to Control the Internet Market in Antiquities? The Need for Regulation and Monitoring." *Antiquities Coalition* 3: 1–15.

Christians for Truth (CFT Team). 2019. "Turkish Police Recover Stolen Jewish Torah Scrolls Decorated with Satanic Illuminati Symbolism." *Christians for Truth.*

Colvin, Jan, and Jane Lanigan. 2005. "Ethical Issues and Best Practice Considerations for Internet Research." *Journal of Family and Consumer Sciences* 97(3): 34–39.

Demant, Jakob, Silje Anderdal Bakken, Atte Oksanen, and Helgi Gunnlaugsson. 2019. "Drug Dealing on Facebook, Snapchat and Instagram: A Qualitative Analysis of Novel Drug Markets in the Nordic Countries." *Drug and Alcohol Review* 38(4): 377–85.

Evans, Harry, Steve Ginnis, and Jamie Bartlett. 2015. *#SocialEthics: A Guide to Embedding Ethics in Social Media Research.* Ipsos MORI.

Google. 2024a. "Sale of Illegal or Regulated Goods." YouTube Help.

Google. 2024b. "Report Inappropriate Content." YouTube Help.

Grafton, Anthony. 1990. *Forgers and Critics: Creativity and Duplicity in Western Scholarship.* London: Collins & Brown.

Handby, Evie. 2023. "Trafficking Fake 'Ancient' Torahs in Turkey: A Media Analysis." *Public Archaeology*, 1–20.

Hashemi, Layla, and Abi Waddell. 2022. "Investigating the Online Trade of Illicit Antiquities." Routledge.

Huffer, Damien, and Duncan Chappell. 2014. "The Mainly Nameless and Faceless Dead: An Exploratory Study of the Illicit Traffic in Archaeological and Ethnographic Remains." *Crime Law and Social Change* 62: 131–53.

Huffer, Damien, Duncan Chappell, Nathan Charlton, and Brian F. Spatola. 2019. "Bones of Contention: The Online Trade in Archaeological, Ethnographic and Anatomical Human Remains on Social Media Platforms." In *The Palgrave Handbook on Art Crime*, edited by Saskia Hufnagel and Duncan Chappell. United Kingdom: Palgrave Macmillan, 527–56.

Huffer, Damien, and Shawn Graham. 2017. "The Insta-Dead: The Rhetoric of the Human Remains Trade on Instagram." *Internet Archaeology* 45: 1–31.

Huffer, Damien and Shawn Graham. 2023. *These Were People Once: The Online Trade in Human Remains and Why It Matters*. Berghahn Books.

Lever, Rob. 2022. "Discovery Claim of Biblical Scroll in Iran is Fake." *AFP Fact Check*.

MacDonald, T. W. 2023. "'How It Actually Works': Algorithmic Lore Videos as Market Devices." *New Media & Society* 25(6): 1412–31.

Markham, Annette, and Elizabeth Buchanan. A. 2015. "Internet Research: Ethical Concerns." In *International Encyclopaedia of the Social & Behavioural Sciences*, 2nd ed.

Meta. 2024. Transparency Center: Facebook Community Standards.

Mohsin, Maryam. 2023. "10 YouTube Stats Every Marketer Should Know in 2023." *Oberlo*.

Sampson, Amy. 2023. "Handling Historic Collections: The Gloves Are Still Off." *National Archives Blog*.

Statista. 2024. "Most Popular Social Networks Worldwide as of April 2024, Ranked by Number of Monthly Active Users."

Swann, Steve. 2020. "Facebook Bans 'Loot-to-Order' Antiquities Trade." *BBC News*.

Tahir, Tariq, and Kamal Tabikha. 2024. "Facebook Trade in Fake Relics Fuels Middle East Looting." The National.

Thompson, Erin. L. 2019. "'Official Fakes': The Consequences of Governmental Treatment of Forged Antiquities as Genuine During Seizures, Prosecutions, and Repatriations." *Albany Law Review* 82: 407–47.

Votey, Maxwell. 2021. "Illicit Antiquities and the Internet: The Trafficking of Heritage on Digital Platforms." *NYU Journal of International Law and Politics* 54: 659–97.

CHAPTER 2

Amateur Archaeology or Looting?

Exploring Heritage Grey Zones on Reddit

Calum Farrar

Introduction

The means to engage with cultural heritage media and discuss it has expanded enormously with the growth of social media platforms since the early 2000s, when the number of users was in the couple of millions (Ortiz-Ospina 2019), to 2024 with over five billion users globally (Statista 2024). Social media has been an important tool for many GLAM (galleries, libraries, archives, and museums) institutions who curate and interpret cultural heritage, allowing them to engage with a broader audience and relay media about collections beyond the confines of their facilities (Booth, Ogundipe, and Røyseng 2020; Griffen and Taylor 2013). However, by their nature, social media platforms have also allowed the general public to communicate on an unprecedented scale independently from traditional authorities.

This has been most clearly observed in relation to the organization of social movements like the Arab Spring (Comunello and Anzera 2012) and Black Lives Matter (Mundt, Ross, and Burnett 2018). Equally, the ability to disseminate views has been matched by social media's ability to consolidate and reinforce them. It is common belief among both users and academics that the way platform design facilitates group organization and content dissemination can result in what is known as *echo chambers*, where users either self-curate or are algorithmically led to only engage in discussions and with media that reinforce their existing beliefs and positions (Cinelli et al. 2021; Terren and Borge 2021). However, some, such as Bruns (2019, 2024), have contested the empirical evidence for echo chambers truly existing, with others finding through quantitative methods that echo chambers were more prevalent on some platforms (e.g., Facebook), but not others (e.g., Reddit) (Cinelli et al. 2020).

How these platforms allow users to engage with cultural heritage, particularly in ways that are ethically ambiguous or illegal, is a niche area of study, even more so when looking at the social media platform Reddit. Reddit is often missed in discussions on social media in academic literature in favor of larger platforms like Facebook and Twitter (X) despite its large and geographically diverse user base, which, according to a 2024 Pew Research Center poll, places it as tied for the ninth most-used social media platform in the United States alongside Twitter (X). No academic publications that focus on material cultural heritage on Reddit have been identified in a review of literature, with only a small sample discussing it tangentially, often in the context of racialized political discussions (Otero, Martin-Rodilla, and Parapar 2021) or as acts of cultural resistance (Dosono and Semann 2020). Only one online publication that discussed the relationship between cultural heritage trade and Reddit was identified (Leeson 2024).

Leeson's article correctly identifies that authentication, selling, and purchasing of artifacts is occurring on some subreddits and that some subreddits take measures to dissuade this kind of activity; however, they do not delve into the nuanced community conversations and reactions to this kind of content. Consequently, this chapter, which examines Reddit communities and users that post items and media and engage in discussions and exchange of material cultural heritage, particularly from archaeological contexts, is novel. Furthermore, it draws in part on the author's own experiences as a longtime active member in Reddit communities that focus on material cultural heritage content, including art, architecture, and history but primarily archaeology.

The primary research questions that this chapter considers are, firstly, where and what kind of content and discussions are occurring on Reddit in relation to material cultural heritage? Secondly, who are the users engaging in these discussions, what are their motivations, and where are they likely to be posting from? Lastly, is there a relationship between ideologies or politics and the discussions of ethics and legality around the cultural heritage content posted on the platform?

To respond to these questions, firstly, an overview and brief history of Reddit as a platform and how it functions is provided to contextualize the methodology and further discussion. Secondly, the chosen methodology to obtain data is discussed, highlighting the challenges associated with the construction of user content and interuser relationships. Following this, a selection of quantitative and qualitative data is presented and discussed, concluding with a summary interpretation and recommendations for future research.

Reddit as a Platform

Reddit, now a mainstream social media platform, was founded in 2005 as a centralized content aggregation platform. Its founders Steve Huffman and Alexis

Ohanian cite frustrations with early content aggregators or bookmarking services like Slashdot and Del.icio.us as their inspiration for creating Reddit (Fiegerman 2014). However, Reddit's primary competitor Digg had been launched the previous year in late 2004, boasting similar features and a head start in gathering users. Reddit would not overtake Digg until 2010 when an unpopular redesign of Digg led to a rapid decline and shift of many users to Reddit (Fiegerman 2014). Reddit users, known as *redditors*, post, comment, and vote on content, which varies considerably.

It was not until 2008 that one of its best-known features, *subreddits*, was added, moving away from a singular stream of posts, allowing users to post and filter content by topics. During this early period, reddit possessed a few key differences from its contemporaries like Facebook, Twitter (X), and MySpace. Firstly, users were largely anonymous, being represented only by their usernames and any personal information they chose to share. Secondly, interuser interactions were almost entirely conducted through the comments section of a post, with user chat functions being added iteratively since 2017 ("Reddit for iOS Version 39 Now Available" 2017; "What I Learned from Chatting with 7000 Strangers on the Internet" 2018). Lastly, the bulk of user interactions with posts and comments come from the *karma system*.

While similar to the various reaction systems on other platforms, the karma system allows users to both positively and negatively react to posts through upvotes and downvotes respectively. The balance of these interactions is represented as a post's or comment's karma, with the exact number of upvotes and downvotes no longer being transparently displayed. Unlike other platforms such as Facebook, where a user's reaction is public, Reddit upvotes and downvotes are anonymous, though this information is stored by Reddit. Karma scores act to determine the position of a comment within the comment section based on default sorting settings (top or best); for example, a comment with ten karma is placed above a comment with five karma.

However, this does not reflect the absolute number of interactions, only their balance. In previous iterations of the user interface, users could see the ratio of upvotes and downvotes; however, in current versions this is only appreciable by sorting with the *controversial* filter. Karma also acts to sort the position of posts on a subreddit or other feed (e.g., Home), but in conjunction with the age of a post, ensuring that older content is eventually replaced by newer content.

What then is it that redditors are posting about? As previously stated, Reddit began as a content aggregator, with users posting links to external web pages on a range of topics. The introduction of subreddits quickly saw the specialization of content as users were allowed to create their own subreddits. Over time, design choices such as allowing text posts—that is, posts entirely of original user text—acted to encourage *original content* (OC). Text post content, while now a major theme on many subreddits, was popularized by subreddits such as r/askreddit and r/IAMA. Original content was further facilitated by the creation of third-party website Imgur, which was built specifically as an image host for reddit users, though it subsequently branched off as its own platform as Reddit began its own image- and later video-hosting service in 2016 ("Image Hosting on Reddit" 2016).

Reddit operates with relatively little oversight from paid staff, generally identified as *administrators* with a red coloring around their username in posts and comments. Instead, it relies on a large cohort of volunteer moderators, who moderate one or multiple subreddits as part of a team of moderators or by themselves. Typically, moderators operate with a great deal of autonomy and without much oversight. The first major public intervention in the conduct of a subreddit occurred in 2011 when r/jailbait was banned after it received attention from journalist and TV host Anderson Cooper for its primary content being sexually suggestive imagery of minors (Centivany 2016).

However, as Centivany (2016) notes, there was nothing explicitly illegal about the content on the subreddit, particularly given the broad speech protections allowed by the First Amendment to the Constitution of the United States. Stricter management of content has continued since; however, the complicity of Reddit's administrators and founders in allowing and at times rewarding what might be characterized as offensive content was apparent (Ohanian 2009). Reddit's laissez-faire approach to moderation was undoubtedly influenced by the ideological positions of its founders such as Alexis Ohanian, or Aaron Swartz, who was famously prosecuted for attempting to download and publicly release the JSTOR academic publication archive, acting upon beliefs espoused in his 2008 manifesto, something strongly linked to his 2013 suicide (Constant 2013; Swartz 2008).

The beliefs of the founders were popular among a vocal portion of the user base, with backlash occurring after bans or acts of censorship by Reddit administrators like in the r/jailbait case (Centivany 2016: 6–7). Between 2014 and 2017 many more waves of subreddit bans came through; however, community backlash peaked when Reddit founder Steve Huffman, or Reddit user /u/spez, was found to be editing the comments of users on the r/the_donald subreddit. In a popular post Huffman (2016) attempted to explain his actions and in the process announced new standards and moderation of subreddits that were acting in a way that Reddit administrators viewed to be disruptive to the rest of the platform.

This was in response to the widespread manipulation of the voting algorithms on Reddit during the 2016 US presidential election campaign by certain subreddit communities, allowing their posts to dominate the r/all feed (Shepard 2020). Another case occurred in 2023, following the announcement that Reddit would be changing its Application Programming Interface (API) policy by charging for access, a large protest was coordinated by subreddit moderators and other users. The changes to the API access portended dire consequences for the sustainability of many third-party applications, including popular apps and tools used in moderation and research data collection.

This protest took the form of subreddits *going dark* by setting their public visibility to private, marking their content as not safe for work (NSFW), or by posting specific troll content (Peters 2023a). Rather than address the concerns, Reddit administrators began issuing ultimatums to moderators, demanding that they end the protest or they would be removed from their position for breaching the code of conduct (Peters 2023b). How the fallout of this event will affect the broader community, beyond the end of support for many third-party apps, remains unclear; however, users have noted the departure of some long-term users and moderators ("Does Anyone Remember the Reddit Blackout?" 2024).

What this brief history highlights is the strong sense of community among the active users and moderators on Reddit, particularly when they feel that their autonomy over their space is being threatened. While this position was initially supported by its founders, Reddit's administrators have increasingly restricted the scope of content and autonomy on the platform as the user base has grown and the nature of some subreddits has become more public, opting to align it with a position that is more amenable to advertising and investment, particularly as they approached initial public offering (IPO) ("Reddit Files Registration Statement for Proposed Initial Public Offering" 2024). In identifying these trends, I do not endorse the subreddits, content, or users banned from the platform; however, it has important implications for how users view and use the platform.

Despite the considerable changes in user autonomy, subreddit moderators retain considerable control over what posts and comments can be made. For example, some moderators or moderation teams operate third-party applications that automatically and often preemptively ban users based on their engagement with other subreddits or use of certain words. While cited as a means to reduce moderation resources being dedicated to dealing with trolls, bots, or spammers, it has the obvious effect of decreasing engagement across polarized communities.

Combined with self-selection by users of which communities to participate in based on which align with their interests and beliefs, there would be an expectation that Reddit would have similar patterns of user base division seen on other platforms. However, Cinelli et al. (2021), using a dataset of user-generated content from three political subreddits, identified that Reddit had very little segregation in what content users were exposed to, particularly in comparison to Facebook users. Firstly, this suggests that the way Reddit exposes users to content by default through r/popular (previously r/all) means users are automatically receiving a less tailored experience than other platforms that encourage greater content curation (e.g., following other users, adding friends, or liking pages) by the user.

The above is a brief overview of how Reddit functions and some notable events in its history, but who are Reddit users, and where are they from? According to data collected in the last quarter of 2023, which appeared in the Reddit SEC filing, 50 percent of site visits come from within the United States, with 90 percent of posts being in English; however, it notes that the number of users from outside the

United States has grown 21 percent from 2022 to 2023 to an average 36.7 million daily active unique users ("United States Securities and Exchange Commission Form S-1/A Registration Statement Registration No. 333-277256" 2024: 5–6). Other notable statistics from this same document are that among US users, 50 percent are male, and 41 percent are between the ages of eighteen and thirty-four and have an average household income on par with the US average.

Furthermore, among the same group, many users were not active on other social media platforms such as Facebook (32 percent), Instagram (37 percent), Snapchat (73 percent), TikTok (41 percent), and X (53 percent). More detailed breakdowns of these statistics are harder to come by, with some third-party data aggregators not clearly identifying the source of their data (e.g., Bianchi 2024; "Reddit.com Overview" 2024) or utilizing their own surveys to identify specific statistics (e.g., "Social Media Factsheet" 2024). The survey conducted by Pew Research ("Social Media Factsheet" 2024) does conflict with Reddit's own self-reported data, suggesting a greater proportion of male users; however it provides some other notable comparisons to other platforms on measures such as tertiary education. In this sense it closely mirrors X prior to 2024, in that most US users have completed or are currently engaged in tertiary education, a ratio that is only surpassed by LinkedIn.

These statistics paint a picture of a user base that is increasingly multinational, tertiary educated, and primarily using Reddit over other platforms. However, given the propensity of subreddits to develop their own demographic quirks (e.g., "Subreddit Demographic Survey 2019" 2019), it is unclear how applicable this data will be to the assessed subreddits.

Methodology

A variety of methods have been used to analyze user content on Reddit, with a systematic literature review by Proferes et al. (2021: 9) identifying that a plurality of methods, where N equals the number of studies (N=273) employed in the studied corpus (N=597) being explicitly reliant on the now prohibitively expensive API. The next largest data collection method (N=59) relied on direct engagement with the Reddit website through screenshots and copying and pasting text. These numbers reflect a bias toward quantitative forms of analysis in the literature, with 183 papers using qualitative methods and only 56 papers employing mixed quantitative-qualitative methods (Proferes et al. 2021: 8). Proferes et al. (2021: 10) reflected on the unlikely long-term sustainability of the quantitative approach given broader trends in API restrictions by social media platforms, a pessimism that proved correct.

As the aim of this study was to identify patterns in user engagement across Reddit in relation to subreddits that deal primarily with cultural heritage, this change in API policy in 2023 introduced limitations in the data available as well as its quality. Firstly, third-party data-presentation applications or websites like

Subredditstats.com, which allow for relationships between subreddits to be quantified, are restricted largely to data collected before July 2023. Secondly, this cutoff point misses key communities that have grown or been created since July 2023. Despite this, quantitative data is still utilized in this study, but conclusions derived from it should be understood in this context.

Before delving into the specifics of the chosen methodology, there are selection criteria that should be discussed that were adhered to in order to narrow the focus of data-collecting activities for both qualitative and quantitative data. These criteria were devised primarily on the personal experience of the author, an active user in a range of communities discussing material cultural heritage, particularly r/archaeology. The criteria are split into two groups. Firstly, subreddits must be focused on or predominantly contain original content relating to archaeological materials. By focusing on aggregations of original content, the motivations of and discussions had by those engaging in collecting activities are more abundant and nuanced.

Secondly, the posts and comments used for qualitative analysis must contain sufficient context or discourse relating to the object or activity. For example, if a user makes a post of an artifact with no accompanying textual information and no comments elaborate on the content, it is discarded. Given the large volume of posts and comments on some of the identified subreddits, this filtering and accompanied using of key term searches significantly reduces the dataset size but increases the average richness of the data being assessed.

Ethical Considerations

Several academics writing on ethical use of Reddit data have identified a general lack of explicit consideration of ethics by researchers (Proferes et al. 2021: 8–9), variable application of ethical frameworks (Fiesler et al. 2024), and inconsistent efficacy (Reagle 2022). In part this comes from a general presumption that a user posting on a public platform such as Reddit has the implicit understanding that their posts or comments are in the public domain. Reagle's (2022) study identified that attempts to anonymize Reddit user data by researchers are rarely effective, with manual search methods such as Google Search or Reddit's internal search engine proving effective in tracing specific users, posts, and comments, even when direct quotes are avoided.

Reagle (2022: 5) found that the most effective anonymizing methods utilized significant rephrasing of quotes, unspecified subreddits, or broad sampling methods, such as many subreddits over large time periods. Furthermore, Reagle agreed with an anonymous academic that the pseudonymous nature of Reddit users still offered considerable protection to their real identities being discovered. Reagle's assessment provides some useful methods that can be proactively employed to minimize harm to users through the use of their data. Given the legally and ethically dubious nature of some user content on the subreddits that met the selection criteria, it is crucial that user identities are protected for two reasons.

Firstly, many users in the assessed subreddits expressed mistrust toward heritage professionals and other authoritative institutions for a variety of reasons discussed later. This observation reflects other literature that has assessed the relationship between amateur archaeological and collector communities and professional archaeologists in the United States (Douglas et al. 2017; Pitblado et al. 2022; Wright 2022). It is worth noting that this turbid relationship is not unique to the United States, with many countries, particularly in Europe, having similar bodies of literature examining the tensions and benefits of engaging with an avid amateur community (e.g., Campbell, White, and Thomas 2019; Winkley 2016). Because of this often-strained relationship, it is crucial that this study does not undermine the efforts of many in both amateur and professional communities to build trust and cooperation.

Secondly, many users engage in highly descriptive discourse that produces identifiable information (e.g., highly specific geographic locations), and furthermore, some users explicitly identify themselves through use of real names, links to third-party platforms with their personal information, or posting media that visually identifies themselves and others. Furthermore, pseudonyms as usernames are still a form of identification, one that can be very valuable to users, and if compromised can cause considerable distress (Bruckman 2002).

Users overwhelmingly provide this information and engage in discussions in good faith, often with the intention of assisting others; therefore, it should not be used in a way that leads to them feeling targeted or harassed. Beyond this, while antithetical to my own understanding of ethical archaeological practice, users engaging in illegal or ethically questionable acts should have the same courtesy extended to them, as in some cases their activity in the community might be a source of income or constitute a valuable source of emotional and mental stability.

Given the above, I have chosen to use a *moderate disguise* as described by Bruckman (2002: 230). To paraphrase, this method combines aspects of *heavy* disguise, such as no use of pseudonyms, not naming subreddits, and no verbatim quotes, together with aspects of a *light* disguise, which accepts that subreddit members may be able to guess who is being discussed. While in-group identification would ideally be avoided in the communities assessed, where there is a high prevalence of original content, context-heavy discourse, and a small cohort of highly active users, this is difficult to avoid.

Quantitative

Numerous modeling methods have been applied to Reddit user data in research settings. A number have focused on identifying user activity overlap between subreddits (e.g., Cinelli et al. 2020; Datta and Adar 2019). Others have used semantic analysis powered by machine learning to quantify less apparent similarities between subreddits (Martin 2017; Partridge et al. 2024). Generally, these methods have all homed in on identifying inter-subreddit relationships, allowing subreddits to be grouped into what have been variously called "cliques" (Hoffa 2015), "countries" (Kashcha 2023), and "interest meta-communities" (Olson and Neal 2015). All these methods, despite their variable results, utilize user commenting and posting as the primary data source. Therefore, they are all limited by the exclusion of what is the main form of user interaction on the platform, the karma system.

The majority of Reddit users fall into a group often known on the platform as "lurkers," being that they rarely, if ever, post or comment, instead only interacting through the karma system. While the influence of lurkers can be inferred to some degree by looking at the karma of a post alongside the upvote percentage accessible via use of the Reddit Enhancement Suite add-on, it is otherwise only accurately observable by the original poster (OP) of the post and the subreddit moderators via the default Reddit interface. Furthermore, the karma of the post does not fully elucidate user engagement with a post. Comments are often of greater interest to users, attracting much greater numbers of user interactions; however, the absolute number of votes on a comment is even more opaque than that of the post.

As previously stated, access to social media data has become a growing issue for researchers as platforms restrict access to APIs, with Reddit being one of the last large platforms to do so in mid-2023. However, data gathered through API access prior to this still offers considerable insight into user-interaction dynamics on Reddit. A number of third-party applications such as Subredditstats and the aforementioned inter-subreddit relationship visualizations utilized the API to publish a variety of statistics and statistical relationships that have been used by some researchers (e.g., Hartzell, Jackson, and Pinchot 2021; Trujillo and Cresci 2022). What these relationships have the potential to reveal is how the user bases of the subreddits targeted in this study might overlap with more overtly ideologically biased subreddits. This can help inform why or how particular views regarding material cultural heritage are formed and propagated.

Qualitative

While this study from its inception was envisaged as utilizing mixed methods, the limitations related to the use of quantitative data have required a greater reliance on qualitative data. The primary benefits to the use of qualitative data in this context is that it allows a more intimate examination of individual users and communities while also allowing for the investigation of communities that have grown in activity and popularity since the API policy change. The two primary subreddits assessed using this method average between twelve to thirty posts a day, with most receiving little engagement in the form of either votes or comments.

These two subreddits have been selected due to their high number of original content posts, not just in the sense that users are posting their own unique media of material cultural heritage, but in how they specifically post material cultural heritage that they have personally acquired through in situ collection, noncommercial or commercial exchange, or inheritance. This presented a unique opportunity to examine those involved in the early stages of ownership chains, a group typically obfuscated deliberately to hide unethical or illegal practices, or by poor documentation. The material culture posted on these subreddits consisted typically of stone tools, with smaller numbers of ceramics and metal objects.

Other subreddits were excluded from more intensive data collection despite containing some content that meets the selection criteria. The primary reason for this exclusion is that the preferred content represents a small and intermittent portion of overall posts. However, some, such as Subreddit 03 (SR03), are included due to their exceptional content that often prompts greater user engagement. Therefore, SR03 stands as a useful point of comparison.

No limitations have been placed on the age of posts and comments recorded; therefore, data collected from a subreddit might reflect nearly a decade of user engagement. It is important to acknowledge that subreddits are constantly evolving through shifts in the user-base demographics, moderation, platform policy changes, and external events. Consequently, subreddits might go through phases where they would meet the criteria set out in this study and other phases where they would not. Equally, attitudes shift toward particular types of post content, such as sales posts and excavation techniques. However, as the user bases of the chosen subreddits have grown as measured by subscriber counts, the frequency of posts and comments has increased, something reflected in the recency of the data collected.

Results

Qualitative

For the qualitative assessment, sixty-two posts were recorded from Subreddit 01 (SR01), fifty-four from Subreddit 02 (SR02), and fifteen from Subreddit 03 (SR03) between December 2023 and March 2024. These posts met the criteria outlined in the methodology section above, representing approximately 20 percent of the total number of posts surveyed. The recorded posts reflect those within their respective communities that received greater levels of engagement through comments and votes, as well as those that addressed the key themes. The vast majority of posts received little engagement, with those receiving the most engagement typically presenting unique media (e.g., a rare or unusual artifact type), containing debate in the comments, or requesting advice, all of which are not mutually exclusive. Posts that received some engagement but did not meet the selection criteria

Table 2.1. Instances of themes identified across recorded posts. © Calum Farrar

Subreddit Code	Themes					Total Recorded Posts
	Ethics	Advice (Not incl. value)	Excavation	Valuations or Exchange	Motivation	
01	16	24	33	16	4	62
02	28	8	17	29	5	54
03	13	13	0	3	0	15

typically contained some comments of congratulations and encouragement to the original poster for finding an artifact. These posts made up the vast majority of media posted to both SR01 and SR02.

Posts that contain photographs or video from excavations or discuss excavations tend to generate substantial user engagement through comments, with more than 50 percent of the recorded posts in SR01 containing implicit or explicit evidence of excavated cultural materials (table 2.1). These posts have a high degree of overlap with posts that discuss the ethics of collecting, with six overlapping posts on SR01, but particularly on SR02 where ten of the posts discussing excavation also discuss ethics, encompassing ~59 percent of excavation posts.

Many of these posts included solicited or unsolicited advice not regarding monetary value from users, instead typically relating to identification or prospection methods. SR02 had a higher proportion of advice relating to the monetary value of material culture heritage with ~54 percent of recorded posts containing comments relating to the valuation of the material culture posted, its sale, or its purchase. It was unclear what proportion of comments by users progressed to the sale or purchase of objects, as these conversations typically transitioned to private messaging between the involved users or it was implied it had moved on to other, unknown platforms.

Ethics

Understanding how users in the target subreddits engaged in discussions around ethics was a key focus of this study. These discussions primarily took place in the comments of posts, with a smaller number of posts directly addressing ethics. Specific reference to "ethics" was rare, with users employing a range of other terms, typically with specific positive or negative inclination (e.g., bad, good, right, wrong). This use of positive and negative language has important implications for understanding user engagement, with several other studies identifying a correlation between the use of negative language and user engagement (Horne et al. 2017; Hiaeshutter-Rice and Hawkins 2022; Segesten et al. 2022; Xia et al. 2020).

Ethics was also a key theme in pinned moderator posts, which outlined rules and guidelines for ethical conduct on the subreddit and what was deemed acceptable content to post. Moderators typically maintained a neutral attitude toward activities that they personally did not support, such as the sale of artifacts and excavations. One moderator cautioned in a formerly pinned post that users should exercise extreme caution when engaging in artifact trading due to the high likelihood of scams.

Wanting to avoid culpability in users being scammed seemed to be a primary motivating factor in the attitude expressed by multiple moderators; however, they did not explicitly ban posts or comments relating to trade. Similar attitudes were found in many active users, with posts enquiring about how to sell or value an artifact were met with many comments encouraging the OP not to engage in commercial exchange of artifacts.

Excavation and prospection methods were commonly embedded in discussion of ethics. Across both SR01 and SR02 there appeared to be three primary schools of thought on what constitutes ethical collection practices. Firstly, there were posters who argued that no artifacts should be collected, regardless of context, without proper application of archaeological methods to ensure contextual information was maintained. These individuals were typically met with negative reactions from others, including moderators at times. The second group of posters broadly argued that collection of "surface finds" (i.e., artifacts) that could be recovered without the removal of sediment were ethically unproblematic for collection.

As one moderator on SR02 argued, artifacts found on the surface are out of context and therefore have no or very limited scientific information that can derive from the application of more intensive documentation standards. This group of posters appears to be the majority across SR01 and SR02 based on the almost exclusively positive reactions to statements or arguments that aligned with this view. A caveat to this group's participation in the subreddit is that they felt strongly bound by the legal requirements applied to artifact collection in the United States, especially that it is illegal on public lands regardless of context and that if collection was to occur on private property, permission was required.

The last group of posters were those who supported the use of excavation techniques to prospect for and gain access to in situ artifacts. While only a small minority of users posted content relating to excavation or indicated that they used it as a method, they were overrepresented in discussions of ethics. Furthermore, the users posting content related to excavation disproportionately identified as conducting the activities in the US state of Texas. Discussion relating to the ethics of excavation tended to attract greater user engagement and the use of more emotive language, including derogatory terms being directed at other users. Critics of users excavating typically focused on the significant loss of contextual information through poor excavation (see figure 2.1) and documentation practices. Furthermore, some users posting excavation content were also accused of potentially

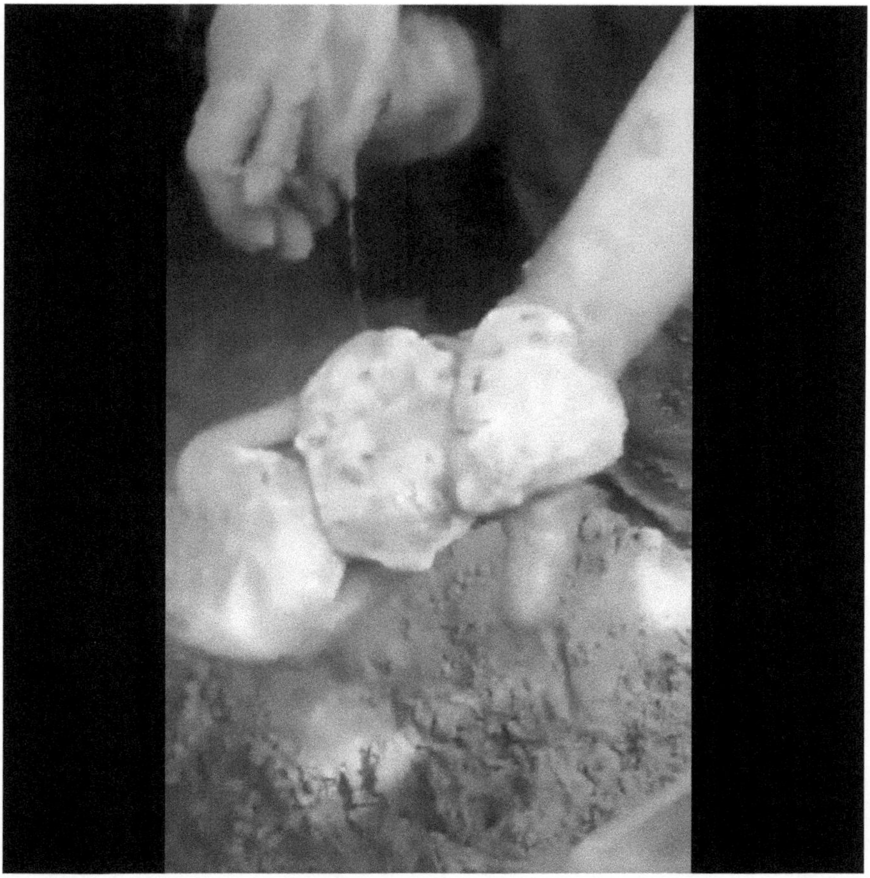

Figure 2.1. A user recovers artifacts from an excavation. Frame from a video posted on Reddit (SR02).

damaging sites containing human remains, with OP responses tending to further inflame outrage expressed by other users.

Recorded posts on SR03 were primarily ethics oriented, with a user base far more likely to discuss the ethics of a post's original content. SR03 users showed a higher propensity to support methods more in line with ethical professional practice in archaeology and explain these to users posting original content. Responses to this advice regarding ethical practice were well received by seven of the OPs on posts where advice to contact heritage professionals was given. However, five of these posts were from users outside the United States, with four posting from the UK. Posters who identified themselves as being from the United States were evenly split between positive and negative reactions to this advice regarding ethical conduct.

Excavation

Excavation posts typically generated more user engagement, not just due to subsequent discussion of ethics, but also to the scale and quality of the artifacts recovered from clandestine excavations. Some users posted image and video media clearly showing the use of various excavation methods, including the use of garden tools and mechanical excavators coupled with sediment sifting as a form of rapid artifact recovery (see figure 2.2).

Those that used mechanical excavators generated intense discussion in all instances, with most users condemning the practice as overtly destructive of both the archaeological record and also potentially the artifacts themselves. Smaller-scale methods, such as test pits, were at times suggested to users as ways to expand their collection efforts. Such suggestions generated less negative feedback. Those who had found artifacts accidentally through excavation (e.g., via gardening or construction) were not met with negative reactions. Despite SR01 being a more

Figure 2.2. Frame from a user-posted video of mechanical excavation for artifact recovery in Texas (SR02).

recently created subreddit, almost twice the number of excavation posts were observed on it compared to SR02, which has very similar subject matter.

Advice

Posts and comments asking other users for advice (excluding those relating to valuation and exchange) were common across both subreddits, with the record for neither subreddit reflecting high frequency due to sampling methods. Many of these posts were users asking for help identifying or authenticating artifacts. Often these posts were classified as "Just a Rock" or JARs because the media posted was not culturally modified material according to users on the subreddit. These posts were disproportionately common in SR03, though there is a more recent trend observed on that subreddit toward not hosting significant original content. User reactions to these posts were often neutral to negative, receiving little positive karma.

This acted as a kind of quality assurance and bar of entry for users to regularly engage with the subreddit outside of what the moderators would do. If you could not demonstrate basic knowledge about the subject matter, your opinion was disregarded and sometimes belittled. Where the media showed something that was not JAR, users often provided quite specific information regarding its stylistic classification. This included at times referring the advice-seeking users to academic literature or other third-party resources. Additionally, users provided advice regarding prospection techniques, sometimes including excavation methods. Of the users providing advice, only two or three across all surveyed posts explicitly identified themselves as current or former professional archaeologists, with there being no way to verify these assertions.

Posts would at times include geographical information of varying specificity, volunteered by the OP or at the behest of other users. The purpose of this was to assist in both identifying artifacts by geographical association and answering the questions of other users. This information was sometimes responded to with advice regarding the legality of their activity if the user implied or explicitly stated that their collecting was taking place in a location where it was not allowed. Consequently, there were some users who would suggest that the OP better hide similar activity in the future by not posting specific locations, or by lying about where they found it. There were no notable instances where the OP obviously heeded this advice, instead most endeavored to report the find to appropriate authorities or academics.

Valuation and Exchange

Posts requesting valuation or advice on how to buy or sell artifacts were common across both SR01 and SR02. Posts requesting valuation advice often received comments along two lines. Either approximations by users were made or users would suggest that the objects were priceless and should not be considered in a monetary sense. Less commonly, users would be directed toward third-party resources such as published pricing guides or known valuation experts. In the rarer cases where the OP had an artifact of great potential value, there was higher user engagement.

Those seeking information on how to sell artifacts were in the majority, with only three posts being identified across SR01 and SR02 that were seeking purchasing advice. Those looking to buy were in all cases requesting help authenticating the artifacts for sale before committing to the purchase. There were some other requests to purchase artifacts; however, these were comments within posts that were either in response to the OP posting a rare artifact or the OP seeking interested buyers.

There was considerable variation in those looking to sell artifacts. In SR02, six posts were identified where users had allegedly inherited artifacts from a family member, three of which were seeking advice on their value or how to sell them. Other users posting about selling artifacts were prompted by financial hardship; in some cases this was an inherited collection or their own that they had developed over time.

Other posts that included discussion in the comments of selling practices were often in response to users expressing interest in buying the artifact in the original post. There were two identified instances of users accusing others of looting for commercial profit, with one OP admitting that they did sell some artifacts, but it was not their primary motivation. SR01, while not condoning the practice of selling or buying artifacts, did offer artifacts as a user raffle prize, the rules of which motivated users to subscribe to and engage with the subreddit. This event was coordinated by one of the moderators and had been repeated at various subscriber milestones to celebrate the growth of the subreddit.

Motivation

At times users would discuss the reason they engaged in the collection of artifacts, with nine posts being identified across SR01 and SR02. These discussions often went into great depth, prompting many users to engage in discussion. Most were positive, with users reflecting on the sense of joy they felt in the process of searching for and finding artifacts. Many felt a great deal of sentimentality in this process as it was something they had started doing with family or had engaged in for a long time. Furthermore, a common expression was that holding and being in the presence of artifacts made users feel a closeness to the past and past people. Many users expressed a desire for their collection to be passed on to family members, something that was reflected in the suggestions given to posts requesting advice on selling, particularly when the collection was inherited.

Conversely, some of these conversations around motivation were negative or in response to negative sentiments from other users. Several users described their collection efforts, including excavation, as an act of saving the artifacts from obscurity or destruction. There were two posts identified in SR01 where the OP described or showed media of their rescue efforts at construction/development sites near to where they lived; they had no known official association with the development. This motivation was often expressed in response to other users accusing them of looting or poor practice, justifying their actions by suggesting that if they did not retrieve the artifacts then they would be permanently lost. While this sentiment was expressed variably, it was often well supported by other users through high positive karma and affirming comments. However, when it was expressed, few users provided explicit and specific reasons for why the artifacts or archaeological sites were under threat.

Although not necessarily a motivation, many users also expressed views about individual rights and private property when discussion of whether collecting actions were justified. Only one user on SR01 was identified as having an explicit monetary motivation for the practice. This was evident in their use of highly destructive but high-turnover methods of collecting artifacts (e.g., heavy machinery). However, this motivation was not supported by the user base of SR01 or SR02, with most suggesting that artifact collection should be a personal endeavor, not a commercial one.

User Information

No formal records were maintained regarding personal information of users to avoid a breach of privacy for the reasons discussed above. However, some details, such as vague geographic location (e.g., US state, or, if outside the United States, country), were recorded. Beyond this, observations were made but not recorded regarding other aspects of user identity. These data were all recorded in an Excel spreadsheet that included hyperlinks to each post, categories it was associated with, and a description of the content of the post and comments. No personal data were recorded in this document; however, it would still be accessible via the links that have not been included here.

Overwhelmingly, the users on SR01, SR02, and SR03 were based in the United States. Within this cohort, users were predominantly posting cultural material they had found in the southern and eastern United States, with posted finds stated to derive from locations in Virginia, across the southern states, to Texas. A smaller number of users identified themselves or their posted material as coming from the Northeast (e.g., New York) and the Southwest (e.g., Arizona), but were often vague and unwilling to divulge specifics. Outside the United States, there was a smaller number of users posting content from the United Kingdom, beyond which there was a smattering of other represented countries, including Canada, Australia, and several from Central America.

More specific information about where users were conducting their collecting activities was often ambiguous. Most posts of in situ or surface artifacts have little geographic contextual information provided, aside from the state or stated proximity to specific cities and towns. When prompted by other users, some OPs would elaborate on whether it was their own property, one they had permission to be on, or somewhere else. Those users that were not on private property typically reveal this information either through naivety of local laws or because they believed their actions were justified.

There were several instances where users posted media of artifacts on public lands but stated that they did not disturb the artifacts. Overwhelmingly, users who revealed such information stated explicitly or strongly implied that they were conducting their activities on private property. However, even those who were acting legally were often reluctant to reveal exact locations for fear of others gaining access to artifacts before them, whether by permission of the same landholder or through trespassing and looting.

Through the use of stated pronouns and what could be inferred from posted media, users were overwhelmingly male, with a smaller number of self-identified female users. Regarding ethnic group affiliation or Indigeneity, little can be said with certainty. Some users identified as being of Native American descent. Those identified visually in media seemed to be predominantly white; however, such assumptions are quite superficial. Furthermore, the age of users was similarly difficult to determine; however, some comments, such as those divulging how long a user had been collecting artifacts, who was involved in the collection (e.g., children/grandchildren), who owned the property the collection occurred on, or how certain collectors complained about age-related difficulty in their work, gave an indication that most active users were above or on the older edge of the most common Reddit age bracket (eighteen to thirty-four).

Tertiary education in archaeology or other cultural heritage studies was infrequently brought up by users, with some self-identifying as archaeologists. Some self-identified archaeologists engaged by helping users determine artifact types and styles; however, most self-identified archaeologists engaged in discussions regarding ethical conduct and suggesting that users alter their practices to better preserve contextual information. Most users did not identify as having any tertiary education in relation to material cultural heritage, with many making negative comments regarding professionals, academics, and particularly those who they felt were intruding on their space in the subreddits and pontificating. This reflected a general negativity toward academic institutions, ideals, and individuals who they felt were in direct competition for access and custodianship over material cultural heritage.

Quantitative

The results of the quantitative analysis of subreddit relationships have relied primarily on the use of the third-party tool Subredditstats; however, this information has been compared with other third-party analyses such as /u/anvaka's (Kashcha 2023) "Map of Reddit." What this comparison demonstrated was that each method produces variable results through variable dataset time ranges and statistical analyses.

The third-party platform Subredditstats is one of several data aggregators that focused on Reddit that have become largely defunct due to the 2023 API policy change. However, Subredditstats still retains some functionality as well as archived data, allowing some user trends between subreddits to be identified. Using its "Subreddit User Overlaps" application, a range of subreddits, including those analyzed in the qualitative section, were examined. This view provides a list of subreddits ordered by an overlap score. This score reflects that a user who posts and comments on Subreddit A will more likely post and comment on Subreddit B compared to the average Reddit user. For example, if Subreddit B is given a score of twenty in relation to Subreddit A, this means that Subreddit A users are twenty times more likely to post on Subreddit B than the average Reddit user.

SR02 showed a strong user overlap, with two subreddits that also focused on or saw regular posted requests to identify material cultural heritage but were not SR01 or SR03. SR02 users were approximately sixty times more likely to post and comment on these two subreddits compared to the average Reddit user. The next three largest overlaps were with two outdoor-activity-oriented subreddits and one dedicated to stock trading, with scores between thirty-seven and thirty-three. Following this, there is a group of what can be characterized as conspiracy- or alternative-knowledge-oriented subreddits with scores ranging between thirty-two and nineteen.

Interspersed within this group are subreddits oriented toward buying and selling products, a specific US state, outdoor activities, and conservative policy advocacy. This association with alternative-knowledge subreddits was poorly corroborated with data from Kashcha (2023), which placed greater emphasis on the relationship between SR02 and other collector- and identification-oriented subreddits.

SR01 does not have sufficient data prior to the 2023 API change to provide useful information for this form of analysis. However, it was noted during the qualitative data collection that SR01 users frequently posted and commented on SR02, sometimes using the cross-post function to share content between the subreddits. SR03 has the highest user overlap with a subreddit dedicated to cats, with a score of 218. Following this is a feminist-oriented subreddit with occult themes, with a score of 142. There are strong associations with a variety of other subreddits after this point, including several dedicated to European countries, media fandoms, and various former default subreddits. The largest overlaps are likely to reflect the long period over which this subreddit has been active, although with low levels of user engagement, allowing a small group of highly active users to strongly skew the data.

In comparison, Kashcha (2023) shows that SR03 has close links to r/archaeology and other ancient-history-oriented subreddits, including several alternate history/knowledge subreddits. These include one devoted to well-known pseudo-archaeologist Graham Hancock. In addition to the subreddits used in the qualitative method, other subreddits with an emphasis on material cultural heritage were assessed with Subredditstats as a point of comparison.

SR02 shared two subreddits with r/archaeology, both of which had high overlap scores and a focus on material cultural heritage. Notably, neither subreddit showed overlap with the other. The other subreddits with high overlap scores with r/archaeology reflect a variety of subject matter, including media fandoms, media-hosting technology, and military subjects for active and former servicepeople. R/archaeology did not show the same association with alternative-knowledge subreddits that SR02 did. However, this is not corroborated by other network visualizations, such as that presented in Kashcha (2023), which does show overlap with alternative-knowledge subreddits.

The largest subreddit devoted to coins, r/coins, has users posting images of coins they have collected or found in situ, but has explicit rules against buying and selling, only allowing users to help authenticate and identify coins. Despite this, it has a strong overlap with two subreddits dedicated to the trading and collection of silver bullion with scores of 184 and 27. The subreddit with a score of 184 contains detailed information from users about how to go about purchasing and selling silver, including coins.

Another subreddit heavily devoted to in situ collection of cultural materials is r/metaldetecting. R/metaldetecting did not show any overlap with the discussed SR01–03. It showed similar relationships to r/coins, which seemed consistent with it having a score of 183 with r/coins. However, this does highlight an oddity of the results generated by Subredditstats, being that r/coins did not show overlap with r/metaldetecting. This may be a product of r/coins having a more diversely engaged userbase compared to r/metaldetecting.

Other larger subreddits, such as r/artefactporn (3.1 million subscribers), were excluded from this analysis because subreddits with larger user bases tend to skew toward other large generalist subreddits, therefore drowning out relationships with smaller, more topic-specific subreddits such as r/coins (~200,000 subscribers). This is in part the product of the karma system, whereby subreddits with high subscriber counts will have a higher initial number of users interacting with posts and commenting, thus making it more likely that the post is promoted to users not subscribed to the subreddit.

Discussion

In examining these results, we return to the research questions asked at the start of this chapter. Firstly, what content and conversations around material cultural heritage are taking place on Reddit, and where can they be found? As for what, most subreddits, including the most popular ones (e.g., r/artefactporn), remain content aggregators, allowing users to share content sourced from elsewhere. However, there are a smaller number of subreddits such as SR01 and SR02 that are almost exclusively spaces for original content from Reddit users. SR03 was unusual in that it represented a transitional state between a long history of third-party link aggregation and a new wave of users posting original content.

As for the where, all the aforementioned subreddits are examples of those dealing primarily with cultural heritage; however, content and conversations regarding material cultural heritage infrequently appear in other subreddits. Examples of these include r/whatisthisthing, r/whatsthisrock, and r/bonecollecting, where cultural heritage is inadvertently posted by users looking for help identifying what they have found. A notable example took place in early 2024 when a user found what they believed to be a fossilized hominin mandible in a travertine floor tile that is now being examined by a group of researchers ("Found a Mandible in the Travertin Floor at My Parents House" 2024).

Despite the vast number of subreddits, posts, and comments where media and discussions on cultural heritage materials might take place, this study has focused on only one small slice. The reason being that SR01 and SR02 specifically represent the push and pull factors of people acquiring and trading artifacts, both producing and consuming media related to artifacts that are largely acquired by standards not ethically or legally permissible in many parts of the world, including in the US states where much posted activity is alleged to have occurred. Therefore, the users of these subreddits produced context-rich discussions regarding cultural heritage and the often-opaque practice of amateur archaeology. The themes identified in the results were *ethics, advice (not valuation or exchange), excavation, valuation and exchange,* and *motivation*. The discussions surrounding these themes provided valuable insight into how active members of these communities understood their practices, justified them, and propagated them.

The results demonstrated that despite overlapping user groups between these subreddits and others, there were clear variations in the frequency and nature of discussions of certain themes. As noted in the results, the major disparity between SR01 and SR02 regarding ethics discussions pertained to posts with an excavation theme. On SR02, 54 percent of excavation posts generated discussion on ethical practices, compared to only 18 percent on SR01. Given that SR01 had almost twice the number of excavation posts compared to the much longer-running SR02, one likely explanation for this disparity is that SR02 users are much more critical of excavation as an artifact-collection technique by amateur archaeologists.

This would then be expected to produce a disincentive for users to post excavation content. Conversely, SR01 users on average reacted much more positively to excavation posts. SR03 users had a high rate of ethical discussion on original content posts, with thirteen of the fifteen containing some kind of ethics discussion. This likely reflects the relatively new arrival of original content posts to SR03, which throughout most of its history as a subreddit has been a third-party link aggregator, not a place for original content. Therefore, those who have subscribed to SR03 prior to the shift in post content are reacting differently to users on subreddits like SR01 and SR02, which have always been explicitly intended for original content.

The exchange of artifacts was a much more nuanced theme in SR01 and SR02, with moderators of both subreddits cautioning, but not explicitly forbidding, users wishing to engage in the practice. In the case of SR01, artifacts were offered by one moderator as raffle prizes to encourage subscriber growth. The issue for moderators then became not the ethics of artifact trade itself but how it might promote destruction of the archaeological record. They were primarily concerned that users might get scammed based on advice provided on the subreddit and then complain to moderators.

Valuation and authentication advice was regularly sought by users; however, it was clear that many users on both SR01 and SR02 believed artifacts were better collected for personal enjoyment rather than commercial gain. In SR02 this was reflected in the quantitative data that demonstrated close user overlap with a number of collection-oriented subreddits, though not ones specifically related to cultural heritage. This overlap, along with observed active user posting patterns, suggests that many users on SR02 were motivated more by the act of collecting, particularly in situ artifacts, rather than what they were collecting.

Explicit discussion of user motivations was rarer, but in the posts where it was discussed, many users would contribute. The frequency of users discussing the thrill of searching for and eventually finding artifacts further supports the above assertion regarding collecting as an activity being the primary motivation. Secondary to this, and likely an origin for this motivation, was users' recollections of being introduced to it by older family members, suggesting a great deal of sentimentality for the activity. Furthermore, many users seem to maintain it as a social activity with friends and family, with the desire of some users to pass on a similar enthusiasm to their children, along with their collections.

This positivity was generally reflected in *advice* theme posts and comments, with most active users happy to provide various kinds of advice ranging from artifact identification, authentication, valuation, trading, and prospection. When users provided advice, academic literature or institutions were often referred to as useful resources. Expanding on this, users regularly complained that museums and archaeologists seemed uninterested in their collection in response to requests that they report their finds. This misunderstanding comes fundamentally from the belief that all value, both monetary and scientific, resides in the artifact. This view acted to fetishize the artifact, something that appeared structural to the function of subreddits like SR01 and SR02. This fetishization seems to have been what drew many users into the practice; however, the pursuit of it often leaves valuable context lost permanently.

This reliance on academic resources was supplemented with considerable personal experience from certain users but stood in contrast to many of the negative attitudes that were voiced toward archaeologists, academia, and government authorities. Given the strong connection many users felt with the activity, those who questioned the ethics of the practice, including several self-identified archaeologists, prompted strong and negative reactions from users. This begins to relate to the third research question of this study, on how user discussions relate to potential political or ideological associations. Examining the complete posting and comment histories of all active users to see if they were also active in politically or ideologically motivated subreddits was not within the scope of this study.

Consequently, the most reliable information for examining the potential link was with the quantitative data and user comments. User-overlap analysis identified SR02 and SR03 as having substantial relationships to alternative-knowledge and conspiracy subreddits, affirming some of the antiauthority rhetoric exhibited by active users in the respective subreddits. However, similar overlap was observed with r/archaeology, which had more stringent moderation regarding posting of and links to alternative-knowledge media and resources. This highlights an issue with user-overlap data, in that it does not elucidate the nature of the user overlap.

Users might be motivated to post and comment on subreddits that are ideologically opposed to their own views as a means of protest or disruption, or to simply engage with opposing points of view. In r/archaeology, users who argued for methods or interpretations that are in opposition to academic best practice were typically met with downvotes and negative comments. Equally, in SR01 and SR02 users who advocated best practice were in most cases met with downvotes and negative comments.

Despite this apparent link to alternative-knowledge and conspiracy-theory subreddits, SR02 users were not observed to partake in pseudo-archaeological theories. The only repeated topic that might vaguely relate to pseudo-archaeological theory was user objection to artifacts belonging to modern Indigenous communities. These users argued that modern Indigenous communities in the United States were not reflective of those present in the past and therefore did not have the right to custodianship over material culture recovered.

It was unclear if this was in reference to the displacement experienced by various Indigenous groups by colonization or precolonization conflict, or if it was a reference to pseudo-archaeological theories of precursor civilizations. Either way, users in SR01 and SR02 seemed to predominantly support a position that alienated modern Indigenous communities from their material cultural heritage. Conversely, those posting original content on SR03 exhibited far less knowledge of artifacts compared to SR01 and SR02 users and a greater propensity to actively discuss pseudo-archaeological theories.

So, what then is the dominant ideology for subreddits like SR01 and SR02? Fundamentally, justifications for the activities promoted on these subreddits hinged on the right of individuals to act freely and without restriction within a certain context. This context heavily aligned with libertarian viewpoints within American political discourse, particularly the right to freely use and enjoy private property without restriction. This was taken to its extreme by a group of users largely from Texas, which has one of the highest proportions of privately owned land in the United States at 96 percent (Lund and Smith 2021) and very limited protections for cultural heritage on private property unless they relate to human remains. These users engaged in and advocated for the most destructive activities observed on SR01 and SR02.

It was also evident that some users from this group were engaging in the same destructive activities outside of Texas. As discussed previously, these users were not universally applauded, particularly in SR02; however, their justifications were largely mirrored by those conducting surface collection of artifacts. In some cases, users who objected to what they believed were overtly destructive methods relented that private property was ultimately a private decision and that it was not the place of others to intercede. What this sentiment suggests is the prioritization of an ethical framework that emphasizes individual freedoms and property rights at the expense of all other interests and concerns.

It is not clear how influential the views of the subreddit moderators are in constructing, propagating, or enforcing this ideology within the subreddits. However, the high degree of moderator involvement in discussions in SR01 and the general regard in which users hold them suggests that their views are respected. This at the very least seems to attract users with similar views to this subreddit, if not encouraging others to support the same view. They are certainly complicit in spreading misleading information about archaeological best practices.

One moderator argued that surface collection was justified due to the artifacts having already lost their context and therefore any valuable scientific data. While there is an element of truth to this position in that exposed archaeological material may be disturbed from its original context, the degree of disturbance is not uniform, nor are disturbing taphonomic processes exclusive to surface materials, and therefore they are still a value avenue of research (Douglass, Wandsnider, and Holdaway 2023). In promoting this view, users might feel their activities are not destroying valuable data when this might have been discouraging them from engaging in the practice.

Conclusion

The results of this study have shown that there are many active and engaged communities on Reddit promoting original content of amateur archaeology, with varying perspectives on ethical conduct. These groups do not demonstrate close ties to pseudo-archaeological theories and movements; rather, many active users show a great deal of knowledge on how to discern and identify archaeological materials. However, there are clear trends within user conduct that suggest users hold political and ideological views consistent with libertarian discourse in the United States relating to private property and personal freedoms.

At the moment there are only a small minority who utilize Reddit as a platform for buying and selling artifacts on the studied subreddits, though many users do seek and provide advice that could be tangential to or in support of artifact trading. With Reddit making it clear that it wishes to provide greater support and officiality to the so called "User Economy" in its SEC filing in early 2024, referring to "collectors [who] sell beloved items" ("United States Securities and Exchange Commission Form S-1/A Registration Statement Registration No. 333-277256" 2024: 8), there is great potential for this minority to grow. Given the growing popularity of subreddits like SR01 and their greater acceptance of more destructive methods compared to more established subreddits such as SR02, there is clearly a growing user base that condones and promotes destructive practices that in most locations outside the United States would be treated as looting. Despite this, users continue to engage in nuanced discussions around ethics and individual motivations, providing valuable insight into a well-known but poorly understood cohort.

Calum Farrar is a research fellow at Griffith University, Australia, specializing in digital archaeology. His work focuses on developing innovative methods for archaeological documentation, including 3D modeling, spatial analysis, and digital survey techniques for Indigenous Australian cultural heritage. Beyond this, his work also explores new ways of communicating archaeological research to both academic and public audiences, leveraging emerging technologies like virtual reality to make the past more accessible.

REFERENCES

Bianchi, Tiago. 2024. "Regional Distribution of Desktop Traffic to Reddit.com as of December 2023, by Country." Retrieved March 2024 from https://www.statista.com/statistics/325144/reddit-global-active-user-distribution/.

Booth, Peter, Anne Ogundipe, and Sigrid Røyseng. 2020. "Museum Leaders' Perspectives on Social Media." *Museum Management and Curatorship* 35(4): 373–91.

Bruckman, Amy. 2002. "Studying the Amateur Artist: A Perspective on Disguising Data Collected in Human Subjects Research on the Internet." *Ethics and Information Technology* 4: 217–31.

Bruns, Axel. 2019. "It's Not the Technology, Stupid: How the 'Echo Chamber' and 'Filter Bubble' Metaphors Have Failed Us." Proceedings of the IAMCR 2019 Conference 2019, Mediate Communication, Public Opinion and Society Section.

Bruns, Axel. 2024. "Filter Bubble: The Dumbest Metaphor on the Internet?" In *Digital Media Metaphors*, edited by Johan Farkas and Marcus Maloney, 65–77. London: Routledge.

Campbell, Stuart, Liz White, and Suzie Thomas. 2019. *Competing Values in Archaeological Heritage*. Cham: Springer International.

Centivany, Alissa. 2016. "Values, Ethics and Participatory Policymaking in Online Communities." *Proceedings of the Association for Information Science and Technology* 53(1): 1–10.

Cinelli, Matteo, Gianmarco De Francisci Morales, Alessandro Galeazzi, Walter Quattrociocchi, Michele Starnini. 2020. "Echo Chambers on Social Media: A Comparative Analysis." arXiv preprint arXiv:2004.09603.

Cinelli, Matteo, Gianmarco De Francisci Morales, Alessandro Galeazzi, Walter Quattrociocchi, Michele Starnini. 2021. "The Echo Chamber Effect on Social Media." *Proceedings of the National Academy of Sciences* 118(9): e2023301118.

Comunello, Francesca, and Giuseppe Anzera. 2012. "Will the Revolution Be Tweeted? A Conceptual Framework for Understanding the Social Media and the Arab Spring." *Islam and Christian-Muslim Relations* 23(4): 453–70.

Constant, Sarah A. 2013. "The Computer Fraud and Abuse Act: A Prosecutor's Dream and a Hacker's Worst Nightmare—The Case against Aaron Swartz and the Need to Reform the CFAA." *Tulane Journal of Technology and Intellectual Property* 16: 231–48.

Datta, Srayan, and Eytan Adar. 2019. "Extracting Inter-community Conflicts in Reddit." *Proceedings of the International AAAI Conference on Web and Social Media* 13: 146–57.

Dixon, Stacy Jo. 2024. "Number of Global Social Network Users 2017–2028." Retrieved March 2025 from https://www.statista.com/statistics/278414/number-of-worldwide-social-network-users/#:~:text=How percent20many percent20people percent20use percent20social,most percent20popular percent20social percent20media percent20platforms?.

"Does Anyone Remember the Reddit Blackout?" 2024. Reddit.com/r/CasualConversations. Retrieved March 2025 from https://www.reddit.com/r/CasualConversation/comments/1g65xn7/does_anyone_remember_the_reddit_blackout/.

Douglass, Matthew, Dennis Kuhnel, Matthew Magnani, Luke Hittner, Michael Chodoronek, and Samantha Porter. 2017. "Community Outreach, Digital Heritage and Private Collections: A Case Study from the North American Great Plains." *World Archaeology* 49(5): 623–38.

Douglass, Matthew, LuAnn Wandsnider, and Simon J. Holdaway. 2023. "Surface Artifact Scatters, Data Collection, and Significance: Case Studies from Australia and the United States." *Advances in Archaeological Practice* 11(1): 29–41.

Dosono, Bryan, and Bryan Semaan. 2020. "Decolonizing Tactics as Collective Resilience: Identity Work of AAPI Communities on Reddit." *Proceedings of the ACM on Human-Computer Interaction* 4(CSCW1) 1–20.

Fiegerman, Seth. 2014. "Aliens in the Valley: The Complete and Chaotic History of Reddit." Retrieved March 2025 from https://mashable.com/archive/history-of-reddit.

Fiesler, Casey, Michael Zimmer, Nicholas Proferes, Sarah Gilbert, and Naiyan Jones. 2024. "Remember the Human: A Systematic Review of Ethical Considerations in Reddit Research." *Proceedings of the ACM on Human-Computer Interaction* 8(GROUP, Article 5): 1–33.

"Found a Mandible in the Travertin Floor at My Parents House." 2024. Reddit.com/r/fossils. Retrieved May 2024 from https://www.reddit.com/r/fossils/comments/1c4hldl/found_a_mandible_in_the_travertin_floor_at_my/.

Griffen, Melanie, and Tomaro I. Taylor. 2013. "Of Fans, Friends, and Followers: Methods for Assessing Social Media Outreach in Special Collections Repositories." *Journal of Web Librarianship* 7(3): 255–71.

Hartzell, Amy, Beau Jackson, and Jamie Pinchot. 2021. "Source Credibility in Social Media: A Case Study of a Reddit Community." *Issues in Information Systems* 22(3): 230–41.

Hiaeshutter-Rice, Dan, and Ian Hawkins. 2022. "The Language of Extremism on Social Media: An Examination of Posts, Comments, and Themes on Reddit." *Frontiers Political Science* 4.

Hoffa, Felipe. 2015. "1.7 Billion Reddit Comments Loaded on BigQuery." Retrieved April 2024 from https://reddit.com/r/bigquery/comments/3cej2b/17_billion_reddit_comments_loaded_on_bigquery/.

Horne, Benjamin D., Sibel Adah, and Sujoy Sikdar. 2017. "Identifying the Social Signals That Drive Online Discussions: A Case Study of Reddit Communities." *IEEE International Conference of Computer Communications and Networks* arXiv:1705.02673.

Huffman, Steve. 2016. "TIFU By Editing Some Comments and Creating an Unnecessary Controversy." Retrieved March 2024 from https://reddit.com/r/announcements/comments/5frg1n/tifu_by_editing_some_comments_and_creating_an/.

"Image Hosting on Reddit." 2016. Reddit.com/r/announcements. Retrieved March 2025 from https://www.reddit.com/r/announcements/comments/4p5dm9/image_hosting_on_reddit/.

Kashcha, Andrei. 2023. "[OC] An Interactive Map of Reddit Built from 330 Million User Comments. 2023 Update." Retrieved May 2024 from https://www.reddit.com/r/dataisbeautiful/comments/12pem68/oc_an_interactive_map_of_reddit_built_from_330/.

Leeson, Madison. 2024. "Reddit and the Illicit Antiquities Trade: Trends in the Online Trafficking and Authentication of Cultural Heritage." Retrieved April 2024 from https://www.meer.com/en/79881-reddit-and-the-illicit-antiquities-trade.

Lund, Alison, and Addie Smith. 2021. "Featured Map: Land Ownership Types across the U.S." Retrieved May 2024 from https://nri.tamu.edu/blog/2021/september/featured-map-land-ownership-types-across-the-us/.

Martin, Trevor. 2017. "Dissecting Trump's Most Rabid Online Following." Retrieved April 2024 from https://fivethirtyeight.com/features/dissecting-trumps-most-rabid-online-following/.

Mundt, Marcia, Karen Ross, and Charla M. Burnett. 2018. "Scaling Social Movements through Social Media: The Case of Black Lives Matter." *Social Media + Society* 4(4).

Ohanian, Alexis. 2009. "You've Decided: Here Are the 2008 Reddit Award Winners." *blog.reddit*. Retrieved March 2024 from https://redditblog.blogspot.com/2009/01/youve-decided-here-are-2008-reddit.html.

Olson, Randal S., and Zachary P. Neal. 2015. "Navigating the Massive World of Reddit: Using Backbone Networks to Map User Interests in Social Media." *PeerJ Computer Science* 1(e4).

Ortiz-Ospina, Esteban. 2019. "The Rise of Social Media." Retrieved March 2025 from https://ourworldindata.org/rise-of-social-media.

Otero, David, Patricia Martin-Rodilla, and Javier Parapar. 2021. "Building Cultural Heritage Reference Collections from Social Media through Pooling Strategies: The Case of 2020's Tensions over Race and Heritage." *ACM Journal on Computing and Cultural Heritage* 15(1): 1–13.

Partridge, Virginia, Jasmine Mangat, Rebecca Curran, Ryan Mcgrady, and Ethan Zuckerman. 2024. "Here Be Livestreams: Trade-Offs in Creating Temporal Maps of Reddit." *Proceedings of the 16th ACM Web Science Conference*, 81–91.

Peters, Jay. 2023a. "Reddit Pressures Mods to End the Blackout as They Find New Ways to Protest." *The Verge*. Retrieved March 2024 from https://www.theverge.com/2023/6/22/23770480/reddit-blackout-protest-pressure-mods-change-rules.

Peters, Jay. 2023b. "Some Subreddits Are Now Filled with Porn to Protest Reddit: Reddit Communities Are Switching to NSFW to Create Some Friction and Rob Reddit of Ad Revenue." *The Verge*. Retrieved March 2024 from https://www.theverge.com/2023/6/20/23767098/reddit-subreddits-porn-protest.

Pitblado, Bonnie L., Matthew J. Rowe, Bryon Schroeder, Suzie Thomas, and Anna Wessman. 2022. "Professional–Collector Collaboration: Moving beyond Debate to Best Practice." *Advances in Archaeological Practice* 10(1): 3–9.

Proferes, Nicholas, Naiyan Jones, Sarah Gilbert, Casey Fiesler, and Michael Zimmer. 2021. "Studying Reddit: A Systematic Overview of Disciplines, Approaches, Methods, and Ethics." *Social Media + Society* 7(2): 1–14.

Reagle, Joseph. 2022. "Disguising Reddit Sources and the Efficacy of Ethical Research." *Ethics and Information Technology* 24(41): 1–11.

"Reddit.com Overview." 2024. Semrush. Retrieved March 2024 from https://www.semrush.com/website/reddit.com/overview/.

"Reddit Files Registration Statement for Proposed Initial Public Offering." 2024. Redditinc Blog. Retrieved March 2024 from https://www.redditinc.com/blog/reddit-files-registration-statement-for-proposed-initial-public-offering.

"Reddit for iOS Version 39 Now Available." 2017. Reddit.com/r/changelog. Retrieved March 2024 from https://reddit.com/r/changelog/comments/75sbky/reddit_for_ios_version_39_now_available/.

Segesten, Anamaria D., Michael Bossetta, Nils Holmberg, and Diederick Niehorster. 2022. "The Cuing Power of Comments on Social Media: How Disagreement in Facebook Comments Effects User Engagement with News." *Information, Communication & Society* 25(8): 1115–34.

Shepard, Ryan P. 2020. "Gaming Reddit's Algorithm: r/the_donald, Amplication, and the Rhetoric of Sorting." *Computers and Composition* 56(102572).

"Social Media Factsheet." 2024. Pew Research Center. Retrieved March 2024 from https://www.pewresearch.org/internet/fact-sheet/social-media/?tabId=tab-5b319c90-7363-4881-8e6f-f98925683a2f.

"Subreddit Demographic Survey 2019: The Results." 2019. Reddit.com/r/childfree. Retrieved May 2024 from https://www.reddit.com/r/childfree/comments/ehjdcx/subreddit_demographic_survey_2019_the_results/.

Swartz, Aaron. 2008. "Guerilla Open Access Manifesto." *Aaron Swartz [Internet]* 5.

Terren, Ludovic, and Rosa Borge. 2021. "Echo Chambers on Social Media: A Systematic Review of the Literature." *Review of Communication Research* 9.

Trujillo, Amaury, and Stefano Cresci. 2022 "Make Reddit Great Again: Assessing Community Effects of Moderation Interventions on R/the_Donald." *Proceedings of the ACM on Human-Computer Interaction* 6(CSCW2): 1–28.

"United States Securities and Exchange Commission Form S-1/A Registration Statement Registration No. 333-277256." 2024. Reddit SEC Filings. Retrieved April 2024 from https://d18rn0p25nwr6d.cloudfront.net/CIK-0001713445/81f89df1-aed9-4a87-8337-514e33015d0a.pdf.

"What I Learned from Chatting with 7000 Strangers on the Internet." 2018. Reddit.com/r/blog. Retrieved March 2024 from https://reddit.com/r/blog/comments/8zwssb/what_i_learned_from_chatting_with_7000_strangers/.

Winkley, Felicity. 2016. "The Phenomenology of Metal Detecting: Insights from a Unique Type of Landscape Experience." *Papers from the Institute of Archaeology* 25(2): 1–15.

Wright, Dennis L. 2022. "How Archaeologists Can Effectively and Ethically Cultivate Responsible and Responsive Stewards." *Advances in Archaeological Practice* 10(1): 114–21.

Xia, Yan, Haiyi Zhu, Tun Lu, Peng Zhang, and Ning Gu. 2020. "Exploring Antecedents and Consequences of Toxicity in Online Discussions: A Case Study on Reddit." *Proceedings of the ACM on Human-Computer Interaction* 4(108): 1–23.

CHAPTER 3

Who Are the Trafficked Dead?

An Examination into Personhood and Postmortem Narratives in Skull Sales on eBay

Christine L. Halling and Ryan M. Seidemann

Introduction

Recent years have witnessed a proliferation of research surrounding the illicit sales of human remains, both in the online and traditional marketplaces (e.g., Huxley and Finnegan 2004; Seidemann, Stojanowski, and Rich 2009; Halling and Seidemann 2016; Huffer, Wood, and Graham 2019; Graham, Huffer, and Blackadar 2020; Graham et al. 2020; Graham and Huffer 2020; Graham, Huffer, and Simons 2022; Breda 2023; Graham, Davidson, and Huffer 2024). This burgeoning area of research spans inquiries in bioarchaeology, biohistory, and osteobiography (Seidemann, Stojanowski, and Rich 2009; Seidemann 2016); the wheres, whats, and whys of selling activity (Huxley and Finnegan 2004; Halling and Seidemann 2016; Breda 2023); and practices such as online image scraping used to monitor the sales of such remains, which researchers such as Huffer and Graham have been pioneering (e.g., Huffer, Wood, and Graham 2019).

What is absent from most of these studies are the "whos." The majority of these sources examine volumetrics of materials that are exchanged and both the means of subverting checks on such sales and the reasons behind the sales. However, what is missing from these studies and what is becoming increasingly important in the event of such remains-trading scandals as that found at Harvard Medical School in 2023 are identities of and agency for those whose remains are being trafficked. In the Harvard situation, a network of people were siphoning wet and dry human remains specimens from Harvard Medical School's body donation program into an anonymized illicit trade in human body parts (Levenson 2023). This scandal, along with other such scandals from funeral homes and others diverting body parts into the illicit trade or donation market (Seidemann 2013), increases the need for the ability to unanonymize these individuals in an effort to return them to family members, restore their dignity, and get them to places of proper disposition.

In this research we have attempted to apply basic bioarchaeological and forensic analyses to a set of human skulls offered for sale on the online eBay marketplace. With two exceptions during this four-year data-collection period encompassing the entirety of 2019 through 2023, these analyses are undertaken on photographic sources alone. The two exceptions were skulls seized pursuant to Louisiana law on which the authors could conduct osteological (rather than photographic) analysis. The primary purpose of this inquiry is to determine whether some amount of identity, and thus agency, can be associated with these anonymized remains. Secondarily, we undertook this research in an attempt to identify, if possible, whether certain peoples are overrepresented in this illicit trade. This latter goal is intended to both inform possible trends in sources of such trafficked material and to provide guidance to lawmakers and law enforcement in identifying areas of focus for potentially at-risk groups for the illicit remains trade or for grave desecration associated with the procurement of such remains.

The Theoretical Context

In 2008 Komar and Buikstra introduced the term *biohistory*. Biohistory has been characterized as "an approach that uses scientific methods applied to materials of biological origin in the analysis of 'historical personages'" (Stojanowski and Duncan 2016: 2–3). In 2016 Stojanowski and Duncan expanded this new term into a practical and theoretical anthropological area of inquiry. This subfield of biological anthropology examines the intersection of bioarchaeological and forensic analyses with a contextual examination of archival evidence and the history of a suspected time and place by searching for a narrative behind otherwise anonymized human skeletal remains. Admittedly, this study blurs the lines between Stojanowski and Duncan's (2016) notion of biohistory as a verification or a disproving of a set of skeletal remains' association with "celebrity dead" (e.g., Richard III and Ötzi) and the osteobiography pioneered by Saul and Saul (1989) in the Maya area in which the latter researchers attempted to create biographic profiles of the anonymous dead from analyzed skeletal remains (see also Seidemann 1999 for another example of this approach in the Maya area).

This study begins with fully anonymous dead, as it does not examine any single "celebrity dead." A few of the sellers make claims regarding aspects of origin or identity of the person being sold, although there is no evidence of the legitimacy of their claims. Therefore, we examine partially anonymous dead, a few of which have gained some manner of celebrity through being featured on television (e.g., several data points in this study were derived from skulls featured on the Netflix series *Dark Tourist*).

Within this rather varied theoretical context, we ask (and attempt to answer) the question of "Who are the commodified dead?" Moreover, combining context from law enforcement perspectives (e.g., Seidemann and Hawkins 2019; Seidemann 2016), we endeavor to answer the further question of "Can already commodified remains tell us anything useful for stemming the illicit trade in these remains in a prospective sense?" The key to answering the latter question lies in the answer to the former question: are the commodified remains, when identified to the extent possible with the available evidence, indicative of theft, looting, or other acquisition trends that might inform future law enforcement personnel regarding where to focus efforts to stem the illicit trade in such materials?

In attempting to answer the above-posed questions, we search for trends in what skulls are being sold—anatomical/archaeological (or medicolegal), male/female, age, and ancestry—in an effort to: (1) determine whether certain demographics occupy the field of illicit skull sales (e.g., Native American, Asian, African American, or others), and (2) attempt to humanize these individuals whose remains are being illicitly traded on this platform.

The latter goal is a variation on the efforts of Stojanowski and Duncan (2016) to identify the individual known as "the Fort King George skull," a calvarium suspected to be (but later determined not to be) a martyred Catholic missionary from sixteenth-century Georgia. Though unsuccessful in finding their quarry, Stojanowski and Duncan (2016) developed an area of scientific inquiry focused not just on the basic biological analysis of a particular set of remains but on attempts to tell a life story of an actual individual. Surely such studies (e.g., Kennewick Man, various Egyptian pharaohs, Ötzi, and others) had periodically occurred prior to Stojanowski and Duncan's (2016) volume (Owsley and Jantz 2014; Aufderheide 2003; Boutin 2012; Capasso 1998), but Stojanowski and Duncan (2016) were the first to attempt a theoretical approach to such analyses. This study attempts to put some of these theories into practice.

Methodology

Indeed, further blurring the lines between fields of study, as Stojanowski and Duncan (2016) note as a common attribute of biohistory, the analytical methods employed here draw heavily on forensic approaches to identifying (or not) individual sets of remains. The methodology for this inquiry is fairly simple and, admittedly, less scientifically rigorous than osteological analysis would be in a laboratory setting. For every human skull offered for sale on eBay during the study period, as much data as possible were gathered from the online listings. For this study, the term *skull* refers to human crania with or without associated calvaria or mandibles.

This information (the total viable dataset is 260 distinct skulls) included description of any demographic data or information regarding the origin of the remains as well as downloading all available photographs of the offered remains.

During the eBay survey period that resulted in this analysis, 260 distinct real human skulls were offered for sale or auction on that online platform. Replicas and fakes were excluded from this dataset easily by closely examining each photograph to identify features that do not replicate well (e.g., foramina, nasal features, etc.). Several offerings of postcranial material were also observed during the data-collection period. These postcranial elements also are not included in this dataset.

When, in 2016, we reported on eBay sales and auction offerings over a seven-month period in 2012 and 2013, we did not capture the numbers of consummated sales versus the numbers of offerings caught by eBay's internal monitoring and canceled before the consummation of sales. For the 260 offered skulls in this dataset, these data were captured. We were able to capture sale cancellation or consummation for 154 out of the 260 skulls in the total dataset (the actual original dataset comprised 396 different listings, but removing fakes and relists reduced that number to 260). It cannot be underscored strongly enough that, in general, eBay's internal monitoring caught and canceled 82 (31.5 percent) of these total 260 skull offerings. The data reflect that, during the survey period, 92 (35.4 percent) of the offered skulls reached sale consummation. The disposition of the remaining 106 (33.1 percent) skull offerings is unknown due to a lack of collectable data.

We are not naïve enough to believe that these cancellations resulted in the end of the commodification of the offered remains. Indeed, our own data revealed that some of the skulls were observed offered again as "replicas," presumably in the hopes of evading cancellation a second time. Moreover, as Breda (2023) has observed, simple intentional misspellings and emojis are often used to evade system checks for illicit sales. Further, as Breda (2023) and Graham, Davidson, and Huffer (2024) have noted, other less visible platforms (e.g., closed Facebook groups and other limited-access corners of the internet) are often a landing place for such illicit sales if the leading services (e.g., eBay) cancel the offerings.

Therefore, while many offerings of illicit remains are made on eBay, many of those items are caught and canceled by that company's internal monitoring. Whether this internal review policy resulted from the media attention following our 2016 publication (e.g., Hugo 2016) is possible but not definitive. With that said, there also exists the risk that such publications and internal system checks and cancellations result in pushing the human remains trade from a visible market like eBay to harder-to monitor platforms. However, the alternative being the unregulated trade in human remains and the potential for capturing some rather than none of those remains, in our estimation, is a lesser evil that outweighs any possible push of illicit sales to the black market.

In terms of actual data collection, we are reliant entirely on the imagery posted by sellers to eBay's platform. We selected eBay as the analyzed platform for this study because it largely won the early 2000s competition for market domination in online auctions (especially in the United States), pushing others operated by Yahoo! and Amazon out of the market (Reynolds and Wooders 2009; Brown and Morgan 2009). As a practical matter, the quality and number of these seller-provided images have greatly improved over the years, allowing us to benefit from multiple high-quality views of most remains offered for sale. Admittedly, the images were seldom taken with an eye toward scientific analysis and publication, so complete demographic data are present for some skulls and are incomplete or nonexistent for others. Because of this, though the total number of skulls reviewed for this research is 260, each of the individual datasets (i.e., biological sex, age, and ancestry) vary in size based upon available imagery as set forth in table 3.1.

To collect all our data points, we kept a running spreadsheet of all listed sale and auction offerings, capturing information on the seller, price, location, and item description, as well as any images posted. To determine which features and how all the data were to be collected, we reviewed major, well-accepted methodologies that are bioarchaeological and forensic standards for the observation of sex, age, and ancestry of the skull (Bass 1995; Buikstra and Ubelaker 1994; Schwartz 2006; Hefner 2009, 2018; Hefner and Ousley 2014). From these methodologies, we selected as many nonmetric methods as possible that could be readily applied to the available photographs and that could contribute meaningfully in some way to our understanding of who these people were whose remains were being trafficked.

These data allowed us, to the extent possible, to extract knowable information from the skulls. In this regard, each set of available imagery was assessed for sex

Table 3.1. Summary of the dataset. © Christine L. Halling and Ryan M. Seidemann

Complete Data	
Category of data	**Number of data points**
Total skulls	260
Total skulls with sex data	223
Total skulls with age data	176
Total skulls with ancestry data	204
Total skulls with age, sex, and ancestry data	142
Incomplete Data	
Total skulls with sex data only	1
Total skulls with age data only	6
Total skulls with ancestry data only	8
Total skulls for which complete biological profile could not be created	118

from cranial features, age via cranial suture closure, and ancestry from cranial features. Basic cranial features that are indicators of biological sex (see table 3.2) were also analyzed. The features are standard for nonmetric analyses and are scored according to each method's guidelines either by a ranking from 1 to 5 or (where applicable) absent or present (Buikstra and Ubelaker 1994; Bass 1995).

Cranial suture closure (vault and lateral) was recorded to estimate the subject's age. As this dataset is limited to photographs of cranial features only, assessment of cranial sutures is the only reliable methodology from which to derive age estimates (Buikstra and Ubelaker 1994). Although there are cranial suture methodologies that incorporate discriminant functions to provide more precise age estimates (Nawrocki 1998), we were not as confident in their application to these photographically derived data, and, accordingly, they were not employed.

Proving most difficult to obtain, information regarding possible ancestry was extracted from the photos (see table 3.2). In order to quickly use these features for assessment of ancestry, the scores were run through the recently released Macromorphoscopic Databank (MaMD) (Heffner 2018). The ancestry data were collected and analyzed using the Optimized Summed Scored Attributes (OSSA) method and the MaMD standards (Hefner 2009; 2018), in which a smaller set of features are observed (with guidelines both written and visual) and captured, however not every value could be captured. Similarly, because the mandible can

Table 3.2. Skeletal features examined to estimate sex and ancestry. © Christine L. Halling and Ryan M. Seidemann.

Features for Sex Analysis	Features for Ancestry Analysis
External Occipital Protuberance (EOP)	Ossicle Bone Presence
Mastoid Process (MDP)	Anterior Nasal Spine (ANS)
Supra Orbital Ridge (SOR)	Inferior Nasal Aperture (INA)
Supra Orbital Margin (SOM)	Interorbital Breadth (IOB)
Mental Eminence (MTE)	Nasal Aperture Width (NAW)
Orbital Size (OTS)	Nasal Bone Contour (NBC)
Zygomatic Ridge (ZGR)	Malar Tubercle (MAT)
Gonial Angle (GOA)	Supranasal Suture (SNS)
	Transverse Palatine Suture (TPS)
	Zygomatic Suture Shape (ZSS)
	Chin Shape (CHS)
	Lower Mandibular Border (LMB)
	Ascending Ramus Shape (ARS)
	Gonial Angle Flare (GAF)

be observed nonmetrically for ancestry, those data were collected where possible; however, there were few mandibles that could be assessed with enough data points to run through any of the discriminant functions (Berg 2015).

We never expected to, and, indeed, could not, positively identify any of the remains in the dataset with a particular individual. However, as indicated by Seidemann (2016), such remains can take on postmortem narratives of their own, thus both creating a biological profile as well as telling a story about what happened to this person after their death. Moreover, as demonstrated below, some of this information can also be used to create basic biological profiles to provide agency in anonymity and death by informing descendant communities of the trafficking of their people.

Any pathological conditions that were observable from the photographs were scored as present or absent. During postprocessing, if data were not present, this indicator helped researchers to understand that data may be missing without requiring them to go back to the imagery. Although not collected to make diagnoses, visible pathology would be a signifier that there may be features obscured, potentially resulting in a lack of analysis of that skull. No further details regarding pathology were collected.

Similarly, indicators of taphonomic changes were collected as present or absent. Again, these data were collected merely to aid in the postprocessing of data where discrepancies in the observations occurred or where missing observations existed. If taphonomic changes to the bone obscured certain demographic features, then those features were skipped in the analysis (and consequently reduced the number of data points for that variable).

To further inform lawmakers and law enforcement, we also collected data regarding the original location of each sale. Such data are not purported to be the location of origin for the remains themselves. Rather, they are merely the locations of the seller. Most of the sale offerings captured during this data collection period originated from the United States (n=196 or 74.4 percent). Of the remaining 36 skulls with known offering origins, nine countries represented the country of origin (table 3.3). Furthermore, a state-by-state breakdown of the United States origins are presented in table 3.4.

Table 3.3. Skull sale offerings by nation of origin. © Christine L. Halling and Ryan M. Seidemann

Country	Number of Skulls
United States	196
Hungary	20
France	4
Germany	3
United Kingdom	3
Spain	2
Portugal	1
Russia	1
Nepal	1
Australia	1
Total of known origins	232

Table 3.4. United States skull sale offerings by state of origin. © Christine L. Halling and Ryan M. Seidemann

U.S. State	Number of Skulls	U.S. State	Number of Skulls
Alabama	0	Nebraska	0
Alaska	0	Nevada	1
Arizona	3	New Hampshire	1
Arkansas	0	New Jersey	10
California	33	New Mexico	3
Colorado	4	New York	11
Connecticut	5	North Carolina	8
Delaware	0	North Dakota	0
Florida	8	Ohio	6
Georgia	2	Oklahoma	1
Hawaii	0	Oregon	3
Idaho	1	Pennsylvania	14
Illinois	6	Rhode Island	0
Indiana	0	South Carolina	6
Iowa	2	South Dakota	0
Kansas	0	Tennessee	4
Kentucky	2	Texas	7
Louisiana	2	Utah	0
Maine	0	Vermont	0
Maryland	1	Virginia	3
Massachusetts	2	Washington	29
Michigan	7	West Virginia	0
Minnesota	4	Wisconsin	4
Mississippi	0	Wyoming	0
Missouri	3	Total known	196
Montana	0		

Based solely upon location of sale-offering origin, these data suggest that law enforcement in California, Washington, and Pennsylvania (among them representing 38.8 percent of all known US state sale-offering origins) should be monitoring eBay and other sales platforms for illicit remains sales. Further, the lawmakers in these jurisdictions should also make efforts to tighten laws prohibiting such activity.

One of the (occasional) data points able to be collected in this research is the seller's claims regarding "who" is being sold. These data are "occasional" because the sellers seldom provided any such claims. Only a few vague references to biological sex (n=10), age (n=3), or ancestry (n=8) existed in the total dataset of 260 (a mere 8.1 percent of the total). Due to this small number, these data were not susceptible to any meaningful analysis or comparison to our own analytical results. Moreover, one recent case worked by the Louisiana Department of Justice alleging that the offered remains were from people who had died violently highlights the often salacious nature of such seller claims that, when not borne out by direct bioarchaeological and forensic analyses (the skull's alleged injuries were simple taphonomic changes to the bone), are apparently simply akin to snake oil claims of nineteenth-century pharmaceutical sellers seeking to enhance the salability of the offering.

Twice during the collection of this dataset skulls were offered for sale that fell within the seizure jurisdiction of the authors (i.e., Louisiana). In cooperation with the Louisiana Bureau of Investigation, skulls were seized prior to consummation of any sale, allowing for actual analysis of remains that otherwise were only visible through online photographs. In this case, the remains were removed from the stream of commerce and will be able to find ultimate disposition. Moreover, these skulls allow for minimal comparison of the analytical methods described above to direct bone analysis.

For comparison to the dataset, these cases were analyzed using only the same methods that allowed for observation of the photographs. The first skull, based upon direct bone analysis, appears to be a possible male, young adult (twenty to forty years old), likely of European or possibly Native American ancestry. After the scores were run on OSSA, the results came back inconclusive, split between Native American (45 percent chance) and European (43 percent chance); however the MaMD analysis results in European ancestry at 65 percent posterior probability. This compares to the photographic analysis as a similar demographic profile. The photographic analysis identified this individual to be a possible male, in their mid-thirties, but of Native American descent.

Regarding the age differences, the direct bone analysis results were broad, but the mandibular third molars were visible in their crypts (a fact not viewable in the photographs for this skull) and partially developed/erupting, which can be indicative of either a younger age or a late eruption. In addition, there were no erupted mandibular third molars in the maxillary dentition; however, there is some antemortem tooth loss, thus the in-person analysis could not fully support the photographic age analysis. This distinction highlights the need for accurate analysis as it helps to determine appropriate collection and disposition under the relevant legal authority (i.e., Native American Graves Protection and Repatriation Act—NAGPRA—or state law). All of this information, taken together, roughly supports the utility of the photographic analytics used in this study, even though nothing substitutes for direct bone analysis.

The second skull, based on direct bone analysis, is a probable female middle-aged adult (thirty-five to fifty years old), of European or Southwestern US Hispanic ancestry. The MaMD analysis places the probability of either ancestry categorization very closely with the posterior probabilities for European and Southwestern US Hispanic ancestry at 44.2 percent and 41.3 percent respectively. This compares closely to the photographic assessment, which returned an indeterminate sex, an age range in the upper forties, and an individual of European descent. The scores for sex actually aligned very similarly. However, many sex scores could be scored as either/or (e.g., scores were a 1 or 2, or a 2 or 3, which leads to ambiguity). A direct bone viewing of the skull provided additional clarity that it likely belongs to a female but was not strongly associated with a female. The age comparisons are directly consistent with each other. The ancestry assessment was more consistent with the OSSA score that classified the skull as European at 95.51 percent likelihood. However, that result does not negate the possibility of Southwestern US Hispanic heritage. This ancestry possibility is nearly as likely, according to this analysis, that the individual may have identified as other than European in life.

Results

Although the study methodology was designed with the intention of capturing all the demographic information for each individual listing offered for sale on eBay, it is impossible for a study to not be limited using summary data. Because of the nature of the data collection for this study, we were limited by the angles and clarity of the photographs that the sellers decided to post. As a result, there are often varying numbers of individuals analyzable for a particular demographic variable. As noted earlier (see table 3.1), 260 skulls were offered for sale during the study period. However, of those 260, some of the associated photographs were not usable for every (and sometimes any) type of analysis. Specifically, based upon angles and clarity, it was only possible to analyze 176 (67.7 percent) for age, 223 (85.5 percent) for biological sex, and 204 (78.5 percent) for ancestry. Indeed, seldom could a complete picture of a decedent be generated based upon the actual data. When all of these variables were collected, a basic biological profile (discussed below) was generated.

One variable that was nearly universally analyzable (n=233 or 89.6 percent) was the original context of the remains. Based on a modified version of the origin context of eBay-sold skulls generated by Huxley and Finnegan (2004) (see Halling and Seidemann 2016), it is possible to state with reasonable certainty, based on the available imagery, that 146 (56.2 percent percent) of the skulls derived from educational (i.e., prepared specimen) contexts, 85 (32.7 percent) from archaeological/desecration contexts, and 2 (0.01 percent) from medicolegal contexts. By and large, the majority of the skulls offered for sale during the study period originated as teaching material, suggesting that colleges, universities, and even some secondary schools need more stringent controls on the decommissioning or deaccessioning of teaching collections to avoid these remains—which were often collected under dubious circumstances in the first instance (e.g., Carney 2011; Agarwal 2024)—from becoming commodified curiosities.

Biological sex was able to be estimated on 85.8 percent (n=223) of the skulls in this sample. Of those estimates, 30 individuals (13.5 percent) exhibited strongly male features, and 10 individuals (4.5 percent) exhibited strongly female features. Individuals whose biological sex was more difficult to determine included 85 individuals (38.1 percent) who were probable males and 47 individuals (21.1 percent) who were probable females. Finally, a total of 51 adult individuals (22.9 percent) were of indeterminate biological sex based upon the analysis of their photographs.

Age was analyzable for 67.7 percent of the sample (n=176). Again, because cranial suture closure was used to calculate average ages at death, the missing 32.3 percent of the ageable skulls in the data sample simply did not present clear enough imagery or imagery from the correct angle from which to be able to undertake these analyses. Not surprisingly, the average age of these 176 individuals was middle-aged ($\bar{x}$=43.73; sd=5.56).

Ancestry was able to be estimated for 78.5 percent (n=204) of the skulls in this sample. Of those, 22 were estimated to be Native American (9.3 percent), 146 European American (71.6 percent), 32 American Asian (15.7 percent), and 7 African American (3.4 percent) (these scores are based on the MaMD results).

For those individuals whose full biological profile was able to be generated from this sample's data, that information is contained in Appendix 1. These individuals' information is included in this chapter because, at least for the time of their online listing and analysis, they were able to be fleetingly identified "somebodies." In this regard, as discussed more fully below, each of these people represents a success of this analytical experiment because, for a time, they had an identity, and because of that identity they have been provided with some amount of agency in these pages and for any readers. For a narrative summary of the data obtained for individuals for which age, sex, and ancestry was available, also see Appendix 1.

In many ways, a casual perusal of the appendix reads much like historic rosters of slaves for sale. We are not comparing the trafficking of human remains to the sale of living humans. Nonetheless, the appendix was intentionally humanized to highlight the reality that these *were* people whose mortal remains are now subject to postmortem enchainment through commodification.

Discussion and Conclusion

What is curiously absent from this dataset are remains whose sale origins are in the areas most known to be the source of trafficked remains: China and India (Carney

2011). This outcome is not a result of the sale platform (i.e., eBay) being based in the United States, as a similar dataset on the sale of human kapalas was running in parallel with this collection, with most of those items being sold from China, Nepal, and India (Wellons, Seidemann, and Halling 2024).

Another curious aspect of this dataset is that groups often considered at risk for structurally violent treatment during life (i.e., women and minorities), though represented in the sample, are represented at levels substantially below those who would represent people in an unprotected class (i.e., white males). This outcome was unexpected. By and large, at least as it relates to eBay, most of the trafficked human remains appear to be of domestic (US) origin and appear to be white males. Although we recognize that there is a preferential bias in anthropology to identify skulls more likely to be male, this result was unexpected as it was assumed that the images would likely diminish the appearance of features.

Interestingly, based upon the age analysis of this sample, it appears that illicitly trafficked human skulls also conform to the inverted life table representation, often referred to as the osteological paradox (Wood et al. 1992), that vexes osteologists. The reason for this similarity can only be speculated about. However, subadult remains are often more difficult to obtain in the human remains trade (there are only five in this sample, or 0.02 percent), so their absence is not unusual. It is possible that the absence of older adults is a function of the roughly 2:1 ratio of teaching specimens versus archaeological specimens that were offered for sale. In the former category, it would be expected that, because of their often virtually complete dentition and absence of age-related pathologies, younger to middle-aged adults would be preferred as teaching material. With the predominance of teaching material in this sample, it is unsurprising that the older adults that may be present in the archaeological specimens are smoothed out by the law of averages (i.e., not necessarily for the same reason as their absence under the osteological paradox).

A simple chi-square test was run to analyze whether the difference in ancestry counts was statistically significant, with the null hypothesis being that the count differences are not significantly different from an even distribution of the four populations across the dataset. This null hypothesis was rejected, finding that there are significantly different distributions of the ancestry data from an expected even distribution ($x^2=234,990$; df=3; $p<0.0001$). This result is unsurprising given the large number of individuals of European ancestry identified in this sample. However, it is surprising when considering that, generally, it is expected that those people who are most susceptible to their remains being commodified or their graves being desecrated trends toward favoring minorities. Such was not the case in this dataset. Again, we acknowledge that there is a distinct bias in anthropological analyses that identifies features as "European" more frequently than other ancestries.

In this regard, because of the absence of direct-bone analyses, it was not possible to mitigate this possible bias. Accordingly, though minority groups should be consulted on the capture of such trafficked remains, their involvement based on this dataset seems less necessary than was originally expected. One possibility suggested by this result in terms of enforcement is that all US jurisdictions need to tighten their statutes and enforcement of human remains trafficking to resemble those in Louisiana. Louisiana has passed explicit and strict laws regarding remains trafficking in recent years (e.g., La. R.S. 8:663; La. R.S. 25:951 et seq.) in order to both attempt to control the market and to eliminate any ambiguity regarding the legality of such activity. Moreover, for these suggestions to matter, law-enforcement must take an interest in human remains trafficking and actively monitor online activity, not just on the eBay platform but beyond. Based on this research, it appears that all sectors of US society are the subject of human remains trafficking.

The idea that this research fits squarely within the biohistory milieu is a bit of a misnomer, but one that is intentionally implemented here. As Stojanowski and Duncan (2016) expound on the potential risks and benefits (but mostly the risks) of unintentional biohistorical analyses revealing of family medical, paternity, or genetic secrets intended to be "taken to the grave," it is precisely these idiosyncrasies that can help to deanonymize and thereby stem the commodification of human remains. Indeed, if an isolated skull or a grouping of trafficked remains can be linked to a descendant group or individual with archived personal records or an identifiable obituary through such analyses, agency is restored for both the dead and their living relatives or descendants. The trafficked dead obtain a partial identity connecting them to some living individuals who are lineally qualified to speak for their rights and protections.

This contextual analysis and the identification of appropriate descendant groups (thus allowing a narrower NAGPRA or NAGPRA-like consultation process to proceed) could not exist outside of a biohistorical context. Moreover, we contend here that successful results in identifying descendant communities or individuals outweigh the potential privacy pitfalls identified by other scholars (e.g., Muramoto 2014; Masterton 2010). Indeed, properly protecting against individualized data privacy breaches and collaborating with Indigenous and other descendant groups to respect sovereignty concerns and to provide for data sharing satisfy most, if not all, the analysis and identification concerns of such interested peoples.

The alternative is that a robust illicit trade in human remains continues to exist, further commodifying those people who most certainly did not intend or consent to becoming curios. Furthermore, we adamantly reject the suggestion by some that modern privacy laws such as the Health Insurance Portability and Accountability Act (HIPAA) applies to or controls interactions with remains such as those analyzed here. While well-intentioned, the application of these inapplicable privacy provisions to those who are otherwise dead and being treated as curios is counterproductive to even the most basic identification and assignment of agency for repatriation to descendant communities.

Ultimately, our analyses of these eBay skulls were only partly able to bridge the gap between analyzing "a skull" and analyzing "the skull" as discussed by Stojanowski and Duncan (2016: 7). In other words, and somewhat unsurprisingly, we were unable to positively identify any of the remains offered for sale on eBay as any one individual person with a clear historical narrative as is often the goal of biohistorical analyses. However, through the application of bioarchaeological and forensic analyses, we were able to generate some individual biological profiles and provide some semblance of personhood to those curios. Moreover, we were also able to generate some aggregate biological profiles of the mass of skulls offered for sale on eBay during the research period. While this outcome does not necessarily or completely conform to the traditional outcome hoped for in biohistorical studies, it does inform a postmortem narrative that can be attributed to the remains, thereby creating and constituting a narrative of the people (individually for some and aggregately for others) of whom these remains once were in a prospective sense (see Seidemann 2016).

In many ways, these postmortem narratives are going to provide the most amount of information for these actively commodified human remains. Unfortunately, unlike many of the individuals discussed in other biohistorical sources (e.g., Richard III, Ötzi), the narratives associated with these eBay analyses here are, by their nature, ephemeral. These people's remains do not (except those removed from the stream of commerce by law enforcement) remain associated with their postmortem narratives generated here. Instead, they disappear into the re-anonymized masses of trafficked human remains that are unlikely to ever find any permanent home where they can reunite with their postmortem (much less premortem) narratives or living descendants or relatives.

In addition, though we were only occasionally able to ascribe but the merest notion of personhood to the studied remains, we are hopeful that this work will join the increasing canon of literature regarding the enchainment of remains (Duncan and Stojanowski 2016)—that is, we hope that the information here, though not identifying a single Jane or John Doe to whom these remains can be attributed (whether famous or not), catches attention, adds some humanity to the human remains trade, thus reminding scholars and the public, as Huffer and Graham's (2023) recent book title asserts: "these were people once." This minimal attribution to otherwise anonymized skeletal remains, it is hoped, will give would-be sellers and buyers pause and attract the attention of lawmakers and law enforcers to the human side of the human remains trade. These were people (and, arguably, still are). They deserve some level of dignity beyond merely being curios, even if that dignity is to help advance research into human identifications and understanding of pathologies, diseases, and the lives of past peoples (even the education of modern physicians and other medical professionals is more respectful than simple commodification). Such realities generally align with various cultural desires (e.g., Dias 2015) and laws (Halling and Seidemann 2016).

Instead of merely serving as macabre curiosities, as is often the case with many illicit sales, this analysis grants the deceased a measure of agency by enabling them to assert aspects of their identity, albeit fleetingly, through an ephemeral online auction. To some extent, this agency can inform modern law enforcement regarding where to look for the most at-risk human remains in the illicit market—based upon these data, among white male teaching specimens. And to be sure, though some scholars (e.g., Marsh as discussed in Schulman-Hall 2023) and many sellers mistakenly believe that human remains sales are broadly legitimate, that legal fallacy has been roundly rejected by Halling and Seidemann (2016). Simply, human remains cannot (lawfully) be owned, and they cannot (lawfully) be sold or otherwise commodified. By analyzing these illicit offerings, some guidelines for enforcement of these ownership and sale prohibitions can be provided to interested law enforcement. In this way, with some amount of identity, these trafficked remains can veritably speak to law enforcement from beyond the grave.

Christine L. Halling, MS, is an archaeologist with Providence Engineering in Baton Rouge, LA. Christine is a registered professional archaeologist (RPA), and previous employment included being the sole anthropologist for the Louisiana Department of Justice as well as teaching anatomy and physiology coursework and serving as the lab director for the Kampsville Human Osteology and Bioarchaeology Field School. Christine's research primarily focuses on pathological conditions, human remains trafficking, and improving disaster response in cemeteries.

Ryan M. Seidemann holds a BA and an MA in anthropology from Florida State University and Louisiana State University, respectively. He holds a PhD in urban anthropology/urban studies from the University of New Orleans and a JD and a BCL from Louisiana State University's Law Center. Dr. Seidemann is the former chief of the Lands & Natural Resources Section of the Louisiana Department of Justice and the former chairman of the Louisiana Cemetery Response Task Force. Now employed as The Water Institute's general counsel, he is also an adjunct professor in University of New Orleans' Departments of Anthropology and Sociology and Planning and Urban Studies, Arizona State University's School of Human Evolution and Social Change, and Southern University's Law Center.

REFERENCES

Agarwal, Sabrina C. 2024. "The Bioethics of Skeletal Anatomy Collections from India." *Nature Communications* 15(1): 1692.

Aufderheide, Arthur C. 2003. *The Scientific Study of Mummies*. Cambridge: Cambridge University Press.

Bass, William M. 1995. *Human Osteology: A Laboratory and Field Manual*. 5th ed. Springfield: Missouri Archaeological Society.

Berg, Gregory E. 2015."Biological Affinity and Sex from the Mandible Utilizing Multiple World Populations." In *Biological Affinity in Forensic Identification of Human Skeletal Remains*, edited by Gregory E. Berg and Sabrina C. Ta'ala, 43–82. Boca Raton, FL: CRC Press.

Boutin, Alexis T. "Written in Stone, Written in Bone: The Osteobiography of a Bronze Age Craftsman from Alalakh." In *The Bioarchaeology of Individuals*, edited by A. L.W. Stodder and A. M. Palkovich, 193–214. Gainesville, FL: University Press of Florida.

Breda, Evelyn. 2023."Bone Collectors: Personhood and Appeal in the Sale and Trade of Human Skeletal Remains on Facebook." Master's thesis, Florida Atlantic University, Boca Raton.

Brown, Jennifer, and John Morgan. 2009."How Much Is a Dollar Worth? Tipping versus Equilibrium Coexistence on Competing Online Auction Sites." *Journal of Political Economy* 117(4): 668–700.

Buikstra, Jane E., and Douglas H. Ubelaker. 1994. *Standards for Data Collection from Human Skeletal Remains: Proceedings of a Seminar at the Field Museum of Natural History*. Fayetteville: Arkansas Archaeological Survey.

Capasso, Luigi. 1998."5300 years ago, the Ice Man used natural laxatives and antibiotics." *Lancet* 352(9143): 1864.

Carney, Scott. 2011. *The Red Market: On the Trail of the World's Organ Brokers, Bone Thieves, Blood Farmers, and Child Traffickers*. New York: William Morrow.

Dias, M. 2015."Dignity after Death and Protecting the Sanctity of Human Remains." *Voices in Bioethics* 1. https://doi.org/10.7916/vib.v1i.6636.

Duncan, William N., and Christopher M. Stojanowski. 2016."Theoretical Facets of Biohistorical Research." In *Studies in Forensic Biohistory: Anthropological Perspectives*, edited by C. M. Stojanowski and W. N. Duncan, 315–27. Cambridge: Cambridge University Press.

Graham, Shawn, Katherine Davidson, Damien Huffer. 2024. "Behind Closed Doors: The Human Remains Trade within Private Facebook Groups. *Internet Archaeology* 67. doi: 10.11141/ia.67.14.

Graham, Shawn, Damien Huffer, and Jeff Blackadar. 2020. "Towards a Digital Sensorial Archaeology as an Experiment in Distant Viewing of the Trade in Human Remains on Instagram." *Heritage* 3(2): 208–27. doi: 10.3390/heritage3020013.

Graham, Shawn, Alex Lane, Damien Huffer, and Andreas Angourakis. 2020. "Towards a Method for Discerning Sources of Supply within the Human Remains Trade via Patterns of Visual Dissimilarity and Computer Vision." *Journal of Computer Applications in Archaeology* 3(1): 253–68. doi: 10.5334/jcaa.59.

Graham, Shawn, and Damien Huffer. 2020. "Reproducibility, Replicability, and Revisiting the Insta-Dead and the Human Remains Trade." *Obradoiro de Historia Moderna* 55. doi: 10.11141/ia.55.11.

Graham, Shawn, Damien Huffer, and Jamie Simons. 2022. "When TikTok Discovered the Human Remains Trade: A Case Study." *Open Archaeology* 8(1): 196–219. doi: 10.1515/opar-2022-0235.

Halling, Christine L., and Ryan M. Seidemann. 2016."They Sell Skulls Online?! A Review of Internet Sales of Human Skulls on eBay and the Laws in Place to Restrict Sales." *Journal of Forensic Sciences* 61: 1322–26.

Hefner, Joseph T. 2009. "Cranial Nonmetric Variation and Estimating Ancestry." *Journal of Forensic Sciences* 54(5): 985–95.

Hefner, Joseph T. 2018. "The Macromorphoscopic Databank." *American Journal of Physical Anthropology* 166(4): 994–1004.

Hefner, Joseph T., and S. Ousley. 2014. "Statistical Classification Methods for Estimating Ancestry Using Morphoscopic Traits." *Journal of Forensic Sciences* 59(4): 883–90.

Huffer, Damien, Cristina Wood, and Shawn Graham. 2019. "What the Machine Saw: Some Questions on the Ethics of Computer Vision and Machine Learning to Investigate Human Remains Trafficking." *Internet Archaeology*. doi: 10.11141/ia.52.5.

Huffer, Damien, and Shawn Graham. 2023. *These Were People Once: The Online Trade in Human Remains and Why It Matters*. New York: Berghahn Books. doi: 10.3167/9781805390862.

Huxley, Angie K., and Michael Finnegan 2004. "Human Remains Sold to the Highest Bidder! A Snapshot of the Buying and Selling of Human Skeletal Remains on eBay®, an Internet Auction Site." *Journal of Forensic Sciences* 49(1): 17–20.

Komar, Debra A., and Jane E. Buikstra. 2008. *Forensic Anthropology: Contemporary Theory and Practice*. Oxford: Oxford University Press.

Levenson, Michael. 2023. "Harvard Medical School Morgue Manager Sold Body Parts, U.S. Says." *The New York Times*. Retrieved 29 July 2024 from https://www.nytimes.com/2023/06/14/us/harvard-medical-school-body-parts.html.

Masterton, Malin. 2010. "Duties to Past Persons: Moral Standing and Posthumous Interests of Old Human Remains." PhD diss., Uppsala Universitet.

Muramoto, Osamu. 2014. "Retrospective Diagnosis of a Famous Historical Figure: Ontological, Epistemic, and Ethical Considerations." *Philosophy, Ethics, and Humanities in Medicine* 9: 10.

Nawrocki, Steven P. 1998. "Regression Formulae for Estimating Age at Death from Cranial Suture Closure." In *Forensic Osteology*, 2nd ed., edited by K. J. Reichs, 276–92. Springfield, IL: CC Thomas Publisher Ltd.

Owsley, Douglas W., Richard L. Jantz. 2014. *Kennewick Man: The Scientific Investigation of an Ancient American Skeleton*. College Station, TX: Texas A&M University Press.

Reynolds, Stanley S., and John Wooders. 2009. "Auctions with a Buy Price." *Economic Theory* 38: 9–39.

Saul, Frank P., and Julie M. Saul. 1989. "Osteobiography: A Maya Example." In *Reconstuction of Life from the Skeleton*, edited by M. Y. Isçan and K. A. R. Kennedy, 287–302. New York: Alan R. Liss.

Schulman-Hall, Juliet. 2023. "Is It Legal to Sell Human Remains? Harvard Morgue Scandal Exposes Lack of Regulations." *MassLive*. Retrieved 29 July 2024 from https://www.masslive.com/news/2023/07/is-it-legal-to-sell-human-remains-harvard-morgue-scandal-exposes-lack-of-regulations.html?outputType=amp.

Schwartz, Jeffrey. 2006. *Skeleton Keys: An Introduction to Human Skeletal Morphology, Development, and Analysis*, 2nd Edition. Oxford: Oxford University Press.

Seidemann, Ryan M. 1999. "Descriptive Analysis of Maya Skeletal Remains from Fighting Conch Mound, Wild Cane Cay, Belize." Master's thesis, Louisiana State University, Baton Rouge.

Seidemann, Ryan M. 2013. "How Do We Deal with All the Bodies? A Review of Recent Cemetery and Human Remains Legal Issues." *University of Baltimore Journal of Land & Development* 3: 1–70.

Seidemann, Ryan M. 2016. "The Influence of the Law on the Postmortem Narratives of Known and Unknown Human Remains." In *Studies in Forensic Biohistory: Anthropological Perspectives*, edited by C. M. Stojanowski and W. N. Duncan, 1–28. Cambridge: Cambridge University Press.

Seidemann, Ryan M., Christopher M. Stojanowski, and Frederick J. Rich. 2009. "The Identification of a Human Skull Recovered from an eBay Sale." *Journal of Forensic Sciences* 54(6): 1247–53.

Seidemann, Ryan M., and William T. Hawkins. 2019. "Acquisition and Disposition Problems and Experiences Policing the Online Marketplace for Human Remains." In *Forensic Archaeology: A Multidisciplinary Approach*, edited by K. S. Moran and C. Gold, 299–312. New York: Springer.

Stojanowski, Christopher M., and William N. Duncan, 2016. "Defining an Anthropological Biohistorical Research Agenda: The History, Scale, and Scope of an Emerging Discipline." In *Studies in Forensic Biohistory: Anthropological Perspectives*, edited by C. M. Stojanowski and W. N. Duncan, 1–18. Cambridge: Cambridge University Press.

Wellons, Sovi-Mya, Ryan M. Seidemann, and Christine L. Halling. 2024. "Tourist Trinket, Religious Object, Human Remains, or Something Else: Kapalas in the Online Market; Presentation in Human Remains." Society for American Archaeology Conference, New Orleans, LA.

Wood, James W., George R. Milner, Hency C. Harpending, and Kenneth M. Weiss. 1992. "The Osteological Paradox: Problems of Inferring Prehistoric Health from Skeletal Samples." *Current Anthropology* 33(4): 343–70.

CHAPTER 4

Online Social Organisation of Cultural Goods Trafficking

New Evidence from Old Forums across Europe

Samuel Andrew Hardy

Introduction

Despite catastrophic looting over the course of decades (Gershkovich 2020) and increased looting of archaeological artifacts in occupied Crimea (Bakalchuk 2019) and the occupied Donbas region (Telizhenko 2019), the pillaging and expropriation of cultural collections (Cultural Resilience Informatics and Analysis (Curia) Lab 2024; Hardy 2023; Hardy and Telizhenko forthcoming; Shydlovskyi, Telizhenko and Ivakin 2023) and possible looting of archaeological sites along the front line (Koropeckyj et al. 2024), since Russia's invasion of Ukraine in 2014, there has not been correspondingly intensive investigation into unscientific extraction, smuggling and trafficking of archaeological resources in eastern Europe and north Asia. This is partly due to the limited capacity of cultural heritage workers in the countries in question, who have been further overstretched by the necessities of national defence, community support and cultural protection in Ukraine and further restricted by the oppressive rule of the Russian Federation, both within Russian territory and in Russian-occupied territories, and Belarus. However, this is also due to an incidental neglect of these situations by cultural heritage workers in western Europe and north America, who have focused on the most prominent objects of demand and supply in their own markets.

This chapter and its companion paper (Hardy forthcoming a) have a particular focus on open-source intelligence from self-organised polls and discussions among artifact hunters in key activity-focused online forums, not only for artifact hunters and antiquities collectors but also for others who engage in artifact hunting such as small-scale drug producers and law enforcement agents (e.g. Hardy forthcoming b), and contact-focused global platforms such as Facebook and vKontakte for extractors in their own markets. This material shows how such OSINT enables the exploration of not only the diverse natures and activities of artifact hunters, but also the attitudes of artifact hunters toward archaeologists and society and/or the state and the law. Specifically, this chapter makes a note of discretion; explains the evidence for activity; and considers the actualities of law and law enforcement. Then, it considers the community's identity, its public representation and its public resistance to legal regulation. Finally, it assesses the demographics of artifact hunters, with regard to nationality, gender, age, religion, politics and economics and so the interactions between demographics and criminal coping economies. Therein, this chapter demonstrates the nature and contribution of data from online forums and social networks to understanding scientifically and socially problematic aspects of artifact hunting, particularly as it varies within and between economies and societies.

A Note of Discretion

Although all of the information in this paper is public, not all of it is polite and some of it is impolitic in a state without the rule of law, as some of its sources explicitly recognised when they shared it. So, user-generated content from online forums and social networks has been pseudonymised.

Publishers and venues of user-generated content have been pseudonymised with categorical alphabetical codes and arbitrary numerical distinguishers. This chapter and its companion paper (Hardy forthcoming a) together cite netnographic data from 282 artifact hunters – thirty-two who were in Belarus (BYAH), 175 who were in Russia (RUAH), fifteen who were probably in Russia yet remained unlocated (UNAH), fifty-five who were in Ukraine (UAAH), one who was in Georgia (GEAH), one who was in Greece (GRAH), one who was in Portugal (PTAH), one who was in Spain (ESAH) and one who was in the United Kingdom (UKAH); two artifact collectors, who were in Russia (RUAC); one citizen, who was in Russia (RUCIT); and five law enforcement agents, who were in Russia (RULEA). They published texts and images across fifty-three online communities – eight that were primarily focused on Belarus (BYOC), twenty-five that were primarily focused on Russia (RUOC), eight that were primarily focused on Ukraine (UAOC) and twelve that were fundamentally international (INOC). In order not to obscure women's activity through pseudonymisation, their pseudonym includes a prefix to highlight their female identity (f).

With regard to the characterisations of constituencies in polls, 0.00% is "absolutely none"; 0.01-5.00% is "almost none"; 5.01-15.00% is "a small minority"; 15.01-

25.00% is "a large minority"; 25.01-35.00% is "a very large minority"; 35.01-45.00% is "an extremely large minority"; 45.01-49.99% is "almost half"; 50.00% is "exactly half"; 50.01-55.00% is "slightly more than half"; 55.01-65.00% is "a small majority"; 65.01-75.00% is "a large majority"; 75.01-85.00% is "a very large majority"; 85.01-95.00% is "an extremely large majority"; 95.01-99.99% is "almost all"; and 100.00% is "absolutely all".

Those fragments of biography and activity are understood in the context of thousands of pieces of information, which have been published over the past fifteen years, by hundreds of other artifact hunters, in hundreds of conversations and tens of polls, in these and tens of other online communities. All of these data points are understood in the light of tens of thousands of data points, which have been published by thousands of artifact hunters and examined in the course of comparable studies by the author (on eastern Europe, e.g. Hardy 2016; 2017b; forthcoming a; forthcoming b; forthcoming c; Hardy and Telizhenko 2023; forthcoming; on south-eastern Europe, e.g. Hardy 2021; on the eastern Mediterranean, e.g. Hardy 2020a; on South Asia, e.g. Hardy 2019a; on Southeast Asia, e.g. Hardy 2020b; on East Asia, e.g. Hardy 2019b; in relation to proof-of-concept studies, e.g. Hardy 2017a; 2018).

Many of those pieces of information are minuscule data points, like photos of ancient coins, historic pieces of religious jewellery and historic pieces of horse harness, which are found so frequently that they are nicknamed "horse meat". Artifact hunters self-deprecatingly query why they continue to feel compelled to collect any fragments that they find (which was itself the subject of a poll by RUAH050 in RUOC001, to which seventy-six responded). These are not cited, because they are simply facts, which are too numerous to cite anyway. (Even when fragments of testimony are cited, long tails of corroboration or agreement are not.) Some of those pieces of information are very specific, like the names of politically-exposed persons (PEPs) who are alleged to have committed serious crimes. These are not published, when they have not been made public through legal proceedings and/or investigative journalism, because they are potentially libelous. See the Appendix for further information.

The Evidence for Activity

Venues of Discussions

There are at least tens of online forums that maintain their own platforms and thousands of social networks that operate on global platforms (at least 2,380 social networks, according to Vasyutin et al. 2020: 309; see also Seleev and Molyarenko 2023; Tuzbekov 2019; Tuzbekov 2020), some of which have fewer than ten members, some of which have tens of thousands of members, some of which are practically defunct (at least in terms of publicly-visible activity), some of which have hundreds of members and hundreds more guests online at any one moment, thousands of members and thousands more guests online over the course of one day. Many have one explicit exclusive or implicit primary language, as a matter of politics or (perhaps more administrative than social/commercial) practicality, but many allow or enable more than one language, again as a matter of politics or (perhaps more social/commercial than administrative) practicality.

There has been a shift toward participation in social networks like Facebook and vKontakte instead of (or, rather, as well as) online forums, at least partly due to the practicalities of everyday life and social life, at least partly due to the greater barriers even public groups in social networks pose to systematic monitoring by law enforcement agents, cultural heritage workers and other concerned citizens. In 2021, UAAH047 notified UAAH049 that, at least in some localities or regions, "everyone" was in groups on smartphone apps like Viber or in social networks like Facebook, rather than in online forums like UAOC001 (which did not display its membership statistics).

Nevertheless, there is still intense activity in at least some online forums (as of 2025) and some artifact hunters explicitly refuse to use social networks or smartphone apps (e.g. RUAH174 in 2022). Just one conversation, about the gender dimension to cultural asset extraction, comprises more than eighteen thousand messages from at least tens of Russian-speaking artifact hunters. Another conversation, about the intensified war in Ukraine, comprises more than ten thousand messages from at least tens of Russian-speaking artifact hunters–and some of those messages are a page long. Even artifact hunters who only contribute content to social networks still use content from online forums and other social media, including to find those social networks in the first place. For instance, in 2015, UAAH034 posted on his blog to encourage readers to shift from online forums to social networks; in 2022, UAAH051 looked in online forums like UAOC001 for directions to social networks such as those on vKontakte.

So, systematic searches with varied wordings in relation to the activity itself and significant aspects of the activity can recover a huge amount of information that has been shared and analyzed by artifact hunters, dealers and collectors. For example, by trawling online forums across Belarus, Russia and Ukraine (externally through Google's search engine and internally through the community's search engine), not only innumerable conversations, but also numerous polls were found, where artifact hunters had asked themselves about their artifact hunting activities and related matters, such as religious belief and political ideology.

User-Generated Content

In a survey of metal-detector-users in Denmark by archaeologists, they 'deliberately chose not to include a number of contentious topics, e.g., irresponsible conduct in the field or heritage crime and/or fraud' (Lykkegård-Maes and Dobat 2022: 5), because they could not be sure that the respondents would not give socially-acceptable, rather than honest, answers. In the anonymous polling processes of artifact hunters by artifact hunters that are considered in this study, there was neither reward nor punishment of any kind for any answer, except insofar as there was an awareness of the hypothetical possibility that overall poll results could be used by cultural heritage workers or law enforcement agents to assist in the targeting of measures for protection of archaeological sites or to advocate for the curtailment of artifact hunting. So, if there was any active bias to indications of the activities or opinions of the community, it reduced indications of social harm, such as cultural destructiveness or political extremism.

For instance, when UAAH028 polled members of UAOC001 about where they found the objects of greatest value (specifically not objects in the greatest numbers), they produced a ranking of targets as fields, forests, farms, settlements, estuaries or inns. Notably, a small minority of voters (n=126) opted for an unlisted type of target and UAAH029 explicitly declined to vote, as "not only artifact hunters" visited the forum.

Several of the self-organised polls and discussions among artifact hunters in online forums and social networks constituted samples of statistically insignificant size, in relation to their particular online community or the general offline community, or otherwise elicited statistically significant yet narrowly differentiated responses with wide margins of error. However, academic/professional-organised interviews, focus groups, polls and (verbal or written unstructured or semi-structured interviews or questionnaire-style) surveys of artifact hunters have relied on relatively small sample sizes, such as (fewer than) five in (Flanders in) Belgium (Thomas and Deckers 2022); seven across Belgium, Denmark, Finland, Lithuania, Norway, Poland and (England in) the United Kingdom (Axelsen, Thomas and Vaitkevičius 2022); seven in Norway (Rasmussen 2014); nine in Norway (Axelsen 2022); twenty-four in Austria (Karl 2011); thirty-seven in Hungary (Ujhelyi 2016); fifty-five in (England and Wales in) the United Kingdom (Robbins 2012); 133 in Austria (Achleitner 2011, unpublished manuscript, cited in Karl 2013: 120); 156 in Denmark (Dobat and Jensen 2016); 156 in Finland (Immonen and Kinnunen 2020); 221 in Finland (Immonen and Kinnunen 2016); 262 in the United Kingdom (Thomas 2012); and 330 in Denmark (Lykkegård-Maes and Dobat 2022). 'Ethnographic poll[s]' and surveys in other fields have had samples such as fifty (e.g. Guzzo and Padley 2021), sixty (e.g. Borba 2008) and 119 (e.g. Davis et al. 2020).

Moreover, divergences between similarly-timed, similarly-sized, similarly-significant polls of the same community highlight the limits of simplistic use of statistical significance as a measure of factual accuracy and practical significance (cf. the poll of RUOC001 by RUAH060 (n=160), who found that a small minority were full-time artifact hunters, and the almost-simultaneous poll of RUOC001 by RUAH052 (n=201), who found that almost none were full-time artifact hunters). Notably, both of those informal ethnographic polls among artifact hunters by artifact hunters achieved larger samples than have been achieved by most ethnographic studies among artifact hunters by academics/professionals.

Usefulness of Content

As primary research studies that have been designed and implemented by the citizens among whom they are conducted, with their own concerns and concepts in mind, these should surely be recognised and addressed as citizen science or participatory science, in the same way that some academics/professionals are now trying to convert records of finds by artifact hunters into archaeological knowledge. At the same time, they must be addressed with awareness of the potential for reputation-managing, policy-influencing manipulation of studies by artifact hunters. This may increase in lockstep with any increase in recognition of those studies by academics/professionals. After all, it would be illogical for artifact hunters to be honest about cultural harm that they cause and other misconduct that they engage in, if they expected that honesty to lead to action to disrupt the very same behaviours that they had chosen not to desist from, in the same way that it would be illogical for artifact hunters to record illegal or otherwise problematic finds (even legal finds from sites that they wanted to empty on their own) in an academic/professional system, unless they could launder or otherwise obscure the origins of those finds through the academic/professional system.

In the publicly pseudonymous discussions among artifact hunters that are considered in this chapter, there may have been a reputational reward or punishment or practical benefit or cost for some answers, particularly as many discussants knew the real private identities of some of the others. So, some biases may have increased rather than decreased indications of social harm. However, there was still an awareness of the possibility that information could be used against discussants, which again militated toward reduced indications of social harm, with regard to both cultural destructiveness and political extremism. There was also the awareness that many discussants knew one another offline as well as online and some engaged in artifact hunting and/or artifact trading with one another offline as well as online, so highly implausible claims or significantly misleading statements were untenable, discussants tended toward self-deprecation rather than self-aggrandisement and implausible claims and misleading statements were challenged when they were made. Such challenges often involved comparisons of contradictory statements online, which enabled independent confirmation of misrepresentations.

This study and its companion draw on testimony from a greater number of artifact hunters than the number of participants in some of the scientific studies by academics/professionals; a greater number of informal studies by artifact hunters than the number of participants in some of the scientific studies by academics/professionals; and informal studies by artifact hunters with sample sizes that are equivalent to or greater than those in the aforementioned scientific studies. Specifically, they cite forty-nine polls of artifact hunters by artifact hunters, with samples that range between twelve and 708 (see figure 1), plus a poll of artifact hunters by lawyers outside social networks, with a sample of 2,479. So, the volume, complexity and span of open-source data – qualitative data in the form of texts and images in

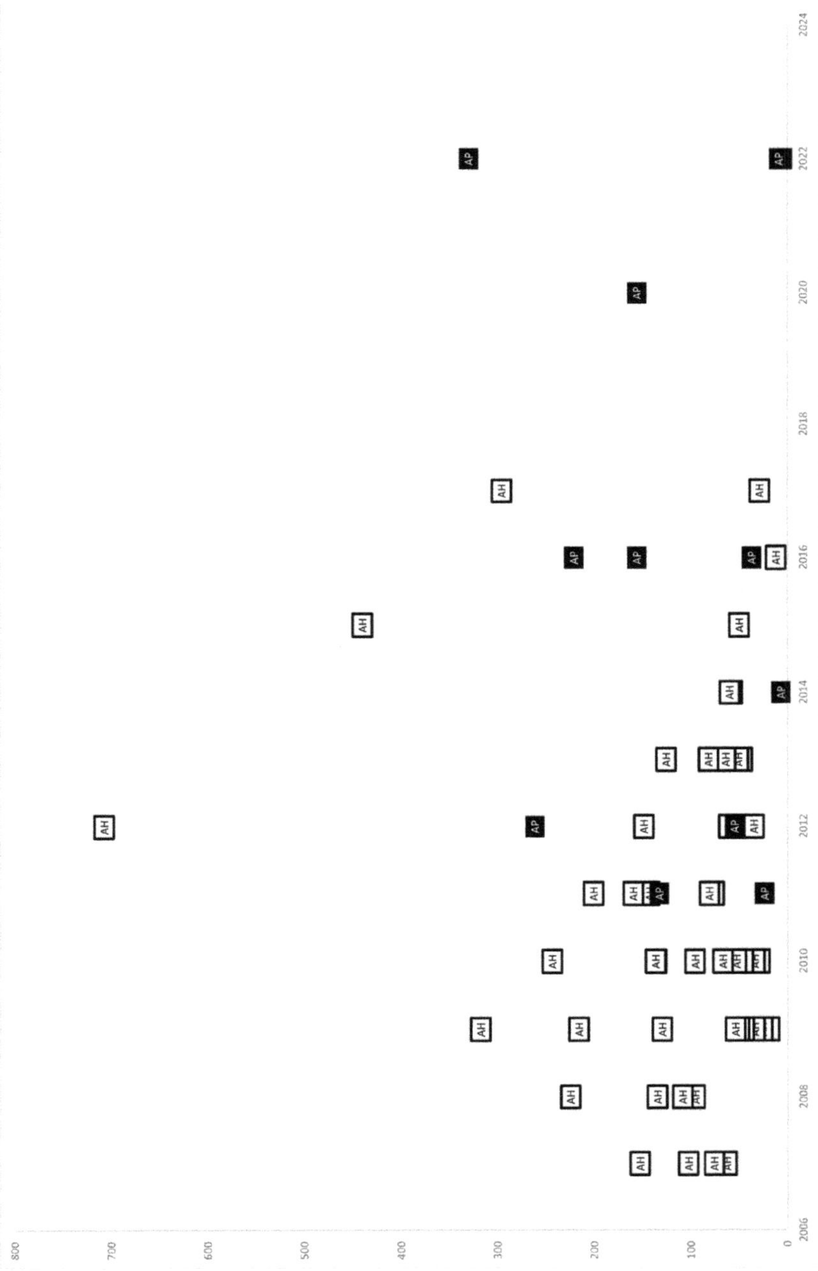

Figure 4.1. Polls by artifact hunters (AH) and by academics and professionals (AP), by size. © Samuel Hardy.

discussions, plus quantitative data in the form of polls and other materials, which were themselves analysed in texts – do give some security to consequent inferences. All of the tables and figures were made by the author.

Law and Law Enforcement

Across the region, laws exert public ownership of archaeological objects, prohibit unlicensed searching for or excavation of archaeological objects and prohibit unlicensed export of archaeological objects (Hardy 2016: 216-218; cf. Respublika Belarus 2016 for Belarus; Rossiiskaya Federatsiya 2013 for Russia; Verkhovna Rada 2004 for Ukraine) – and they have done so since before the emergence of intensive and extensive looting with metal-detectors (cf. SSSR 1986, for the Soviet Union). Yet in Belarus (according to archaeologist Vadim Koshman, cited by Tania 2016), in Russia (according to a search center for missing persons cited in Iskatel 2013) and in Ukraine (according to Rafaliv village head Vasyl Sovgut, cited by Skibchyk 2019), artifact hunters have long enjoyed 'impunity [beznakazannost / beznakazannosti / bezkarnist]'.

Even when criminals are caught and convicted, the punishment may be too little, too late, to have any deterrent effect. For instance, one metal-detector-using artifact hunter in Russia who supplied private collectors, who was found to still possess 1,484 historic coins with a market value of more than 50,000 euros, was fined around 1,000 euros (and those remaining coins were confiscated, see Prokuratura Vladimirskoi Oblasti 2019). Looting has 'not [even] disappeared [ne znykla]' since Russia's intensification of its invasion of Ukraine, 'only hidden [lyshe prynyshkla]' (according to the acting director of the Historical and Cultural Reserve of Davniy Plisnesk, Volodymyr Shelep 2022).

Even with regard to any community "law" of social *etiquette*, there is little honor among thieves. When UAAH022 polled members of online forum UAOC001, a very large majority of voters (n=137) stated that they would target locations that other artifact hunters had not named yet had revealed enough information to identify, while a small minority claimed that they would ask for the permission of the finder first and almost none claimed that they would not do it. Still, there is some honor – or at least enlightened self-interest – in the equitable distribution of finds between metal-detector-bearing finders and shovel-bearing diggers (as documented in comments by UAAH024, RUAH011, UAAH026 and UAAH025).

The Community's Identity and Its Public Representation

Community Identity

When RUAH083 polled members of online forum RUOC001, a small majority of voters (n=61) characterised it as digging, while a large minority characterised it as amateur or otherwise non-specific searching. Artifact hunters preferred "searching", sometimes only because "digging" was legally problematic (e.g. RUAH088), although searching is legally problematic as well, sometimes because they wanted to distinguish their activity and themselves from "professional searching" by archaeologists (e.g. RUAH089 and RUAH090). Despite the commonality of the term in community names, only a small minority characterised the activity as treasure-searching, while almost none characterised it as archaeology-searching and absolutely none characterised it as archaeology, sometimes because all of those terms were legally problematic (e.g. RUAH081 and RUAH087, who thought that it was a bad idea to advertise a prohibited activity), sometimes because archaeology implied science and at least some participants in the trade are dismissive of the conception of hobbies as sciences (e.g. RUAC002 in artifact collecting forum RUOC002, who argued that the extraction and collection of coins or medals were not scientific practices, any more than hunting or fishing were scientific practices).

Notably, too, absolutely no-one characterised it as metal-detecting, even though metal-detecting for scrap metal was a common excuse (e.g. UAAH033) and a common supplementary income (e.g. RUAH139; RUAH138; UAAH053; UAAH053) and the term is commonly used by artifact hunters and archaeologists to characterise the activity in western Europe and north America. Some observed that this and all of the other terms were euphemisms that obscured the intention of the activity (e.g. RUAH084 and RUAH085). Some suggested that they should instead be characterised as marauders, plunderers, grave-robbers or mass grave-diggers (e.g. RUAH082; RUAH086). Regardless of the word games that they recognised that they were playing, almost all characterised their own activity as unscientific extraction of cultural goods.

Community Interests and Marketable Cultural Goods

Any thought that they might have been ridiculing negative characterisations of an innocent hobby would be dispelled by the sight of grave goods and uncomplicated celebrations of finds of grave goods, which are visible across the social media of artifact hunters. Indeed, "gravedigging (grobokopatelstvo)" or "burrowing (bugrovshchichestvo)" into kurgans (burial mounds), by 'burrowers [bugrovshchiki]' or 'burial mounders [kurganshchiki]', is a long-documented line of artifact-hunting activity (e.g. Artsibasheva 2015: 7). Finds of human remains and uncomplicated collections/trades that involve human remains are much less celebrated and much less visible. Nonetheless, 'skull-digging [kop po cherepam]' is another long-documented undercurrent of artifact-hunting activity (e.g. Tsitsagi 2021), even if deals are made for purported 'copies of bones', which are 'indistinguishable from the originals', as they are 'made to order from the originals' with 'synthetic bone matter' (as was advertised by UNAH013), or if goods are marketed privately.

This is the case, partly since they are uncovered in the process of unearthing grave goods and other artifacts, particularly military artifacts that are often found on or around fallen soldiers at historic battlefields; partly since disembodied skulls, other bones and bloodstained artifacts can hold the same grim fascination as pierced helmets (as illustrated by UNAH015 with the battle-damaged helmet in figure 4.2, which had belonged to a soldier who was killed in the Second World War, and by UNAH014 with the bloodstained patch in figure 4.3, which had belonged to a fighter who was killed during the intensification of Russia's invasion of Ukraine, although some artifacts, such as 'helmet[s] with parts of brain attached',

Figure 4.2. Auction by UNAH015 of a battle-damaged helmet from the Eastern Front of World War II. Blurring is intentional for anonymity. © Samuel Hardy.

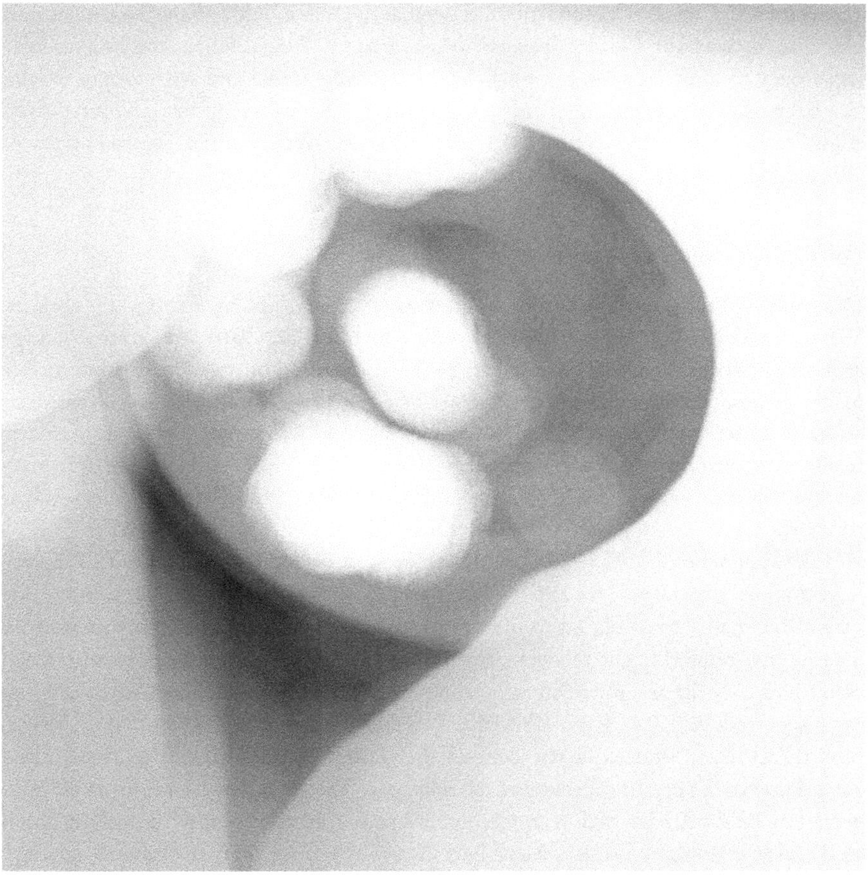

Figure 4.3. Auction by UNAH014 of a bloodstained fighter patch from Russia's war on Ukraine. Blurring is intentional for anonymity. © Samuel Hardy.

are rejected by some handlers, as documented by the Economist, 2024); and partly since some artifacts such as musical instruments are carved out of human bones and others such as ornate weapons include decorative carvings of human bones (e.g. voxpop_66 2019). The most common purchasers are collectors and the most common destinations are elsewhere in Europe and North America (according to the Economist 2024).

Meanwhile, war trophy-hunting/trading is such an intense undercurrent in the subculture around Russia's war on Ukraine that false accusations of trading in cultural products of human remains by Ukraine's fighters are a feature of Russia's propaganda (as documented by Escrivá and Barber 2023). For instance, although one apparently authentic trading account, which publicly declared that the associated fighter 'looted' and 'sold' the possessions of 'dead Russians' and which was publicly 'recommended' by a collector who had been active since before Russia's invasion of Ukraine (so was not a sock puppet whose account had been fabricated to lend false legitimacy to another sock puppet), was apparently associated with a fighter who had been accused of trading in cultural products of human remains. The purported evidence could not be traced beyond disinformation outlets and there was no traceable evidence of any human remains at all in his trading records.

Community Self-Presentation

Different options, with different audiences in mind, produce different choices. When BYAH014 polled members of online forum BYOC001, an extremely large majority of voters (n=440) wanted an NGO for artifact hunters, with an audience in the general public as well as in the artifact hunting community, to have one or another name that related to history or heritage (which are legally unproblematic terms that obscure the legally problematic activity), while only a small minority wanted another name, perhaps a more literal name like the Instrument Search Enthusiasts' Club (as suggested by BYAH015 and BYAH013).

Likewise, when BYAH020 polled members of online forum BYOC001, a very large majority of voters (n=296) wanted an NGO for artifact hunters to have one or another name that related to history or heritage, while a large minority wanted a name that related to the recovery of missing persons and almost none wanted another name, perhaps a more literal name that related to metal-detecting or digging (as suggested by BYAH017, BYAH019, BYAH018, BYAH021 and BYAH022, plus BYAH025, who explicitly echoed the names of associations in the United Kingdom) or a very literal name that related to kurgans (burial mounds, as suggested by BYAH023, which was deemed too provocative). Meanwhile, others (such as BYAH024) warned that it was a bad idea to advertise their prohibited activity.

To put these deliberations in context, when RUAH016 polled members of online forum RUOC001, a large minority of voters (n=103) straightforwardly identified as black (market) diggers; a small minority identified as more black than white; an extremely large minority identified as grey; a small minority identified as more white than black; a small minority identified as white diggers; and only a small minority identified as archaeologists (see figure 4), which is unsurprising, when it is normalised for them to identify archaeologists as parasites (e.g. UAAH038; BYAH027). Elsewhere, as is common among artifact hunters in restrictive jurisdictions, RUAH019 celebrated that "diggers" in the United Kingdom were "officially recognised as amateur archaeologists" and were "almost equal in rights to [professional] archaeologists".

So, by their own reckoning, a large minority explicitly identified themselves as wholly-criminal actors, a very large majority explicitly identified themselves as wholly or partly-criminal actors and some of the remainder may have been falsely arguing that their reading of the letter of the law allowed their activity or falsely arguing that

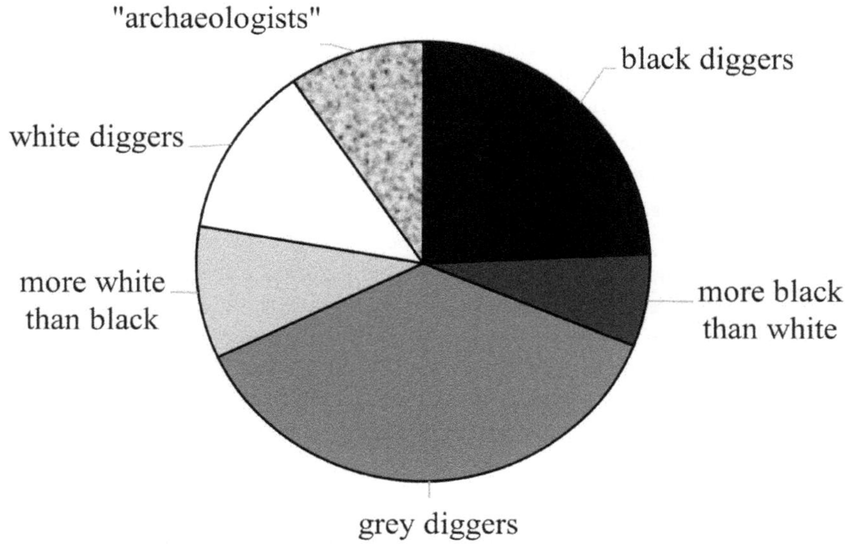

Figure 4.4. Poll by RUAH016 of self-identification of members of RUOC001. © Samuel Hardy.

they recovered missing persons rather than looted historic artifacts. For instance, recently, in the Russian exclave of Kaliningrad in one month alone (May 2020), police intercepted twenty-nine black diggers who were pretending to be white diggers (Chereneva 2020). Likewise, after a 529-message conversation about legal regulation of artifact hunting in online forum BYOC001, BYAH026 concluded that the two practical options were the one that existed elsewhere, where it was expensive but legal, and the one that existed in Belarus, where it was free but criminal.

Notably, elsewhere, a modern militaria-focused, self-identified "black digger", RUAH137 (who has his own social media channel, RUOC004), told an ostensibly-reformed financial criminal with multiple social media channels (including at least two that advertised his former criminal enterprise), RUOC005, that he and "many" others trained themselves in cultural artifact extraction through volunteering with "white diggers" of missing persons. The video has had hundreds of thousands of views. Elsewhere again, RULEA001 stated that he participated in white digging for missing persons, then engaged in black digging for artifacts in the spare time around those activities. Others may train themselves through volunteering with professional archaeologists. RUAH119 suggested that a relative had participated in an archaeological expedition as a metal-detectorist and had embezzled finds in the process.

When (f)UAAH027 polled members of online forum RUOC001 in anticipation of the amendments in 2013 to the law for suppression of illegal activities in relation to archaeological goods (Rossiiskaya Federatsiya 2013), a small minority of voters (n=708) claimed that they would finally obey the stricter ban and stop artifact hunting and a small minority stated that they were undecided, yet a very large majority insisted that they would not stop (see figure 4.5). Likewise, when RUAH108 polled members of online forum RUOC001, in an albeit humorous response to the law of 2013, almost all of the voters (n=60) said that they could not stop themselves from digging and almost none said that they could not dig, wherein those few joked that they could not dig *because it was midwinter* (e.g. lawyer RUAH100 and RUAH105). Most perfectly phrasing the collective response, RUAH106 observed that "we are not obliged to shit on the laws, but we are obliged to get around them". Indeed, now, whenever the law is amended, artifact hunters laugh at the fact that they have been "banned again" (e.g. RUAH133 in RUOC006).

Such attitudes at the source end are underpinned by similar attitudes at the market end. When RUAC001 polled members of a coin-collecting forum RUOC007, a large minority of voters (n=29) did not approve of black market digging and almost none did not care, yet a large majority approved and believed that they owned whatever they could acquire. Since a large majority were enthusiastic about buying illicit cultural goods, and a certain proportion of the ostensibly disapproving minority would buy undocumented cultural goods as long as they were not explicitly advertised as illicit cultural goods, looters would not have found any serious obstacle to offloading their loot.

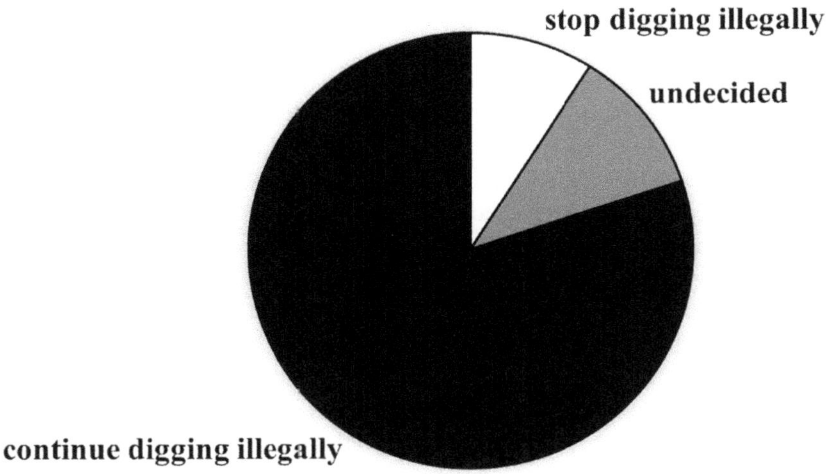

Figure 4.5. Poll by (f)UAAH027 of criminal intent of members of RUOC001. © Samuel Hardy.

The Community's Public Resistance to Legal Regulation

Petitions

In this region as elsewhere, there are intermittent attempts to legalise or deregulate metal-detecting for cultural objects and other searching for archaeological materials. For instance, there was a campaign to access a free consultation with a legislative lawyer about a legal justification of metal-detector-assisted artifact searching as a hobby, which was widely circulated (e.g. by RUAH068 in RUOC008; RUAH069 in RUOC002, which, notably, is a primarily artifact collecting community, which wanted to maximise the commercial supply of archaeological goods by "hobbyists" to private collectors; gaming-nicknamed RUAH070 in RUOC009; RUAH071 in RUOC010; RUAH072 in RUOC011; RUAH080 in RUOC001).

A similar, laxly designed petition to lift the ban on metal-detector-assisted artifact searching was not visibly widely spread within Russia (e.g. by RUAH095 in RUOC006). Nonetheless, it was widely spread, as demonstrated by the assistance of artifact hunters in Belarus, who were able to sign, despite not being resident in Russia (e.g. BYAH006, BYAH009, BYAH005, BYAH003, BYAH004, BYAH010, BYAH008 and BYAH011 in online forum BYOC001). They signed to support their "brethren" in Russia (e.g. BYAH006); to prevent increased transnational looting by artifact hunters from Russia and so increased competition for cultural resources in Belarus (e.g. BYAH007, BYAH006 and BYAH002); and/or to prevent retaliatory protectionism that would deprive artifact hunters in Belarus of their own opportunities for transnational looting in Russia (e.g. BYAH012). Another similar petition was not visibly widely spread (e.g. by RUAH093 in RUOC006).

All of those, plus an effort to skew an opinion poll by, and so the political programme of, the Communist Party of the Russian Federation with regard to the law of 2013, failed (according to RUAH132 and RUAH101), despite the fact that the effort had been undertaken by members (and spouses of members) of internal regional and national communities (according to RUAH102 in RUOC012). Yet, as RUCIT001 observed in gaming forum RUOC014, foundational claims by campaigning artifact hunters that they "do not dig into listed monuments" and "do not trade in archaeological artifacts" were "lies" that could be disproved by "anyone who has not been banned" from accessing the internet.

Campaigning artifact hunters never achieved the thousands or tens of thousands of signatures that they desired, at least partly because would-be signatories knew that the state was keeping lists of known – yet unprosecuted – cultural property criminals (e.g. BYAH002, who had been caught in the act and put on the lists of at least one law enforcement agency and one intelligence agency) and any petition was akin to a voluntarily-offered list. Their attempts demonstrated the futility of trying to secure the 100,000 signatures that would have been required to trigger a review by a panel of politicians and officials, who could have recommended a bill for consideration by parliament, under Decree 183 on petitions by Russian citizens through the Russian Public Initiative, which has been in place since 4 March 2013, which RUAH104 worried would be akin to a voluntarily-offered list *and* enable the geolocation of signatories while committing cultural property crimes.

Regardless of the merits of the case in this particular instance, already around the time of the passing of the law of 2013, such futility had intensified political disengagement and legal nihilism. RUAH0100, RUAH103 and RUAH104 had openly warned other artifact hunters that politically-inconvenient votes would be ignored. RUAH100 had actively encouraged other artifact hunters to disengage from politics: "We won't change anything, vote or no vote. Look at Putin, sitting there, like a fat scavenger, eyeing things up. He doesn't care about the people."

Associations

Before and since the most intense period of petitioning, artifact-hunters have considered forming citizens' associations of artifact hunters or NGOs for artifact hunting. When RUAH018 polled members of artifact hunting forum RUOC001, an extremely large minority of voters (n=135) supported the establishment of an organisation of artifact hunters, because they could defend their activity, yet a small majority believed that it would be reckless, because they would advertise their prohibited activity. Like so many others, RUAH051 desired the deregulated system of England and Wales (cf. Barford 2020; Brodie 2020; Daubney 2017), wherein artifact hunters in Russia could operate through private agreements with landowners, where common finds would be shared equally with landowners, while rare finds would be surrendered to the state in return for market-rate monetary compensation that would be shared equally with landowners.

Later, when RUAH063 polled members of RUOC006, a large minority of voters (n=56) supported the establishment of a national federation of people who hunt for artifacts with metal-detectors, such as RUAH065, who believed that the increase in artifact hunters and the decrease in finds necessitated licensing, in order to enable the licensed artifact hunters to continue to extract a satisfying number of archaeological objects. However, overall, a very large majority rejected it. Specifically, a large minority dismissed it as practically irrelevant or practically incompetent, such as RUAH066, who judged that any organisation would have no power. A small minority dismissed it as personally irrelevant, because they did not want to be a member of an organisation, such as RUAH062, who did not want to be burdened with obligations to others. An extremely large minority rejected it, because it would be practically restrictive. For instance, RUAH064 claimed to have found an ancient Greek helmet, and was willing to consider refraining from targeting registered archaeological sites and honouring the rights of the landowners, yet was not willing to accept the licensing of artifact hunting or the prohibition of artifact trading. RUAH123 concluded that any attention would be harmful, because they were in Russia. RUAH067 refused to pay tax or donate finds.

Contrarily, in-between those two polls, when UAAH021 polled members of UAOC001, an extremely large majority of voters (n=318) supported the formation of a citizens' association of artifact hunters, which had been designed to echo legislative lines that encouraged civil society, while almost none were undecided and a small minority opposed it. Again, regardless of the merits of the case in this very particular instance, the opposite results in Russia and Ukraine may reflect the opposite states of democratic government and civil society in Russia and Ukraine (even then, after the Orange Revolution but before the Revolution of Dignity), wherein citizens in Ukraine were sufficiently free that they were able, willing and ready to mobilise for social change.

Discussion

Nationality

Ostensibly and even explicitly ethnicity or citizenship-based national communities often have *some* international members, whether they are members of that nation in other countries (the diaspora), members of other nations who visit that country to hunt for artifacts or members of other nations who trade or collect cultural goods from that historic culture. Typically, particularly in large national communities, international members are insufficiently numerous to materially affect membership statistics.

However, there are also transnational communities and transnational organised crime groups that span the region and sometimes engage in cross-border crime. For instance, there is an online community of more than 5,000 artifact hunters (plus artifact traders and artifact collectors), where around 50% are based in Ukraine, 46% are based in Russia and 4% are based elsewhere (as documented in Hardy 2016: 222); the administrators have since withdrawn public access to poll results, but they had not expelled (or tried to expel) any national community in response to the invasion in 2014, they have not expelled any national community in response to the intensification of the invasion in 2022 and the population has not grown or shrunk significantly. Some national communities have actively facilitated international participation. For instance, UAOC001 offers navigational functions in four regional languages and one global language.

Gender and Sexuality

Gender

The gender dimension of cultural property crime, within the region and elsewhere around the world, must be analysed separately – and there is now enough qualitative and quantitative data to begin doing so. Nevertheless, it is already possible to show that women constitute perhaps 7-11% of artifact hunters in Russia (Tuzbekov 2019; 2020: 110). This appears to be more than among metal-detectorists in the former Yugoslavia (0.86-5.45%, according to Hardy 2021: 183), more than among metal-detectorists in Finland (4%, according to Immonen and Kinnunen 2016: 170), approximately the same as among metal-detectorists in the United Kingdom (7.6%, according to Thomas 2012: 51) and less than among metal-detectorists in Denmark (15%, according to Lykkegård-Maes and Dobat 2022: 5). Women constitute perhaps 17-25% of smugglers in Ukraine (according to Mishchenko 2017: 192). Their increasing numbers and increasing seniority are visible in open-source evidence and their activity is threaded throughout the research presented in this chapter and a forthcoming paper (though the 'physically strenuous and demanding' nature of the activity may mean that it continues to be mostly 'men who dig', according to Sezneva 2007: 23).

Sexuality

Sexuality is a similarly interesting matter, but there is much less evidence and much of the available evidence may be more reflective of community attitudes than individual identities and activities. For instance, when UNAH012 polled members of INOC008 about non-heterosexuality, an extremely large majority (almost all) of voters (n=51) expressed virulent homophobia; only a small minority (almost none) expressed indifference and absolutely none identified as anything other than heterosexual. At that time, "only" a large majority of the citizenry had any negative attitudes toward the LGBT+ community, which encompassed a very large minority who felt disgust at or fear of LGBT+ people, a large minority who felt wary of LGBT+ people and a large minority who felt irritated by LGBT+ people; a large minority were indifferent; and "only" almost half believed that LGBT+ people should not have the same rights as heterosexual members of society (cf. Yuri Levada Analytical Center 2021).

Age

When RUAH016 polled members of RUOC001 (n=63), the median age was in the thirties and a very large majority were under forty-two. When RUAH030 polled members of RUOC018 (n=130), the median age was in the twenties and an extremely large majority were under forty. When UNAH003 polled members of INOC008 (n=216), the median age was in the thirties and a very large majority were under forty-one. When RUAH109 polled members of RUOC018 (n=57), the median age was in the thirties and a small majority were under forty. Likewise, in a preliminary assessment of samples of data from profiles in three communities, KB, KBU and KBKUM (after Tuzbekov 2019; 2020: 110), the median age was in the thirties and a very large majority were under forty-one.

Meanwhile, when Thomas (2012: 51) surveyed rally-goers in the United Kingdom (n=262), the median age was in the late forties or early fifties and a large majority were over forty-four (Thomas 2012: 51). When UKAH001 polled members of INOC009 (n=64), the median age was in the forties and a very large majority were over forty. When Lykkegård-Maes and Dobat (2022: 5 – fig. 3) surveyed members of social networks in Denmark (n=262-330, where the number of answers varied with the nature of the question), the median age was in the forties and a very large majority were over thirty-nine.

All of the communities in eastern Europe (cf. table 1 and table 2) have significantly younger age profiles than artifact hunters in western Europe (cf. table 3). Around the time of the polls in eastern Europe, life expectancy at birth was around sixty-seven or sixty-eight in Russia, as it had been around sixty-five or sixty-six when those people had been born; it was sixty-eight in Ukraine and had been sixty-eight; and it was seventy in Belarus and had been sixty-eight. By contrast, in the United Kingdom, for example, it was seventy-nine and had been around seventy or seventy-one, which may partly explain the younger age profile of artifact hunters

Table 4.1. Age profiles of artifact hunters in Eastern Europe, based on polls of RUOC001 by RUAH016, RUOC018 by RUAH030, INOC008 by UNAH003, and RUOC018 by RUAH109 and UKAH001 in INOC009, where narrower ranges have been amalgamated to enable comparison and median age ranges have been highlighted. © Samuel Hardy.

RUOC001 by RUAH016		RUOC018 by RUAH030		INOC008 by UNAH003		RUOC018 by RUAH109	
over 51	4.76			over 50	6.9	50–59	3.5
42–51	15.87	39–45	12.31	41–50	17.6	40–49	31.58
32–41	**30.16**	33–39	20.77	**31–40**	**41.2**	**30–39**	**45.62**
22–31	31.75	**21–32**	**54.61**	21–30	31.9	20–29	15.79
15–21	7.94	16–20	11.54	under 21	2.3	15–19	3.51
under 15	9.52	under 16	0.77				

Table 4.2. Age profiles of artifact hunters in Eastern Europe, based on reviews of profiles in social networks in Russia by Tuzbekov (2019; 2020: 110), where median age ranges have been highlighted. © Samuel Hardy.

KB by Tuzbekov		KBU by Tuzbekov		KBKUM by Tuzbekov	
over 40	20	over 40	22	over 40	20.5
31–40	**45.5**	**31–40**	**55**	**31–40**	**52.5**
21–30	28.7	21–30	21	21–30	22.5
under 21	5.7	under 21	2	under 21	4.3

Table 4.3. Age profiles of artifact hunters in Western Europe, based on a survey of a rally in the United Kingdom by Thomas (2012: 51), a poll of INOC009 by UKAH001, and a survey of social networks in Denmark by Lykkegård-Maes and Dobat (2022: 5, fig. 3), where median age ranges have been highlighted. © Samuel Hardy.

Rally in the United Kingdom by Thomas		**Poll of INOC009 by UKAH001**		**Social networks in Denmark by Lykkegård-Maes and Dobat (n.b. men)**		**Social networks in Denmark by Lykkegård-Maes and Dobat (n.b. women)**	
				71–83	3.2	71–83	0
over 64	12.6	over 60	6.25	60–70	13.6	60–70	22.9
55–64	22.14	51–60	25	50–59	25.8	50–59	22.9
45–54	**32.06**	**41–50**	**45.31**	**40–49**	**32.6**	**40–49**	**35.4**
35–44	26.72	31–40	15.63	30–39	16.8	30–39	14.6
25–34	4.2	21–30	6.25	20–29	4.7	20–29	2.1
16–24	1.53	under 21	1.56	15–19	3.2	15–19	2.1
under 16	0.76						

in eastern Europe. The difference in age profiles may also be influenced by greater activity online among younger artifact hunters, but it has also been attributed to the physical and financial requirements of the activity in Russia (Tuzbekov 2020: 110), which would complement testimony of artifact hunters about the intensity of their activity in eastern Europe, which is presented in this study.

Religious Belief and Artifact Hunting Practice

When UNAH006 polled members of INOC008, a small majority of voters (n=53) identified as Orthodox Christians (and almost none were non-Orthodox Christian), some of whom expressed their faith during their artifact hunting (see figure 4.6), a large minority indicated no faith, a small minority were atheist, a small minority were pagan (and absolutely none were old-believers or cultists), almost none were Muslim and absolutely none were Jewish. Meanwhile, when RUAH118 polled members of online forum RUOC024, a large majority of voters (n=50) believed in God; almost none professed another religion, which appeared to encompass monotheism outside organised religion and paganism; a small minority were agnostic; and a small minority did not believe. Around that time, aggregating numerous descriptive categories, a small majority of Russians appeared to be theist; a small minority appeared to be spiritual; a small minority appeared to be agnostic; and a small minority appeared to be atheist (cf. Yuri Levada Analytical Center 2020). As documented in a 1,494-message conversation that was initiated by RUAH002 on RUOC001 and a 231-message conversation that was initiated by RUAH061 on RUOC001, there are pagans and double-believers (of traditional as well as organised religions), as well as deists and theists.

Further highlighting a religious diversity that appears to be more common among artifact hunters in Eastern Europe (and, it should be reiterated, North Asia) than it is among those in Western Europe and North America, there were numerous Muslim artifact hunters in online communities (e.g., in RUOC001, RUAH058; RUAH059; RUAH057; RUAH073; RUAH092; RUAH054; RUAH122; in RUOC003, RUAH117, who discussed community tradition and disrespectful treatment by police officers). Non-Muslim artifact hunters spontaneously congratulated their Muslim peers on religious holidays (e.g. RUAH035; RUAH093) or otherwise observed that Muslims also dug (e.g. RUAH121). However, there may still be disproportionately few among artifact hunters, since Muslims constitute a small minority of the citizenry (Pew Forum on Religion and Public Life 2011: 127).

An ultraconservative Islamist car dealer and artifact hunter in his early forties, RUAH170, had been publicly active online until at least late 2020, but had deleted his artifact hunting profile by mid-2022. Since he had at least two others, where he maintained connections with family, friends and colleagues and displayed a range of personal information, including his political and religious views, yet did not display any indication of involvement in artifact hunting, he appears to have decided to obscure his involvement in that activity.

Religious belief appeared to have some meaningful effect on artifact hunting practice, though it appeared not to have any effect on most religious artifact hunters and may have had even less of an effect than was professed. When RUAH038 polled members of artifact hunting online forum RUOC001 about what they would do if they found a church bell in the attic (while specifically drawing parallels with other Christian objects that they extracted and collected or sold every day without a second thought), a very large minority of voters (n=136) said that they would (or would be willing) to donate it to the Church, but a large majority said that they would keep or sell the bell as was their right. By contrast, when RUAH091 polled members of RUOC001, a small minority of voters (n=149) supported the idea of reusing tombstones in walls; a small minority could not decide; a small minority did not care; and a very large majority considered it blasphemy.

On one of her *two* social media channels, (f)RUAH140 rejected the idea of donating a historic icon to a monastery. On one of *her* two social media channels, (f)RUAH165 defended the collecting of pectoral crosses from Byzantine, medieval and other periods as theologically responsible, in order to prevent a symbol of faith from being dirtied or otherwise damaged. This echoes broader self-justifying arguments for extraction to prevent physical damage by human action and the environment. However, the argument for extraction to prevent spiritual pollution

Figure 4.6. Meme of a cross of shovels, with a coin in the scoop of the shovel, within a circle of coins, shared by BYAH032. Blurring is intentional for anonymity. © Samuel Hardy.

alongside the rejection of donation to a community or public institution such as a church also echoes the narrative of private "rescue"-by-purchase alongside the rejection of donation to a community or public institution such as a museum. Notably, it is a rejection of donation to a spiritual institution within the country of origin by residents of that country. This may reflect distrust of all institutions as organs of power – especially institutions that are instruments of power that are wielded by the state.

Politics of Artifact Hunters in Eastern Europe

Trends

When (ironically latterly banned) RUAH029 polled members of RUOC001, an extremely large minority of voters (n=50) supported bans on discussions of politics, diplomacy and religion; exactly half opposed bans; and a small minority abstained. Thanks to balances of opinion like this, or the whims of administrators, there are numerous polls and innumerable discussions of politics online. There is tentative evidence that the politics of artifact hunters in Eastern Europe resemble those of wider society in some ways (e.g. in relation to vaccination, as documented by Hardy 2022a), yet diverge from those of wider society in other ways.

Sometimes, such evidence only evinces the breadth of opinion in the community. For instance, when RUAH131 polled members of RUOC022, about the nature of the Russian nation, the identification of the Russian nation and the rights of Russian nationals, minority preferences among voters (n=12) spanned the options of defining the Russian nation by language; state; Russian ethnicity; territory; indigenous ethnicity; religiosity, including Islam and Buddhism as well as Orthodox Christianity; and internationalism, including equality of rights; but absolutely none chose atheism. A large majority wanted the nation to be identified as Russian by ethnicity; a small minority did not care; and a small minority as Russian by citizenship. Exactly half believed that everyone should have equal rights; a very large minority believed that indigenous peoples should have exceptional rights; a large minority believed that ethnic Russians should have exceptional rights; and absolutely none did not care.

Other times, the evidence is more instructive. When UNAH006 polled members of INOC008 about attitudes toward homeless people, exactly half of voters (n=34) felt disgust (and almost none, yet not absolutely none, felt a desire to destroy them); an extremely large minority felt pity or sympathy; and almost none felt a desire to help. Albeit more recently, a more in-depth survey indicated that only a small minority of the citizenry felt disgust; a very large majority felt pity or sympathy; and an extremely large minority felt a desire to help (cf. NAFI Analiticheskii Tsentr 2022). When UNAH002 polled members of INOC008 about the death penalty, an extremely large majority of voters (n=50) supported capital punishment. Around that time, only a large majority of the general public supported it (cf. Semukhina and Galliher 2009: 143).

In INOC008, when UNAH006 held a poll about state systems, minority preferences among voters (n=19) spanned the options of democracy, socialism, anarchy, parliamentarism, republicanism, monarchy and dictatorship; when UNAH008 held a poll about Lenin, a very large minority of voters (n=29) approved while an extremely large minority disapproved; and when UNAH002 held a poll about Stalin, a large majority of voters (n=45) approved while a very large minority disapproved. However, when UNAH011 held a poll about voting intentions, it suggested distinct political trends among the artifact hunting community, since almost none of the voters (n=143) opted for the ruling United Russia party while almost half opted for the Communist Party of the Russian Federation, whereas almost half of the citizenry voted for United Russia while only a large minority voted for the Communist Party (cf. Centre for the Study of Public Policy 2011).

Opposition

Despite narrower community tendencies and broader societal trends in circumstances of intolerance and oppression in Russia, there are smaller and larger expressions of nonconformity and dissent, on issues of history as well as archaeology. For instance, on one occasion, an outraged museum journalist in Ukraine reported that 'antique barons [Antykvarni baryhy]' were auctioning a silver Grivna ingot from Kyivan Rus that had been either 'stolen and exchanged [with a counterfeit] in [a] museum [kradena-pidminena v muzeyakh]' or, most likely, 'quietly dug up somewhere by black [market] archaeologists, smuggled to Moscow, [then] from there to the United States [des tykho vykopana chornymy arkheolohamy, contraband no perevezena do Moskvy, a zvidtydo SShA]' (Trygub 2017). He observed that the 'seller [was] obviously from Russia [Prodavets – yavno z Rosii]', 'because they are the ones who are actively promoting Putin's schizophrenic ideological message that Kievan Rus belongs to Russia [Bo same vony aktyvno prosuvayut shyzofrenichniyi putinskiyi ideolohichniyi posyl, shcho Kyiyvska Rusnadezhyt Rosiyi]' (Trygub 2017), and the provenance in the auction catalogue attributed the origins of the object to 'RUSSIA[,] Kiev' (Stack's Bowers Galleries 2017). In response, an ethical artifact hunter in Belarus, BYAH016, who refrained from targeting known archaeological sites and had intervened to stop looting in a historic neighbourhood in his city, shared the news without comment, in apparent agreement with the tone of the report. Following an estimate of USD 1,500-2,000, the ingot sold for USD 1,800.

Likewise, there are some matters of preservation of archaeology that unite artifact hunters with archaeologists. For instance, on one occasion, an infrastructural development company from Chechnya, Interbiznes-55, dug channels for water and sewage works in occupied Crimea, 'without the consent or presence of archaeologists [bez sohlasovaniya y prysutstviya arkheolohov]'; exposed (then disregarded) some human remains and other archaeological remains; and mixed and dumped other archaeological deposits as waste in the moat around the Genoese fortress in Feodosia (Polyakova 2020). In response, an artifact hunter there, UAAH047, informed artifact hunters in Belarus that the ancient city was being "mercilessly destroyed"; that there were also mass graves of thousands of prisoners of war and civilians from the Russian Civil War and the Second World War; and that this evidence of "war crimes had never been properly investigated".

Economic and Political Insecurity and Criminal Coping Mechanisms

Economic and Political Insecurity

Economic insecurity is known to intersect with artifact hunting (Hardy 2016: 215), and to be reflected in an intersection between artifact hunting and cannabis farming (as documented by Hardy forthcoming c), in Eastern Europe. When UNAH005 polled members of INOC008, almost none of the voters (n=96) were students; almost none were pensioners; a small minority were unemployed; a small minority worked on flexible or freelance contracts; a large minority were self-employed (when only a small minority of the citizenry were self-employed, cf. International Labor Organization, cited by World Bank n.d.); a small minority worked on a shift basis, twenty-four hours on, three days off; almost none worked on a shift basis, twelve hours a day, six days a week; and an extremely large minority were full-time employed (when a very large majority of the citizenry were full-time employed, cf. Karabchuk 2012: 23). Ethnographic research suggested that, at least in Kaliningrad, 'most' artifact-hunters were 'temporarily unemployed', while 'some' others had abandoned regular working-class labour to 'make a living by digging and selling' (Sezneva 2007: 26). When UNAH005 polled members of INOC008, a coincident, extremely large minority of voters (n=26) paid tax on their legal income, possibly simply because the identifiable income from their full-time employment could not be hidden, yet a small majority either evaded tax on their legal income or earned an entirely illegal income.

Between 2020 and 2021, as Russia became more insecure in terms of both economics and politics, search queries for metal-detectors increased by 50% nationwide (as researched by VseInstrumenty.Ru and reported by New Retail 2021). Although there are many factors in developments within regions and across the country, there are indications that an acute sense of economic and political insecurity contributed to the increased interest in artifact hunting. Notably, searches for metal-detectors increased even more in the southwestern city of Kazan (150%), which is the capital of the relatively poorer Tatarstan oblast. Tatarstan has been a disproportionate source of volunteer soldiers and has become a disproportionate target for mobilised soldiers; and they increased yet more in the far-southern city of Rostov-on-Don (267%), which is across the border from the long-occupied territories of Ukraine and has become a military center for Russia. Now there is a shortage of metal-detectors even for the Armed Forces of the Russian Federation, which is accepting home-made, hand-built devices from volunteers (according to a Russian soldier who was testing a device, cited by Hotrico 2024).

Meanwhile, according to Russia-based, eBay-equivalent, online marketplace Avito, there was a 13% decrease in the price of metal-detectors, a 54% increase in adverts and a 65% increase in purchases (as reported by MFD 2021). As had been noted in a previous study by Avito, 'due to the high cost of metal-detectors, income is also generated from their rental [yz-za visokoyi stoimosti metalloiskateleyi uslekhom polzuetsya i ikh arenda]' (as reported by Vasilenko 2019).

Criminal Coping Mechanisms

Attitudes toward the war and activity during the war are extremely complex and deeply intertwined. They have been the subject of tens if not hundreds of thousands of messages among artifact hunters since 24 February 2022 alone and must be analysed separately. Still, some comments exemplify sentiments among artifact hunters and developments in relation to the war.

While it was complicated by inflation (according to RUAH159 and RUAH150), anti-war Belarus-based Russian BYAH006 and anti-war Russia-based Belarusian RUAH153 informed their pro-war peers that suppliers had raised the prices of metal-detectors by 10-40% at the moment of the intensification of the invasion, so it would become difficult for them to sustain their activity. BYAH031 was cashing in on the insatiable demand amid the crisis, asking for 65% more for a used device than the original price for a new device.

Pro-war Russian RUAH157, who had volunteered to serve in the invading forces and was waiting to be called up, suggested that they could cope by buying equipment from China instead. However, anti-war Russian RUAH156 mocked his pro-war peers, because he believed that the realisation of their desire for war would collapse the collecting market along with the rest of the economy, so their finds would be worth nothing at all in practice and, therefore, they would not have an income to reinvest in equipment, even if they had access to a supplier in China in theory.

At the time of writing, more than three years into the intensified invasion, pro-war cultural property criminals appear to have been proven correct by the course of events. Among artifact hunters, arguments continue, ranging from the state and sustainability of Russia's economy, to problems with personal payments for devices from international enterprises, to differences in life expectancy between the Russian Federation and the European Union. Nevertheless, Russia's economy is still growing albeit slowly; inflation is rising quickly, yet incomes are rising even more quickly (according to Prokopenko and Kolyandr 2024). There is even a risk of an 'association of Putin's wartime leadership with prosperity and economic growth, and peace with decline and humiliation' (according to Prokopenko 2024). Even worse, as documented with OSINT (e.g. Hardy 2022b), even more cultural property criminals have taken up positions in the armed forces, paramilitary organisations, private military companies, occupying administrations and collaborationist networks of the invading forces.

Conclusion

Over the course of decades, a complex ecosystem of local, national and international online forums and social networks has evolved around the unscientific extraction and consumption of archaeological goods from Eastern Europe and North Asia. For those involved, it facilitates online social organisation of and participation in looting, dealing and collecting. For those outside, its user-generated content facilitates analysis of the development and functioning of those markets, the challenges of policing, the demographics and politics of their participants, and the politics and economics of the activities.

Looking in, we see that artifact hunters tend to be self-consciously criminal, yet publicly defensive of their premeditated hunting and opportunistic taking of various arrays of ancient, historic and modern artifacts (if not their handling of human remains), in a way that is not mirrored by other criminal communities, except perhaps by handlers of soft recreational drugs such as cannabis and hallucinogenic mushrooms. Artifact-hunters' behaviour reflects a combination of various factors, particularly the inevitable difficulties of policing and the societal challenges of weak rule of law and consequent legal nihilism.

Despite women's advances in artifact hunting specifically and in society generally, due to the physical demands of the activity and the business leanings of the participants that intensify the physical demands (even among the self-professed hobbyists), it is a (seemingly specifically heterosexual) young man's game. They appear to maintain distinctly precarious livelihoods, at least sometimes, by choice, due to a prioritisation of freedom over security. Furthermore, they appear to hold disproportionately extreme right-wing views. As a consequence of the confluence of these factors, they may play a disproportionate role in state violence and other violent political extremism. Hence, illicit trafficking of cultural goods is not only a cultural and economic problem, but also a political and security problem. Open-source research can augment efforts to combat it on all of these fronts.

Dr. Samuel Andrew Hardy is a researcher at Rey Juan Carlos University (URJC), for work on destructive exploitation and care of cultural objects and professional/public education for sustainable heritage management (DECOPE), with funding from the Joint Programming Initiative on Cultural Heritage and Ethics. He is also an expert in the Alliance to Counter Crime Online and an honorary lecturer at the Institute of Archaeology, University College London.

REFERENCES

Artsibasheva, Tatiana. 2015. 'Klad i Kladoiskatelstvo v Etimologii, Tipologii i Sovremennoyi Zhizni [Treasure and Treasure Hunting in Etymology, Typology and Modern Life]', *Uchenie Zapiski. Elektronniy Nauchniy Zhurnal Kurskogo Gosudarstvennogo Universiteta* 1(33): 1–9.

Axelsen, Irmelin. 2022. 'Collaboration and Communication between Hobby Metal Detectorists and Archaeologists in Norway', *Advances in Archaeological Practice* 10(3): 295–310.

Axelsen, Irmelin, Thomas, Suzie and Vaitkevičius, Vykintas. 2022. 'Digital Archaeological Knowledge Production and Communication among Metal Detectorists: a Web Focus Group Discussion', *Journal of Community Archaeology and Heritage* 10(2): 90–106.

Bakalchuk, Vladyslava. 2019. 'Zberezhennya ta Okhorona Kulturnoyi Spadshchyny v Krymu: Aktualni Vyklyky ta Problemy [Preservation and Protection of Cultural Heritage in Crimea: Current Challenges and Problems]', *Stratehichi Priorytety* 50(2): 46–52.

Barford, Paul. 2020. 'Some Aspects of the Collection-Driven Exploitation of the Archaeological Record in England and Wales', *Revista d'Arqueologia de Ponent* 30: 101–125.

Borba, Valdinéa. 2008. 'A Expressão da Afetividade na Educação Infantil: Concepções de Algumas Docentes [the Expression of Affectivity in Early Childhood Education: Conceptions of Some Teachers]', *Nucleus* 5(1): 40–47.

Brodie, Neil. 2020. 'What Is This Thing Called the PAS? Metal-Detecting Entanglements in England and Wales', *Revista d'Arqueologia de Ponent* 30: 85–100.

Centre for the Study of Public Policy. 2011. 'Duma Voting Behaviour: 2011 – Final Result of the Duma Election, 4 December 2011', *Russia Votes*, 15 December. Retrieved 28 July 2024 from https://web.archive.org/web/20120111174030/http://www.russiavotes.org:80/duma/duma_today.php.

Chereneva, Vera. 2020. 'Pochemu Obshchestvo tak Sniskhoditelno k Deyatelnosti "Chernikh Kopateleyi"? [Why Is Society so Lenient toward the Activities of "Black Diggers"?]', *Ekonomika Severo-Zapada*, 30 June. Retrieved 28 July 2024 from https://rg.ru/2020/06/30/reg-szfo/pochemu-obshchestvo-tak-snishoditelno-k-deiatelnosti-chernyh-kopatelej.html.

Cultural Resilience Informatics and Analysis (Curia) Lab. 2024. *Documenting the Appropriation of Cultural Assets from Kherson Art Museum – a Conflict Observatory Report*. Charlottesville: Cultural Resilience Informatics and Analysis (Curia) Lab.

Daubney, Adam. 2017. 'Floating Culture: the Unrecorded Antiquities of England and Wales', *International Journal of Heritage Studies* 23: 785–799.

Davis, Dan, Morgan, Brian, Burns, Daniel, Barnhill, David and Davis, Mark. 2020. 'Populating a Virtual Conversation Database: Community Data Collection and Analysis', in National Training and Simulation Association (ed), *Proceedings of MODSIM World 2020*. Norfolk: National Training and Simulation Association. Retrieved 28 July 2024 from http://www.modsimworld.org/papers/2020/MODSIM_2020_paper_7_.pdf.

Deckers, Pieterjan, Dobat, Andres, Ferguson, Natasha, Heeren, Stijn, Lewis, Michael and Thomas, Suzie. 2018. 'The Complexities of Metal Detecting Policy and Practice: a Response to Samuel Hardy, "Quantitative Analysis of Open-Source Data on Metal Detecting for Cultural Property" (Cogent Social Sciences 3, 2017)', *Open Archaeology* 4: 322–333.

Dobat, Andres and Jensen, Astrid. 2016. '"Professional Amateurs": Metal Detecting and Metal Detectorists in Denmark', *Open Archaeology* 2: 70–84.

Economist. 2024. 'Dealers Are Selling War Trophies to Buy Weapons for Ukraine', *The Economist*, 9 May. Retrieved 22 March 2025 from https://www.economist.com/europe/2024/05/09/dealers-are-selling-war-trophies-to-buy-weapons-for-ukraine.

Escrivá, Ángeles and Barber, Ferran. 2023. 'El Soldado Muerto Español (Según los Rusos) Estaba Muy Vivo... y Nos Manda una Prueba de Vida Irrefutable [The Spanish Soldier Who Was Dead (According to the Russians) Was Very Much Alive... and He Sends Us Irrefutable Proof of Life]', *El Mundo*, 20 February. Retrieved 22 March 2025 from https://www.elmundo.es/cronica/2023/02/20/63eff176fdddffe5488b4583.html.

Gershkovich, Yakiv. 2020. 'Embezzlement and Destruction of the Archaeological Heritage in Ukraine: Real Scale and Catastrophic Results', *International Conference on Handling of Cultural Goods and Financing of Political Violence, Online, 22–23 October 2020*. Rome: Norwegian Institute in Rome, University of Oslo.

Guzzo, Siria and Padley, Roxanne. 2021. 'New Practices in Academia: Moving towards Hybridity', *I-LanD* 2: 92–112.

Hardy, Samuel. 2016 [2018]. '"Black Archaeology" in Eastern Europe: Metal Detecting, Illicit Trafficking of Cultural Objects and "Legal Nihilism" in Belarus, Poland, Russia and Ukraine', *Public Archaeology* 15(4): 214–237.

Hardy, Samuel. 2017a. 'Quantitative Analysis of Open-Source Data on Metal Detecting for Cultural Property: Estimation of the Scale and Intensity of Metal Detecting and the Quantity of Metal-Detected Cultural Goods', *Cogent Social Sciences* 3(1). http://dx.doi.org/10.1080/23311886.2017.1298397.

Hardy, Samuel. 2017b. 'Illegal Finders of Antiquities in Ukraine: Do Digital Data Indicate Grassroots Growth, Coincidence, False Advertising, Astroturfing, Trolling or Sockpuppetry?', *Ukrainian Archaeology* 2016: 3–14.

Hardy, Samuel. 2018. 'Metal Detecting for Cultural Objects until "There Is Nothing Left": the Potential and Limits of Digital Data, Netnographic Data and Market Data for Analysis', *Arts* 7(3). https://doi.org/10.3390/arts7030040.

Hardy, Samuel. 2019a. 'To Get a Good Price, "You Have to Sell in International Bidding Sites": Trafficking of Metal-Detected Cultural Goods from South Asia', in Saskia Hufnagel and Anton Moiseienko (eds), *Criminal Networks and Law Enforcement: Global Perspectives on Illegal Enterprise*. London: Routledge, pp. 93–119.

Hardy, Samuel. 2019b. '"Paint It Black": "Simple" and Increasingly "Professional" Looting of Antiquities with Metal Detectors in East Asia', in Valsamis Mitsilegas, Saskia Hufnagel, Anton Moiseienko, Yanan Shi and Mingxiang Liu (eds), *Transnational Crime: European and Chinese Perspectives*. Abingdon: Routledge, pp. 103–126.

Hardy, Samuel. 2020a. 'Treasure-Hunters "Even from Sweden", Organised Criminals and "Lawless" Police in the Eastern Mediterranean: Online Social Organisation of Looting and Trafficking of Antiquities from Turkey, Greece and Cyprus', *Revista d'Arqueologia de Ponent* 30: 215–240.

Hardy, Samuel. 2020b. '"You Just Have to Wear It": Trafficking of Metal-Detected Antiquities from South-East Asia', in Saskia Hufnagel and Anton Moiseienko (eds), *Policing Transnational Crime: Law Enforcement of Criminal Flows*. London: Routledge, pp. 63–95.

Hardy, Samuel. 2021: 'It Is Not against the Law, If No One Can See You: Online Social Organisation of Artifact-Hunting in Former Yugoslavia', *Journal of Computer Applications in Archaeology [Special Issue on Fighting Illicit Trade in Antiquities with Digital Technology]* 4(1): 169–187.

Hardy, Samuel. 2022a. 'Attitudes to Personal and Public Health Precautions among Artifact-Hunters amid the Covid-19 Pandemic', *Conflict Antiquities*, 1 August. Retrieved 28 July 2024 from https://conflictantiquities.wordpress.com/2022/08/01/artifact-hunters-social-attitudes-personal-public-health-precautions-covid-19-coronavirus-pandemic/.

Hardy, Samuel. 2022b. 'Looting of Antiquities from Ukraine by Soldiers, Collaborators and Ordinary Criminals, Trafficking to and through Russia and Dealing and Collecting in Western Europe, since 2014', *Scientific and Practical Seminar on Protection and Preservation of the Archaeological Heritage of Ukraine, Kyiv, 2 December 2022*. Kyiv: Taras Shevchenko National University of Kyiv, the State Institute of Cultural Heritage of the Ministry of Culture and Information Policy of Ukraine, the Institute of Archaeology of the National Academy of Sciences of Ukraine and the Municipal Center for Conservation of Archaeological Objects.

Hardy, Samuel. 2023. 'Looting and Trafficking of Antiquities during Russia's War on Ukraine', *Globalization, Illicit Trade, Sustainability and Security (GLITSS) Webinar, 2 May 2023*. Groningen: Globalization, Illicit Trade, Sustainability and Security (GLITSS).

Hardy, Samuel. Forthcoming a. 'Theft and Destruction of Knowledge in Ukraine, Russia and Belarus', in Gill, David and Barford, Paul (eds), *Knowledge Theft, Artifact Hunting and Archaeological Context in Europe*. Oxford: Archaeopress.

Hardy, Samuel. Forthcoming b. '"If We Just Stopped Stealing, We Would Have Enough Money for Everything": Cultural Property Crime by Police Officers and Legal Nihilism among Professional Criminals and Ordinary Citizens in Russia', *Forensic Archaeology, Anthropology and Ecology*.

Hardy, Samuel. Forthcoming c: 'Criminal Choices for Precarious Livelihoods: Antiquities Looting by Cannabis Cultivators in Poland, Russia and Ukraine'. *Public Archaeology*.

Hardy, Samuel and Telizhenko, Serhii. 2023: 'Russia Was "Doomed to Expand [Its] Aggression" against Ukraine: Cultural Property Criminals' Responses to the Invasion and Occupation of the Donbas since 20th February 2014'. *The Historic Environment: Policy and Practice* 14(3): 286–307.

Hardy, Samuel and Telizhenko, Serhii. Forthcoming. '"This Is All My Own, My Motherland, Russia": Cultural Property Criminals' Responses to the Invasion and Occupation of Crimea Since 20th February 2014', in Francisco Romeo Marugán (ed), *Expolio y Tráfico Ilícito de Bienes Arqueológicos; Redes, Estrategias y Procedimientos*. Zaragoza: Gobierno de Aragón.

Hotrico. 2024. 'Due to the Lack of Metal Detectors in the Russian Army, Soldiers Are Having to Rely on Homemade Detectors Made by Russian Volunteers, Detectors Whose Quality and Reliability Can Vary, a Variation that Can Be Very Dangerous', *Reddit*, 7 August. Retrieved 27 March 2025 from https://www.reddit.com/r/UkraineWarVideoReport/comments/1emav0t/due_to_the_lack_of_metal_detectors_in_the_russian/.

Immonen, Visa and Kinnunen, Joonas. 2016. '"Quidditching" and the Emergence of New Heritage Identities – Amateur Metal Detecting in Finland', *Public Archaeology* 15(4): 163–185.

Immonen, Visa and Kinnunen, Joonas. 2020. 'Metal Detecting as a Social Formation: a Longitudinal Survey Study from Finland', *Journal of Social Archaeology* 20(3): 313–334.

Iskatel. 2013. 'Tulskie Poiskoviki Podderzhivayut Pravitelstvennii Zakonoproekt o Borbe s Nezakonnimi Raskopkami [Tula Searchers Support the Government Bill on Combating Illegal Excavations]', *PoiskoviiTsentr 'Iskatel'*, 27 February. Retrieved 1 October 2017 from http://www.iskateltula.ru/novosti/tulskie-poiskoviki-poderzhivayut-pravitelstvenyi-zakonoproekt-o-borbe-s-nezakonymi-raskopkami.html.

Karabchuk, Tatiana. 2012. 'Part-Time and Temporary Workers in Russia: Winners or Losers?', *Journal for Labour Market Research* 45: 23–39.

Karl, Raimund. 2011. 'On the Highway to Hell: Thoughts on the Unintended Consequences for Portable Antiquities of § 11(1) Austrian Denkmalschutzgesetz', *the Historic Environment: Policy and Practice* 2(2): 111–133.

Karl, Raimund. 2013. 'Do As We Say, Not As We Do! Archaeological Heritage Protection and the Excluded Austrian Public', in Agneta Lagerlöf (ed), *Who Cares? Perspectives on Public Awareness, Participation and Protection in Archaeological Heritage Management*. Jambes: Europae Archaeologiae Consilium, pp. 115–122.

Koropeckyj, Damian, Greenland, Fiona, Harrell, Katherine, Jasparro, Chris, Munevar, Santiago and Hardy, Samuel. 2024. *Documenting Russian Military Activity in the Vicinity of Ancient Ukrainian Burial Mounds: Fortification, Destruction, and Possible Looting. A Conflict Observatory Report*. Charlottesville: Cultural Resilience Informatics and Analysis (Curia) Lab.

Lykkegård-Maes, Mette and Dobat, Andres. 2022. 'Hunters of the Past – a Study of Demography, Attitudes, and Values among Danish Metal Detector Users', *Danish Journal of Archaeology* 11: 1–22.

MFD. 2021. 'Rossiyane s Maya Stali Chashche Interesovatsya Pokupkoyi Metalloiskatelya Dlya Poiska Kladov [Since May, Russians Have Become More Interested in Buying a Metal Detector to Search for Treasures]', *MFD*, 18 June. Retrieved 28 July 2024 from https://mfd.ru/news/view/?id=2430320.

Millan, Francesc. 2024. 'Se Vende Uniforme de Soldado Ruso Muerto: Entrega Rápida a Barcelona [Dead Russian Soldier's Uniform for Sale: Fast Delivery to Barcelona]', *Ara*, 27 May. Retrieved 22 March 2025 from https://es.ara.cat/internacional/europa/vende-uniforme-soldado-ruso-muerto-entrega-rapida-barcelona_130_5041587.html.

Mishchenko, Maryna. 2017.'Kryminolohichna Kharakterystyka Osoby Zhinky, Yaka Vchynyaye Kontrabandu Kulturnykh Tsinnosteyi [Criminological Characteristics of Female Persons, Who Smuggles Cultural Property]', *Visnyk Penitentsianoyiasotsiatsiyi Ukrayiny* 1: 190–195.

NAFI Analiticheskii Tsentr. 2022.'Bolshinstvo Rossiyan Sochuvstvuyut Bezdomnim, i Tolko Edinitsi Ikh Boyatsya [Most Russians Sympathize with the Homeless, and Only a Few Are Afraid of Them]', *NAFI Analiticheskii Tsentr*, 1 February. Retrieved 28 July 2024 from https://nafi.ru/analytics/bolshinstvo-rossiyan-sochuvstvuyut-bezdomnym-i-tolko-edinitsy-ikh-boyatsya/.

New Retail. 2021.'VseInstrumenti.ru: Polovina Rossiyan Mechtaet Nayiti Klad i Razbogatet [VseInstrumenty.Ru: Half of Russians Dream of Finding Treasure and Getting Rich]', *New Retail*, 18 June. Retrieved 28 July 2024 from https://new-retail.ru/novosti/retail/vseinstrumenty_ru_polovina_rossiyan_mechtaet_nayti_klad_i_razbogatet5383/.

Pew Forum on Religion and Public Life. 2011. *The Future of the Global Muslim Population: Projections for 2010-2030*. Washington, D.C.: Pew Research Center.

Polyakova, Vera. 2020. "V Feodosii Bezzhalostno Unichtozhayut Istoriyu Goroda [the History of the City Is Being Ruthlessly Destroyed in Feodosia]", *Kafa News*, 17 December. Retrieved 28 July 2024 from https://kafanews.com/novosti/174029/v-feodosii-bezshalostno-unichtoshayut-istoriyu-goroda_2020-12-17.

Prokopenko, Alexandra. 2024.'Russia's Economic Gamble: The Hidden Costs of War-Driven Growth', *Carnegie Politika*, 20 December. Retrieved 27 March 2025 from https://carnegieendowment.org/russia-eurasia/politika/2024/12/russia-economy-difficulties.

Prokopenko, Alexandra and Kolyandr, Alexander. 2024.'The Russian Economy in 9 Graphs', *the Bell*, 20 December. Retrieved 27 March 2025 from https://en.thebell.io/the-russian-economy-in-9-graphs/.

Prokuratura Vladimirskoi Oblasti. 2019.'Vstupil v Silu Prigovor Yuev-Polskovo Prayionnovo Suda po Delu o Nezakonnom Poiske i Izyatii Arkheologicheskikh Predmetov iz Mest Zaleganiya [the Verdict of the Yuryev-Polsky District Court in the Case of Illegal Search and Removal of Archaeological Objects from Burial Places Has Come into Force]', *Prokuratura Vladimirskoi Oblasti*, 22 March. Retrieved 28 July 2024 from https://web.archive.org/web/20190323044104/http://vladprok.ru/vstupil-v-silu-prigovor-yurev-polskogo-rajonnogo-suda-po-delu-o-nezakonnom-poiske-i-izyatii-arheolog.

Rasmussen, Josephine. 2014.'Securing Cultural Heritage Objects and Fencing Stolen Goods? A Case Study on Museums and Metal Detecting in Norway', *Norwegian Archaeological Review* 47(1): 83–107.

Respublika Belarus. 2016.'Kodeks Respubliki Belarus ab Kulturi [413–3] [Code of the Republic of Belarus on Culture [413–3]]'. *Respublika Belarus*, 20 July. Retrieved 28 July 2024 from https://web.archive.org/web/20170123074053/http://www.pravo.by/document/?guid=12551&p0=Hk1600413&p1=1.

Robbins, Katherine. 2012. *From Past to Present: Understanding the Impact of Sampling Bias on Data Recorded by the Portable Antiquities Scheme, PhD Dissertation*. Southampton: University of Southampton.

Rossiiskaya Federatsiya. 2013. 'Federalnii Zakon o Vnesenii Izmeneniyi v Otdelnie Zakonodatelnie Akti RF v Chasti Presecheniya Nezakonnoyi Deyatelnosti v Oblasti Arkheologii [245-FZ] [Federal Law on Amendments to Certain Legislative Acts of the Russian Federation Regarding the Suppression of Illegal Activities in the Field of Archaeology [245-FZ]]', *Rossiiskaya Gazeta*, 23 July. Retrieved 28 July 2024 from https://rg.ru/2013/07/26/arch-dok.html.

Seleev, Sergei and Molyarenko, Olga. 2023: '"Metalloiskatel Kupil, i Poneslos. . .": Ustroyistvo i Praktiki Pribornogo v Rossii ["I Bought a Metal Detector and Things Are off and Rolling. . .": Organization and Practices of Metal Detecting in Russia]'. *Mir Rossii* 32(3): 28–51.

Semukhina, Olga and Galliher, John. 2009. 'Death Penalty Politics and Symbolic Law in Russia', *International Journal of Law, Crime and Justice* 37: 131–153.

Sezneva, Olga. 2007. '"We Have Never Been German": The Economy of Digging in Russian Kaliningrad', in Craig Calhoun and Richard Sennett (eds), *Practicing Culture*. London: Routledge, pp. 13–34.

Shelep, Volodymyr. 2022. 'Maroderstvo, Tak Zvana "Chorna Arkheolohiya", Nabula Vseosyazhnosti ta Bezkarnosti [Looting, So-Called "Black Archaeology", Has Acquired Comprehensiveness and Impunity]', *Galinfo*, 1 July. Retrieved 28 July 2024 from https://galinfo.com.ua/news/maroderstvo_tak_zvana_chorna_arheologiya_nabula_vseosyazhnosti_ta_bezkarnosti_387127.html.

Shydlovskyi, Pavlo, Telizhenko, Serhii and Ivakin, Vsevolod. 2023. 'Archaeological Monitoring in War-Torn Ukraine', *the Historic Environment: Policy and Practice* 14(2): 154–180.

Skibchyk, Serhii. 2019. 'Vidchuvayuchy Bezkarnist, "Chorni Arkheolohy" Vzhe Rozkopuyut Mohyly na Bakhoviyi Hori [Sensing Impunity, "Black Archaeologists" Are Already Excavating Graves on Bachova Gora]', *Holos Ukrayiny*, 7 March. Retrieved 28 July 2024 from http://www.golos.com.ua/article/314573.

SSSR. 1986. 'Instruktsiya o Poryadke Ucheta, Obespecheniya Sokhrannosti, Soderzhaniya, Ispolzovaniya i Restavratsii Nedvizhimikh Pamyatnikov Istorii i Kulturi [Instructions on the Procedure for Recording, Ensuring the Safety, Maintenance, Use and Restoration of Immovable Monuments of History and Culture]', *Ministertva Kulturi SSSR*, 13 May. Retrieved 28 July 2024 from https://web.archive.org/web/20220522044543/https://zakon.rada.gov.ua/laws/show/v0203400-86#Text.

Stack's Bowers. 2017. 'RUSSIA. Kiev. Grivna Ingot, ND (ca. 11th–13th Century). VERY FINE. [Lot 21314, Ancient Coins and World Coins Part 2 (Haiti-Yemen), 3 December 2017–13 January 2018, Stack's Bowers Galleries, New York, United States.]', *Stack's Bowers Galleries*, 3 December. Retrieved 28 July 2024 from https://auctions.stacksbowers.com/lots/view/3-96D45/russia-kiev-grivna-ingot-nd-ca-11th-13th-century-very-fine.

Tania. 2016. 'Ishchut Arkheologi, Ishchet Militsiya: Kladoiskatelstvo Obyavleno Vne Zakona [Archaeologists Are Looking, Police Are Looking: Treasure Hunting Is Outlawed]', *Mayak Prydnyaproyiya*, 4 March. Retrieved 28 July 2024 from https://www.bykhov.by/?p=109270.

Telizhenko, Serhii. 2019. 'Sytuatsiya z Akheolohichnoyu Spadshchynoyu v Zoni Provedennya Boyiovykh Diyi (Luhanska Oblast) [the Situation of Archaeological Heritage in the Area of Hostilities (Luhansk region)]', *Seminar on Archaeology in Occupied Territories and in Zones of Armed Conflict [Arkheolohiya na Okupovanykh Terytoriyakh ta u Zonakh Zbroyinykh Konfliktiv], Kyiv, 16 May 2019*. Kyiv: VHO Spilka Arkheolohiv Ukrayiny ta Institut Arkheolohiyi NANU.

Thomas, Suzie. 2012. 'Searching for Answers: a Survey of Metal-Detector Users in the UK', *International Journal of Heritage Studies* 18(1): 49–64.

Thomas, Suzie and Deckers, Pieterjan. 2022. 'And Now They Have Taken over: Hobbyist and Professional Archaeologist Encounters with the Material Heritage of the First World War in Western Belgium', *International Journal of Heritage Studies* 28(1): 1–15.

Trygub, Viktor. 2017. 'V SShA prodayut hryvnu Kyivskoyi Rusi! Minkult ne znaye? [The Hryvnia of Kyivan Rus Is Being Sold in the USA! Does the Ministry of Culture Not Know?]', *Muzeyi Ukrayiny*, 21 December. Retrieved 28 July 2024 from https://www.museum-ukraine.info/?p=2965.

Tsitsagi, Nikita. 2021. 'Iskat-Kopat: V Poiskakh Predmetov Vtoroyi Mirovoyi s Chornim Kopatelem [Search-Dig: In Search of Objects from the Second World War with a Black Digger]', *Zapovednik*, 27 May. Retrieved 22 March 2025 from https://zapovednik.space/material/iskat-kopat.

Tuzbekov, Ainur. 2019. 'Sotsialnie Seti Kak Rekurs v Issledovanii Deyatelnosti "Kladoiskateleyi" (Primer Respubliki Bashkortostan) [Social Networks As a Resource in the Study of the Activities of "Treasure Hunters" (the Case of the Republic of Bashkortostan)]', *Sotsiodinamika* 12: 126–133.

Tuzbekov, Ainur. 2020. '"Kladoiskatelstvo" Kak Faktor Razrusheniya Arkheologicheskikh Pamyatnikov Novovo Vremeni (Primer Respubliki Bashkortostan) ["Treasure-Hunting" As a Factor of Destruction of Modern Age Archaeological Sites (the Case of the Republic of Bashkortostan)]', *Rossiiskaya Arkheologiya* 2020(1): 107–116.

Ujhelyi, Nóra. 2016. *The Relationship between Archaeology and Metal Detecting in Present Day Hungary, Master's Dissertation*. Budapest: Central European University.

Vasilenko, Andrei. 2019. 'Zhiteli Saratova v 2019 Godu Nachali Aktivnee Iskat Kladi [in 2019, Residents of Saratov Began to Actively Search for Treasures]', *Bez Formata*, 31 October. Retrieved 28 July 2024 from https://saratov.bezformata.com/listnews/nachali-aktivnee-iskat-kladi/78922328/.

Vasyutin, Sergei, Marochkin, Aleksei, German, Pavel, Sizyov, Aleksandr and Gorlyshkin, Nikita. 2020. 'Osnovnie Vizovi Sokhraneniyu Arkheologicheskogo Naslediya Kuzbassa. Chast 1: "Arkheologicheskoe" Kladoiskatelstvo [Key Challenges of Archaeological Heritage Preservation in Kuzbass. Part I: "Archaeological" Treasure Hunting]', *Vestnik Kemerovskogo Gosudarstvennogo Universiteta*, 22(2): 307–317. https://doi.org/10.21603/2078-8975-2020-22-2-307-317.

Verkhovna Rada. 2004. 'Law on Protection of Archaeological Heritage', *Vidomosti* 26: 361. Retrieved 28 July 2024 from https://web.archive.org/web/20210514024227/https://en.unesco.org/sites/default/files/ua_law_protection_archaelogical_heritage_engtof.pdf.

voxpop_66. 2019. 'Chastnaya Kollektsiya Oruzhiya Igorya Altushkina [Private Collection of Weapons of Igor Altushkin]', *Livejournal*, 15 April. Retrieved 22 May 2025 from https://voxpop-66.livejournal.com/2191881.html.

World Bank. N.d. 'Self-Employed, Total (% of Total Employment) (Modeled ILO Estimate) – Russian Federation', *World Bank*, no date. Retrieved 28 July 2024 from https://data.worldbank.org/indicator/SL.EMP.SELF.ZS?locations=RU.

Yuri Levada Analytical Center. 2020. 'Attitudes to Religion', *Yuri Levada Analytical Center*, 19 March. Retrieved 28 July 2024 from https://www.levada.ru/en/2020/03/19/attitudes-to-religion/.

Yuri Levada Analytical Center. 2021. 'The Attitude of Russians to the LGBT Community', *Yuri Levada Analytical Center*, 19 October. Retrieved 28 July 2024 from https://www.levada.ru/en/2021/10/19/the-attitude-of-russians-to-the-lgbt-community/.

CHAPTER 5

Cybercrimes and Chinese Cultural Relics

Status Quo, Legal Issues, Future Criminal Legislation, and Regulations

Hao Liu

Introduction

Understanding and resolving issues around the cybercrime of cultural relics is an interdisciplinary, complex, and ongoing research topic. However, it is far from complete. It is necessary to continue grappling with the dynamic evolution of this criminal phenomenon; applying multidisciplinary research methods from sociology, archaeology, economics, criminology, and law; and prudently reviewing the actual status of the application and implementation of domestic law and even international uniform substantive law to regulate against online heritage crime comprehensively.

As a traditionally identified source nation (Merryman 1986: 832) and emerging market nation within the global art market (Hao 2017: 381), the People's Republic of China (PRC)[1] (Bull 2009: 26; Polk 2000: 82) overtook the United Kingdom to move back into position as the second-largest global art market, ahead of the United States of America, in the first half of 2025.[2] Given this change in position within the global art market, the Chinese physical art market is also experiencing a significant transformation from the state-owned monopoly of cultural relics shops, as well as cultural relics auction enterprises and the rather limiting privately owned cultural relics shops, as well as cultural relics auction enterprises under the legal permit issued by the administrative departments of cultural relics of people's governments at different levels, to more popular and open-ended online trading platforms. The above dynamic evolution process reflects that the majority of commercial activities concerning the trade in cultural relics and its societal impacts were gradually extended to the portion of the Chinese art market occurring on emerging various online platforms and blockchain applications (Artzt and Richter 2020: 32–44) in the digitization of cultural heritage. As such, active primary (the trade between investors and online platforms) and secondary online art markets (the trade between different investors) have been going beyond the traditional transaction framework in the Chinese multi-jurisdictions, along with the ever-evolving development of non-fungible token (NFT) marketplaces and their potential for further investment, which witnessed a process of emergence and accelerated evolution by a new combination of online transactions and the use of NFTs (He and Zhang 2024: 19). In addition, such highly fluid and continuous Chinese trading marketplaces, with few barriers to entry, attract highly speculative buyers primarily focused on buying and reselling cultural relics (or NFT digital collectibles) in a concise amount of time for financial profit that derives from the direct impetus of further connecting society's economic activity to the application of high-tech digital technology so that the buyers will be endowed with an irrevocable digital certificate of ownership and authenticity for collecting and purchasing a unique cultural asset that cannot be duplicated or exchanged by others based on the protection of their digital copyrights.

However, as of this writing, Chinese official policies still adopt a scrupulous attitude toward applying NFTs through the lens of compliance under the existing legal system without being expressly forbidden. By contrast, as another outcome of blockchain technology, due to the risks of virtual currency trading and further suspected of disrupting the financial market and undermining financial security, the People's Bank of China has already issued a *Notice on Further Preventing and Resolving the Risks of Virtual Currency Trading and Speculation* to a blanket ban on virtual currency trading headed by Bitcoin, Ethereum, and Tether since 2021,[3] emphasizing that they do not enjoy the same status as legal tender and cannot be circulated as legal currency in the Chinese market.

Based on the current Chinese social environment and recent trends in cybercrimes, the research background of this chapter stems from the following three impetuses: firstly, the external impetus lies in the factual scenario that there is a high incidence of upstream crimes, such as illegal excavation and theft, with subsequently hidden downstream behavior such as the dumping and sale of stolen cultural relics. These activities are spreading to online platforms, and there is a need to fight against and stem the flow of such potential cybercrimes in light of the current trend of gangsterization, professionalization, and intellectualization of Chinese cultural relic crimes. Unfortunately, the National Administration of Cultural Heritage (NACH) and the Supreme People's Procuratorate jointly released the first batch of five typical cases of punishing crimes involving cultural relics in 2023, and there is no case concerning the cybercrimes of cultural relics.[4] Secondly, rational reflection on Chinese judicial practice summarizes that cybercrimes in Chinese jurisdictions have witnessed four different forms of crime: (1) that the network or a computer is the primary medium and carrier for the target of a crime (Grabosky

2007: 48) so that perpetrators launch an attack on a personal computer or network to destroy information systems;[5] (2) that a computer or network is an instrument of crime for producing, reproducing, publishing, selling illegal information, and disseminating erotic material for profit;[6] (3) that cybercrime is an incidental outcome to Chinese computer-related offenses, infringing on the interests of a network headed by real or virtual asset theft, and stolen public and private accounts, deriving other related crimes;[7] (4) that the network or online platforms themselves are criminal spaces or the locality of the crime.[8] Although the above four forms of cybercrime mutually coexist in Chinese jurisdictions, considering a computer network as a location of criminality has gradually extended traditional crimes involving cultural relics into cyberspace. In addition, neither Chinese legislation and judicial prosecution of crimes involving cultural relics nor existing judicial interpretations of the Supreme People's Court and the Supreme People's Procuratorate are carried out considering tangible cultural relics and digital collectibles as new tradable objects under the fourth form defining cybercrime.[9] It should be noted that the traditional criminal offenses involving cultural relics in mainland China can be charged with the six crimes of disrupting the administration of cultural relics under the existing Criminal Law. However, there are no new approaches or legal efforts to regulate cybercrime within the Chinese criminal legal context. Third, the internal impetus from the theoretical research shortage puts judicial courts in an awkward position, which consequently indulges the discretion of the judges. In addition, although cybercrime involving cultural relics has the potential to be a novel and flexible category of crime in China, Chinese judicial practices and professional practitioners of cultural relics are much more concerned about protecting Chinese cultural relics from the existing Law of the PRC on the Protection of Cultural Relics (LPCR) under the administrative legal framework rather than randomly adding the new criminal regulations on such relatively niche online crimes to damage the authority and stability of the Criminal Law from the public legal perspective.

The literature review presented below identifies that the existing published academic research contains significant discussion of the criminal punishments and regulations on cultural relics crime in general, but much less research examining the cybercrime of cultural relics. Thus far, research has mainly revolved around a limited threefold analysis: first, a range of studies focus on the Chinese criminal regulation and legislation on the crimes of disrupting the administration of cultural relics without relation to cybercrimes of cultural relics (Wang 2018; Yang 2015; Yu 2016; Ma 2008); second, the latest published papers tend to explore the issues involved in the digital collectibles headed by the NFTs from both angles of civil liability and intellectual property law rather than concern about criminal legal matters in this field (Tao 2022; Zhang 2024; Deng and Li 2022; Yu 2022; Zhang and Qi 2022); third, another few bits and pieces of the chapter examine the motivations, characteristics, and implications of cybercrimes regarding fraud, real asset theft, virtual asset theft, stolen accounts, and smuggling in China without considering the criminal offenses of cultural relics (Cai et al. 2018; Zhuge et al. 2009; Sun 2011). Such research outputs are much more classified as commerce-related civil matters or traditional economic crimes represented by white-collar crimes. However, existing studies have given very limited attention to cybercrimes involving cultural relics. The few that do exist concentrate on the general protection of cultural relics, without examining how to identify and detect crimes in which cultural relics are treated as subject matter and actual scenarios where online platforms are used to trade these cultural objects, thereby facilitating opportunities for the involved parties to commit such crimes. Given the above, academics and judicial practitioners have yet to consider what kinds of administrative regulation and criminal legislation are needed to tackle China's complex and evolving cybercrime landscape.

The following sections discuss the Chinese criminal legal context in a noncomparative way, exploring the specificities of online cultural relics crime. The first section presents an overview of a wide range of online cultural relics crime, as revealed by qualitative research represented by case studies. It aims to present the status quo regarding online cultural relics crime in China and why this category of crime is distinct under criminal law from traditional crimes against cultural relics offenses and to explore the motives for committing such a cybercrime. Due to the intrinsic defects of existing laws and weak criminal regulations applied to cybercrimes, the second section explores the legal issues involved in criminal adjudication and the regulation of cybercrimes relating to cultural relics. The final section addresses how laws and administrative regulations will be applied to cybercrime of cultural relics to ensure the sustainability and efficient operation of legal online transactions over the long term, which provides decision-makers and lawmakers with practical approaches to market regulations and suggestions for legislative reform to aid the fight against cybercrime of cultural relics when future cases involving Chinese cultural relics come to light.

The Status Quo on Cybercrimes of Cultural Relics

The following empirical research, centered around the case study methodology of qualitative research, can be divided into four parts. These cover the historical evolution of cybercrimes of cultural relics, the interpretation of terminology, research methodology, and results. Taken together, they objectively reflect the status quo of knowledge concerning cybercrime and Chinese cultural relics.

The Historical Evolution of Cybercrimes of Cultural Relics

In general, the history of cybercrimes on cultural relics is later than the history of the crimes disrupting the administration of cultural relics through offline forms of organized crimes. The latter can be dated back to the period of the policy of reforming and opening up initiated by the late Deng Xiaoping in 1978 (Grose 2006: 40–41) that led to increased economic activity and international engagement, which brought huge profits from the transnational business to the involved grave robbers and thieves as well as art dealers and smugglers. In addition, with the forming of a smuggling chain, many state-owned cultural relics have been stolen from unknown ancient tombs, cellars, and underwater cultural sites. Although the specific number and situation of crimes against cultural relics have not been grasped up to now, the means, objects, categories, and probabilities of these crimes have changed at that time, so it is imperative to adapt to the situation of these crimes in a specific period and adopt appropriate criminal policies to prevent and control them effectively. The single crime of smuggling has been developed into the crimes of intentionally destroying cultural relics, destroying state-protected places of historical interest or scenic beauty, destroying cultural relics through negligence (Article 324); the crime of illegally selling or privately giving valuable cultural relics prohibited by the state to foreigners as presents (Article 325); the crime of reselling cultural relics to reap profits (Article 326); the crime of illegally selling or privately giving cultural relics (Article 327); the crimes of robbing any site of ancient culture or ancient tomb of historical, artistic, or scientific value (Article 328); and the crime of seizing and stealing state-owned records (Article 329). The above six crimes are generally categorized as disrupting the administration of cultural relics under the 1979 Chinese Criminal Law.

Tracking back to the historical evolution of cybercrimes of cultural relics in China can be divided into three periods from Chinese judicial practices. From the late 1990s to 2002, although internet technology in China was rapidly popularized and developed at that time, there was a lag in domestic legal regulation and technical supervision, resulting in the gradual transformation of cultural relics crimes from the physical art market to the virtual spaces. This embryo period of cybercrime presents three typical features: First, technology-driven cybercrime was dominant and represented the criminal pattern of committing a white-collar crime. Criminals used early Chinese internet platforms (such as BBS forums, e-mail, and self-built websites) to release false information on cultural relics to implement fraud. Second, the characteristics of such cybercrime were cross-regional; criminals used online platforms to break through physical geographic limitations and gradually formed a model of contacting each other online and reaching a deal offline. Third, the criminals made full use of the loopholes in domestic laws, such as the 2002 revised LPCR, which did not specify the details of online cultural relics trading, and the 2015 Amendments to the Criminal Law (IX) lacked specific application of the criminalization and sentencing of online cultural relics fraud. Given this, the criminal group of the earliest online shopping fraud case of imitation bronzeware in 2001 self-built the Central Plains Cultural Relics Network and issued forged Shang Zhou bronzes and false authentication certificates to lure overseas buyers at a high price, involving an amount of 1.2 million yuan.[10] In this case, the court punished the principal offender with seven years' imprisonment for fraud and selling cultural relics.

The second rapid development period from 2003 to 2013 witnessed cybercrimes and fraud evolve in tandem with emerging e-commerce platforms and interacted with the establishment of the most significant social media, Weibo. With the launch of Taobao in 2003, the rise of C2C e-commerce, and the initial dissemination of Alipay in 2004. In 2010 a People's Court of Zhejiang Hangzhou prosecuted a group selling counterfeit Ming dynasty porcelain through the online platform Taobao. The defendants used stock images from museum catalogs and forged excavation permits, defrauding over 20 buyers of ¥500,000 before TaoBao's nascent monitoring systems flagged the store.[11] This case exposes the loopholes in the regulation of online platforms. Taobao was beginning to become a new channel for the outflow of cultural relics, so resale and smuggling crimes showed organized characteristics. Since the establishment of Weibo in 2009, it has gradually become a new venue for cultural relics fraud and cybercrime of cultural relics, with its characteristics of instant dissemination and social trust. In 2012 Weibo began appearing in the marketing scam's archaeological discovery. The parties involved in the case took advantage of the loopholes in real-name authentication in the early days of Weibo to register associated accounts in bulk, create public opinion hotspots, and claim to have discovered unregistered Han Dynasty jade artifacts by forging pictures of the field archaeology site and the Weibo accounts of experts certified by the Weibo company (e.g., @Huaxia Archaeology Team); users were lured into entering external phishing websites and induced to pay deposits.[12] However, this case from the early days of Weibo could not have been brought to justice or dealt with as other offenses because of the immaturity of the technology or the difficulty of detecting them.

Applying new technology and promoting diversified cybercrime scenes within the networks marked the third period from 2014 until now. On the one hand, some criminals used not only the existing Weibo to transform information into third-party platforms like WeChat and QQ to implement cross-border illicit trafficking of cultural relics but also, for the first time, blockchain technology to initiate the cybercrime of cultural relics. The principle of technological neutrality is being challenged as artificial intelligence deep forgery techniques begin to be applied to the production of forgeries. On the other hand, the cybercrime phenomenon boomed with the rise of the Chinese version of TikTok (DouYin). Short videos and live broadcasts on DouYin involved grave robbery, tomb exploration, forgery of archaeological sites, and illegal identification of unearthed cultural relics. Some video bloggers and anchors pursue traffic one-sidedly, deliberately distorting the value of archaeological work; using "treasure hunting" and "exploration" as gimmicks; promoting feudal superstitions, overnight wealth, and other undesirable values; or facilitating information for illegal and criminal activities such as excavation of ancient tombs and burials. By contrast, DouYin generally adopts a self-operated model and an open platform model to generate profits. This former one, self-supporting goods procurement, warehousing, distribution, and after-sales service, is solely responsible for DouYin. The latter is a third-party retail platform that gives merchants much more autonomy to operate, allowing them to be more flexible in developing sales strategies and activity programs through DouYin. Given the latter model, some merchants adopt the latter model through online networks to disseminate false propaganda in the disguise of "Sky-high price" and "antique appreciation", facilitating the offline sale of cultural relics and thereby misleading the public, disrupting the management of cultural relics, and endangering the safety of these cultural relics. Therefore, on 28 October 2024 the NACH and the Central Internet Information Office deployed a special administrative action to crack down on illegal short videos and live broadcasting activities related to grave robbery, tomb exploration, and illegal appraisal on the internet to regulate the Chinese version of TikTok administratively.[13] However, as of this writing, there is no criminal trial case related to DouYin.

Terminologies

It is crucial to first clearly define the terminologies involved to ensure accurate and objective research results. This is a key requirement of purpose-driven research, which examines not only the nature, scope, and legal definition of cybercrime but also other involved proper nouns and their interrelationship to the subject matter of cultural relics with substantive discussion in Chinese contexts.

Cybercrime

Although the battle of adopting the terms *cybercrime* and *cyber crime* has long existed, the distinction between both terms is purely orthographic and stylistic, with no difference in the exact meaning. Major dictionaries, led by the *Oxford English Dictionary* and *Merriam-Webster*, recognize *cybercrime* as the primary and standard term to ensure clarity and uphold professional standards in modern usage. In addition, it is also a challenge to define the term *cybercrime*, which raises many conceptual complexities and semantic interpretations from different disciplines since the millennium celebrations of 2000 (Crang, Crang, and May 2001: 1–18; Williams 2001: 152–53).

As a common English compound word, the term *cybercrime* originated from the term *cyberspace* (Smith, Grabosky, and Urbas 2009: 21). The former term always describes criminal offenses, especially related to computers and telecommunication, or the crimes that occur within the latter term (Chatterjee 2001: 81). However, neither is there an explicit, precise, and agreed-upon definition of cybercrime, nor is it treated as strictly legal terminology in academic research. By contrast, criminological academic research defines a wide range of illegal activities regarding cyberterrorism (EveryCRSReport 2008), cyberextortion (Lepofsky 2006), ransomware (Palo Alto Networks 2022), cybersex trafficking (Carback 2018), online harassment (Seitz 2024), drug trafficking (Arora 2020), fraud (Lehman and Phelps, 2005), identity theft, data breaches (Gordon 2006), and computer scams (Richet 2022). The above descriptive categories of crime overlap to a certain degree with cybercrimes under both international and national legal frameworks. Specifically speaking, from the early implementation of the Budapest Convention on Cybercrime in 2004[14] to the latest United Nations Convention against Cybercrime adopted by the General Assembly of the United Nations in 2024,[15] *cybercrime* has been widely used in international legal instruments. In light of the national perspective, early legislative practices of developed countries, headed by Italy[16] and Australia,[17] adopted the term "Cybercrime" to regulate the involved illegal activities. As a result, the developing nations represented by the Philippines,[18] Nigeria,[19] and South Africa[20] began using this term in domestic legislation. It can be seen that both categories of nations share common interests in this field, as reflected by the substantive and procedural contents of their domestic legal systems. Such domestic legislative trends in this field explain why the term "cybercrime" was chosen. Unfortunately, the Standing Committee of the National People's Congress (NPCSC) of China has not yet developed specific legislation on the fight against cybercrime and the related criminal offense of cultural relics, but through the fragment provisions (Articles 285–287) of the existing Criminal Law to regulate them.

Given that the motivation for cybercrime in Chinese legal and academic discourse centers around the vast profits cybercriminals earn from crimes related to computers, communication technologies, and networked services, the existing Chinese legal regulations focus more on the previous four forms of crimes. Therefore, the following sections have adopted a narrow definition of *cybercrime*, focusing on criminal offenses involving tangible cultural relics and digital collectibles, specifically crimes facilitated by new technology that can be interpreted as technology-facilitated or cyber-enabled crime conducted via online platforms.

Networks

Given that this chapter repeatedly mentions *networks* and *online platforms*, it is necessary to define these two terms from the Chinese criminal perspective of their practical application rather than the technical angle. The definition of *networks* in this chapter can be narrowly interpreted as the primary internet portals and computer information systems supporting applications and services that not only carry the main benefits of the computer network but are also the stakeholders that gain from the "network" and the victims of a criminal offense directly against the network itself. Given this, such highly technical and frequently used applications of "networks" have evolved from being used as information mediums or integrated information carriers of an online platform for daily life and work to being used as a location of criminality for the potential offenders.

The manifestation of the social attributes of the network is due to the deep socialization possible on the internet through the establishment of virtual communities to create the multiplicity and mobility of involved identities and social capital accumulation. The rise of platform economies like cross-border e-commerce led to complexities in the reconstruction rules in cyberspace that force the legislatures to consider criminal compliance to hedge the risks from the interaction between buyers and sellers and other involved parties. However, the legal nature of cyber-spatialization involves the migration of social relations to the network and the interactionalization between social relations and criminal offenses.

Online Platforms

Like the term *cybercrime*, the term "online platform" not only faces the difficulties of distinguishing between scholarly discourse and accessible explanation, but also manifests in different theoretical reflections and practical applications across multiple disciplines. Although past literature has frequently used the terms "digital platforms" and "online platforms" interchangeably, a challenge still exists in distinguishing between these two terms from a single discipline, which naturally covers a wide range of meanings. Although academia always uses the term *digital platform* to convey distinct concepts that create semantic confusion within the different disciplines (Zeamari and Laurier 2024: 59), the connotation and denotation of the term *digital platform* keep expanding in parallel with the dynamic development of "digital platforms" to instead of a concrete and concise definition of this term.

As an indispensable component of the interactive medium and the related online activity that facilitates cybercrimes involving Chinese cultural relics, the term *online platforms* can be defined as digital services or websites that allow users to interact with one another, share information, and conduct business over the internet to facilitate the development of interaction patterns such as Weibo, QQ, and DouYin. For this reason, "online platforms" can also be considered marketplaces (such as Taobao and Tianmao, as well as other self-built websites) for arts, cultural relics, and many other items, rather than merely digital shops. As a foundational digital space that enables connections and transactions between various users and services, the aforementioned online platforms facilitate the development of the platform economy. Criminal activities are carried out through their websites and outside of them, facilitated by links to prompt, efficient, and modern services such as social media channels or app stores, which provide the necessary external conditions for the transnational organized cybercrime of cultural relics and fraud.

Digital Collectibles

Although the previously mentioned Chinese policies produced two very different attitudes to the two outcomes (cryptocurrency production and NFTs) of blockchain technology, the Chinese government has shown a pragmatic approach and a moderately cautious attitude toward the application of NFTs, indicating that China is willing to adapt to NFT-related advances and explore innovations in blockchain technology. Explicitly speaking, this process began with the largest third-party payment platform, Alipay[21], which initially issued eight thousand limited-edition NFT artworks based on Dunhuang frescoes. Subsequently, leading social media firms and NFT companies, such as Tencent, launched innovative NFT platforms.[22] This development culminated in the official launch of China's first national and regulated NFT marketplace, the "China Digital Collectibles Trading Platform," on 1 January 2023.[23]

"Digital Collectibles" is a special NFT, combining digital ownership with artistic and creative expression. NFT is a technical realization of digital collectibles, but not all digital collectibles are NFTs. The specific technological construct of an NFT not only solves the problem of representing unique ownership in a digitally standardized way, but also serves as an open-standard, blockchain-based asset, solving the problem of enabling cross-platform circulation and potential interoperability by freeing ownership proof from any single platform's control. Although these NFTs can be treated as digital collectibles in Chinese art marketplaces and are the only virtual items able to become limited-quantity collectibles for further distribution and transfers in ownership via the blockchain, the online transaction of the digital collectibles inevitably arose from the risks of theft and fraud (Kshetri 2022: 60), market offenses(Saskia and King 2023: 1–20), authenticity (Adler 2023: 706), and money laundering (Chambers-Jones 2022: 23). Therefore, "digital collectibles" can be regarded as another subject of this chapter to explore the illegal results of interaction between this subject and online platforms from the Chinese perspective.

Cultural Relics

Regarding the protection of a tangible object of cultural and historical value in a legal context, a series of dictions have been adopted in international conventions since World War II. The 1954 Hague Convention for the Protection of Cultural Property in the Event of Armed Conflict[24] and the 1970 UNESCO Convention on the Means of Prohibiting and Preventing the Illicit Import, Export, and Transfer of Ownership of Cultural Property[25] have successively adopted the term *cultural property* to express a deep concern about the legal protection. *Cultural objects* was first used by the 1995 UNIDROIT Convention on Stolen or Illegally Exported Cultural Objects.[26] However, *cultural relics* is mainly used in existing Chinese legal instruments represented by the PRC on the LPCR 2024.[27] Article 2 of the latest revised version of this domestic law first offers a legal definition of *cultural relics,* which refers to the following material remains of historical, artistic, and scientific value created by human beings or related to human activities. It also lists five categories of protected cultural relics.

Although the LPCR belongs to the administrative legal system, the ownership of cultural relics and legal transactions within the Chinese jurisdiction are stipulated by the LPCR. Both state-owned and privately owned cultural relics are highly protected and strictly regulated on the import and export controls under the legal framework of the LPCR. The general transaction of cultural relics is tangible and movable cultural relics in practices, which are not only related to entities and qualifications for cultural relics transactions but also involve the prohibited types of cultural relics and transaction regulation and legal liabilities under the LPCR. To be specific, Chinese citizens and organizations other than cultural relics collection entities may collect cultural relics obtained through the following five ways under Article 67: (1) legal inheritance or acceptance of donations; (2) purchasing from cultural relics sales entities; (3) purchasing through auction enterprises engaged in the auction of cultural relics; (4) exchanging or transferring cultural relics legally owned by individual citizens by the Chinese law; (5) other legal methods provided for by the state. Concerning the legal transaction channels, cultural relics sales entities shall not carry out auctions of cultural relics or form enterprises carrying out auctions of cultural relics and vice versa. It is prohibited to buy or sell the following five categories of cultural relics within China via online or offline approaches: (1) state-owned cultural relics, except those of which trading is permitted by the state; (2) mural paintings, sculptures, and construction components, among others, included in state-owned immovable culture relics, with the exception, however, of the mural paintings, sculptures, and construction components, among others, included in state-owned immovable culture relics that have been dismantled according to the law, and those do not fall within the range of cultural relics that shall be collected by culture relics collection entities as provided for in paragraph 4 of Article 31 of this LPCR; (3) non-state-owned valuable cultural relics in museum collections; (4) stolen cultural relics notified or announced by the relevant departments under the State Council and other cultural relics whose sources do not comply with the provisions of Article 67 of this LPCR; (5) lost cultural relics notified or announced by foreign governments or relevant international organizations in accordance with relevant international conventions.

In addition, the existing Regulations on the Administration of Online Transactions 2014 and the Measures for the Administration of Cultural Relic Auction 2016 conditionally offer the right to trade cultural relics to the involved parties through online platforms. Given this, the sellers and the online platform have a legal duty to check the provenance and provenience of the subject matter and the certificate of legal title, and the potential buyers are responsible for performing due diligence in the following auction.

Research Methodology

The case study methodology of selected qualitative research includes all previously decided cybercrime cases derived from the government's judicial platform for verified accounts within Mainland China, referred to as China Judgments Online,[28] as well as Guiding Cases published by the Cases Database of the People's Court,[29] which aims to list all existing cases exhaustively. Taking case studies from these two databases not only manifests a mutually reinforced relationship between aspects of the Chinese judicial system but also reflects that the former offers case sources to the latter, and the latter has value for reference and demonstration based on publicized judgments. Accordingly, this study excludes cases that involve the five computer-related cybercrimes under the provisions of Articles 285–287 of Criminal Law due to their irrelevance to the subject matter. Instead, given that China Judgments Online was established in 2013 and first opened to access for searching only in 2014, the following case studies include decided cybercrime cases from 2014 to 2024 as the sample duration at the time of writing this chapter. However, the other cases mentioned in previous sections of this chapter have to be cited from the official reports and the Chinese academic references.

Based on the definitions of cybercrimes given in this chapter and the stated focus on criminal offenses against tangible cultural relics and digital collectibles after deleting duplicate and misclassified cases, this study first employed keyword searches of *cultural relics, cybercrime, online platforms, NFTs, digital collectibles,* and *criminal cases* that are relevant to criminal cybercrime cases involving cultural relics in the abovementioned two databases. The selected cases will be deeply analyzed from a legal perspective to clarify how and why cybercrime involving cultural relics in China differs from traditional crimes that disrupt the administration of cultural relics and address the relationship between cultural relics trafficking and online platforms, and why cybercriminals adopt the online transactions of tangible cultural relics and digital collectibles to fund other related crimes.

Research Results

Investigating the cybercrime of Chinese cultural relics via searches of the databases mentioned above resulted in two main conclusions. In the compiled dataset, only 5 of 1,383 cases directly related to tangible cultural relics and digital collectibles as a component of Chinese cybercrime. The remainder involved white-collar crime in the physical art market, specifically frauds (8), sham transactions (4), money laundering (96), fraudulent fundraising (5),[30] unlawfully raising funds (5),[31] smuggling (1), theft (89), and organizing and leading pyramid schemes (1,175). Regarding criminal case categories, cybercrime involving Chinese cultural heritage is quite different from the six crimes of disrupting the administration of cultural relics (Articles 324–329) under the legal framework of Criminal Law.

Case Study Methodology of Qualitative Research

The following case studies do not adopt a legal textbook-writing style to address individual elements in the format of case briefs.[32] However, the following five representative case studies, presented in chronological order, will introduce the extent to which existing Chinese Criminal Law determines the conviction and sentencing of disputes concerning cultural relics trading through online platforms and how cultural relics and digital collectibles constitute new forms of cybercrime.

Case 1: Online Fraud Involving Cultural Relics (2020)

This case involved 6,628 deceived victims and total monetary losses of up to 419 million RMB. It was the first case to dominate Chinese headlines due to the fabrication of an online platform in the guise of managing financial affairs to implement online fraud. This case was once dubbed the largest-ever case of fraud in financial futures platforms.

One of the codefendants (Mr. Jia) sponsored the launch of the Guangdong Creative Cultural Property Rights Trading Center Co., Ltd (Company), and became the biggest shareholder, with 85 percent of the equity in 2014, to develop a profitable business model of charging transaction fees with other codefendants. In March 2016 this company successively organized personnel, paid rent for office space and a website server, and purchased the trading software in order to establish an online futures trade platform with fictitious cultural relics like "Dunhuang Flying Apsaras" and "Chinese Zodiac Silver Medal" for attracting potential investors to deposit money into this company for the sole purpose of selling these fictitious cultural relics rather than the transaction of actual existing subject matters after organizing tier-one operators and extending membership options. Since then, the remaining thirty co-defendants have established over thirty tier-one operators to establish their membership. Following the above model, these tier-one operators then sought out potential investors to achieve and cheat these potential investors by arranging for the personnel to act as "profited investors" who have already gained the profits from this company and its membership. Since then, the remaining thirty codefendants have established over thirty tier-one operators to recruit members. Following the same model, these tier-one operators sought out potential investors. To lure and ultimately cheat them, the operators arranged for associates to pose as "profited investors"—individuals falsely claiming to have gained profits from the company and its membership. This tricked new investors into contributing the contractually mandated 3 percent of the underlying total, lured by the promise of high returns from expected price fluctuations. The illusion was further perpetuated through the use of legitimate online platform transactions to manipulate the price of fictitious cultural relics, thereby misleading the investors. The series of actions misled investors, who then continued investing money into this online futures trade platform and paying a high commission.[33]

The case was finally tried and sentenced as fraud by the Guangdong Provincial Higher People's Court of the Second Instance, which reflected that an organized cybercrime group operated exclusively via a self-built website to commit the substantive offense and fully use network technologies to facilitate their criminal conduct.

Cases 2–3: Two Cases Concerning the Resale of Cultural Relics Online (2020)

Case 2 occurred when two residents of Guan Nan County in Jiangsu Province, Mr. Liu and Mr. Sun, met a like-minded resident of Heilongjiang Province named Mr. Feng through the network to trade cultural relics in pursuit of financial gain. The former two successfully bought several unprovenient and unprovenanced tangible cultural relics in 2015 from Mr. Feng to help him realize his "assets." After that, Liu and Sun began to recognize the value of leveraging the networks to facilitate the commission of cybercrime. Therefore, they resold these tangible cultural relics through self-managed online stores to create favorable opportunities for themselves to reap profits until their arrest in 2020.

The following investigations not only revealed and confirmed the authenticity and provenance of these cultural relics as state-owned relics from the illegally excavated archaeological sites but also calculated that this case involved nine hundred pieces of tangible cultural relics, including only about 10 grade-three cultural relics with relatively important historical, artistic, and scientific values.[34] In terms of the identification of Mr. Feng, although he did not participate in the original theft and excavation, he had been legally identified as a "present possessor" of cultural relics that had passed through several hands before reaching him. Although he did not participate in the original theft and excavation, he has been legally identified as a "present possessor" of cultural relics that had passed through several hands before reaching him under an unnamed loose collective collaborating to achieve the illicit trafficking of cultural relics at the final stage, so that he also became a "final buyer" in the initial trading relationship of this case.[35] As a "present possessor" of the subsequent transaction relationship, Mr. Feng was naturally a member who knowingly bought the subject matters under the traditional organized crime groups of cultural relics and offered the source of subject matters so that the following organized cybercrime groups could use online platforms to enhance illegal transactions and related criminal activities. Given this, the three suspected offenders were charged as codefendants and finally tried in a People's Court for reselling cultural relics.

Case 3 represents a transprovincial and mixed form of organizing offline and cybercrimes involving 42 suspected offenders and more than 160 items of tangible cultural relics. Although the 42 suspected offenders always provide a one-stop service based on the supplies and demands of the art market expectations that there be a highly sophisticated division of labor within the trafficking network of Chinese cultural relics till finally closing the deals, they have multiple identities to create legal barriers for the following conviction and sentencing.

These persons not only initially "scope" ancient tombs and archaeological sites before the illegal theft and excavation of cultural relics but also perform the following steps to obtain stolen cultural relics or "contract out" a specific task to specialist groups of grave robbers. In addition, they also seek "middlemen" to act as antiquities dealers to extend the approaches of the art business so that those selling the stolen cultural relics through online art trading platforms can order public sales.[36] However, the problem with convicting such cybercrimes is determining whether the suspected offenders shall be convicted of reselling cultural relics or robbing an archaeological site or ancient tomb of its historical, artistic, or scientific value. This case highlights how to handle overlapping offenses under Chinese Criminal Law and shows that the pervasiveness of networks and technologies promotes the probability of committing both organized cybercrimes and offline heritage crimes.

Case 4: Organizing and Leading a Pyramid Scheme Involving Cultural Relics (2021)

In early 2019 codefendants Zhang and Li jointly operated a physical art gallery and sold paintings and calligraphy to the public. In the first half of 2020, the codefendants established an e-commerce company based on their privately owned art gallery, providing a self-managed website for buyers to purchase paintings and calligraphy online. As a legal representative, Zhang performed the overall management of this online platform and provided cashback deals (rebates) and discounts to promote the sharing economy model. Simultaneously, Li was responsible for constructing, maintaining, and upgrading the online platform and performing other technical work. They priced each painting and calligraphy and posted them online to sell.

Such "dummy" websites sell paintings and calligraphy as bait to recruit members for an external investor referral program. These members pay dues and fees, and then profit by recruiting potential participants, convincing them to scan invitation codes to access this online platform. After that, participants are required to buy a painting or calligraphy after receiving membership. Meanwhile, these new members must buy paintings and calligraphy and pay a so-called listing fee to the online platform's administrators to sell their paintings and calligraphy. The next day, the online platform displays the former purchase price, floating a certain percentage of this price, and then lists it on the platform for resale. The members and online platform administrators each earn 2 percent and 4 percent of the commission for each painting and calligraphy transaction, respectively. In this way, existing members need to attract entry-level members to accumulate online transaction amounts of 3 ‰ as cashback deals.

Unfortunately, the new members did not receive physical paintings and calligraphy after finishing the above transactions. Given that the online platform lacks substantial business activities and does not generate real profits, the primary income for the administrators is the listing fee. Therefore, the prosecuting jurisdiction, the Jining High-Tech District Procuratorate of Shandong Province, held that the online platform operated in violation of Article 224 of China's Criminal Law, which defines illegal pyramid schemes as operations that: (i) use business activities as a pretext, (ii) set entry thresholds, (iii) organize hierarchical structures, and (iv) remunerate participants based on recruitment numbers.—in other words, the platform disrupted the economic and social order by organizing and leading a pyramid scheme. On these grounds, the two were indicted.

Case 5: The Case of Criminal Fraud in the Financing of Digital Collectibles (2023)

In June 2022, the codefendants Zhang and Liu successively purchased low-quality images or downloaded them for free from the internet. Soon after, they jointly established an online trading platform called "Tonggu" by adopting blockchain technology to mint the physical images into NFTs for sale. Meanwhile, the codefendants also promoted these digital collectibles to the public through social media platforms such as QQ and WeChat. They even falsely promised potential buyers that if the digital collectibles were purchased, they could regularly buy back specific items at double the price and enjoy the platform's dividends, priority purchase rights, and other exclusive membership rights and interests.

To enhance credibility, Zhang also opened the secondary market to buyers so that self-buying and selling artificially inflated amounts of digital collectibles at inflated prices created the illusion that commerce on their website was "hot" and there was room for appreciation. With people paying attention to Tonggu, the online platform absorbed thousands in funding, a total of more than 1.34 million RMB from buyers, resulting in a total loss of more than 410,000 RMB for victims.

At the end of September 2023 Zhang stopped paying the fee to renew the server. He closed the online platform, preventing buyers from withdrawing funds from accounts or checking the status of their digital collectibles. Later, during the trial in this case, the two defendants voluntarily pleaded guilty, accepted punishment, and withdrew all illegal proceeds to compensate for victim losses. The Minhang District People's Court of Shanghai held that the codefendants were guilty of ill-gotten gains (money), fraudulent methods, and illegal fundraising; their behavior constitutes fundraising fraud and is classified as a joint crime.

Short Summary

Although there are a relatively limited number of Chinese judicial cases concerning cybercrime and cultural relics, the five cases discussed above illustrate what this chapter refers to as the status quo for such cybercrimes, summarized as follows.

First, the abovementioned cases hold tangible cultural relics (Cases 2–4) and digital collectibles (Case 5) as a new class of tradable objects under current definitions of cybercrime in the Chinese legal system, except for the subject matter of Case 1, which had never existed. The perpetrators simply created fictitious relics to further commit the fraud. A computer network is a location of criminality for the potential offenders, indicating that the direct motivation for such cybercrimes is financial gain, achieved by carrying out traditional financial crimes that have already defined under Chinese criminal statutes, which readily apply to online platforms (Cases 1, 4–5). It can be concluded that such new forms of cybercrime within the Chinese legal context are always incidental to traditional white-collar crimes such as financial fraud. It cannot be surmised that traditional financial crimes, such as theft, market offenses, money laundering, forgery, and copyright crimes, occurring on online platforms are likely to occur as a follow-up to cybercrimes, demonstrating a high degree of convergence between cybercrimes and white-collar financial crimes. Other comparisons should be noted, such as the similarities of and distinctions between general cybercrime stipulated under Chinese Criminal Law and cybercrime involving cultural relics. The similarities between general cybercrime and cybercrime involving cultural heritage under the Chinese judicial practices are that they cannot be accomplished without the technical and communications support of networks or leading online platforms.

The distinctions are as follows: general cybercrime under Chinese Criminal Law can be classified as computer-related crime, which requires the perpetrator to be subjectively intentional (directly or indirectly), and thus negligent acts do not constitute crimes in this category. The objective behaviors of computer-related crime stipulate that such crime be implemented by technical means (e.g., intrusion, destruction, interference with the system) or by directly targeting technical carriers (e.g., data and programs). The criminal regulation of computer-related crimes aims to maintain the security of computer information systems and public order in cyberspace and protect the security of personal information, property rights, and other private legal interests, reflecting the diversification of the protection of legal interests. By contrast, cybercrimes related to cultural relics typically involve acts of dishonesty and deception targeting providers or users of online platforms and payment technologies through networks. These acts may occur concurrently with wrongful civil acts for online transactions under the Chinese legal system, centered on fault-based liability for rights infringement, with the online platforms being held responsible for fraud and white-collar crime rather than focusing on disrupting the administration of cultural relics.

Second, and importantly, cybercrimes overlap with traditional crimes, leading to ambiguity in categorization and law enforcement (Wall 2007: 100). Therefore, there is no precise or concrete definition of cybercrimes involving cultural relics within Chinese and international legislation. However, cybercrimes of cultural relics, newly recognized in Chinese courts, have three outstanding features, as reflected in the above five cases. The first implies that criminal networks treat the global internet system as an instrument of cybercrime and online platforms and networks as criminal spaces derived from the creation and rapid development of the internet. The second implies that cybercriminals in China mainly view tangible cultural relics and digital collectibles as general objects sellable purely for their monetary value and potential for profit. The last feature shows that digital collectibles such as NFTs have also been viewed as "trading objects" with which to commit cybercrime, albeit less so for their "cultural" value compared to physical cultural relics within the NFT creator community. In fact, the legal status of digital collectibles such as NFTs should be clarified, and future determinations of the value of digital collectibles under Chinese criminal law will need to draw on arguments for digital collections within existing civil jurisprudence after a verdict is issued in the first criminal case involving NFTs in China. According to China Judgments Online, Chinese civil cases involving digital collectibles have begun to be tried since 2023, with many cases focusing on disputes over infringements of the right to disseminate information networks and disputes over contracts to sell and purchase information networks. The Hangzhou Internet Court is an example of the reasoning for handed-down verdicts,[37] given that a recognized value confirmation system has not yet been formed in China. The prices of digital collectibles fluctuate considerably, easily inducing stakeholders to collude with one another and participate in bidding, speculate on prices, and induce uninformed bidders to make impulsive contributions. Therefore, civil judges adjudicating such cases have adopted the view that digital collectibles are a form of virtual cultural property under network law, providing Chinese courts with their first reference for defining the legal nature of digital collectibles as virtual cultural property, which first offered the Chinese courts a reference for the precise positioning of the nature of the virtual property of digital collectibles.

Third, there is considerable overlap in the characteristic features of the cybercrimes of cultural relics in China, as illustrated by the five cases above, and organized, offline cultural relics crime. Specifically:

(1) Organized crime groups trafficking in cultural relics generally use publicly available online platforms or visible offline venues to engage in these highly profitable illegal activities.

(2) The abovementioned case studies demonstrate the essential characteristics of organized cultural relics crime when applied to cultural relics cybercrime in the Chinese context. These groups can be treated as organized crime groups that have sometimes merely targeted transactions involving cultural relics and sometimes focused on seeking high profits. The abovementioned cases specifically involve exchanging money for purchased cultural relics via an online platform.

(3) Any transactions carried out via online platforms and involving cultural relics are illegal in China, where Criminal Law states that the buying and selling of cultural relics may constitute a crime, meaning that cultural relics are not legally permitted to be freely commodified. By contrast, the LPCR stipulates that natural persons, legal persons, and other organizations, as well as the collection entities of cultural relics like museums, art galleries, and libraries, may only have five approaches to obtaining cultural relics, including legal inheritance or accepting dona-

tions, purchasing from cultural relics shops and cultural relics auction enterprises, exchanging or transferring cultural relics legally owned by individual citizens, and other legal approaches provided for by the state.

(4) The abovementioned cases involving online platforms established that more than one individual would need to be involved in such a case, reflecting the complex division of labor that emerged, which meets the requirements of constituting traditional organized crime and organized cybercrime. It also proved that criminals exploit the network or online platform as an instrument and target of organized crime, which has become increasingly common with the pervasiveness and popularity of digital technology.

Legal Issues Involved in Criminal Adjudications

The similarity in Chinese Criminal between the two categories of cybercrime of cultural relics and the six traditional crimes that disrupt the administration of cultural relics offline Law is that cybercrime of cultural relics solely involves resale and illicit trafficking (Cases 2–3), thereby infringing on the legal interests in ownership of state-owned cultural relics. The distinction between the crimes that disrupt the administration of cultural relics offline and cybercrime of cultural relics in China is reflected in three aspects:

(1) When prosecuting offline cultural relics crimes, the first question concerns the administrative identification of different ratings of cultural relics, their authenticity, provenance, and provenience. Based on this, identifying the specific charges and penalties to be levied depends on whether the transactions of cultural relics meet the essential requirements stipulated under Chinese Criminal Law. This law lists the crime of intentionally destroying cultural relics from the perspectives of constitutive elements of crime. Crimes that disrupt the administration of cultural relics have various objective forms. The victim and perpetrator of cybercrime can be either legal or natural persons. By contrast, the victim and perpetrator of the six categories of offline cultural relics crime can be natural persons and units. There is also the question of intent to destroy or negligence in the care of cultural relics in terms of the subjective elements of crimes that disrupt the administration of cultural relics. However, there only exists an intent to commit cybercrimes; defendants cannot argue negligence.

(2) An outstanding feature of cybercrime involving cultural relics is that it has to rely on online platforms to gain profits and does not aid in the destruction of cultural relics themselves. Cybercrime of cultural relics treats tangible cultural relics and digital collectibles as a new category of profitable commodity that is exchanged online. Given the long period of lax attention to regulating cybercrimes of cultural relics in China, levying specific charges and penalties is generally within white-collar crime legislation.

(3) Three criteria are followed when determining sentencing for any of the six crimes that disrupt the offline administration of cultural relics. First, whoever commits the act of smuggling, stealing, or unlawfully reselling immovable cultural relics shall be subject to sentencing in accordance with the grade of the item in question; Second, where cultural relics of various grades are involved in a case, the sentencing shall be based upon the range of sentencing applicable to the items of the highest grade, and if several cultural relics of the same grade are involved, five items of the same grade shall be deemed as one item of a higher grade, unless the value is obviously equivalent; third, where conviction and sentencing are subject to the value of the cultural relics, their value shall be determined according to the valid price certificate of the items involved, and if there is no valid price certificate or it is obviously irrational to determine the value according to a price certificate, the value shall be determined according to the amount required to dispose of the stolen items, or in light of a value prescribed by an Interpretation of the Supreme People's Court and the Supreme People's Procuratorate on Several Issues Concerning the Application of Law in the Handling of Criminal Cases Concerning Hampering the Administration of Cultural Relics.

By contrast, the common consensus regarding sentencing for the cybercrime of cultural relics in which fraud, or organizing and leading a pyramid scheme, is involved is that guilty parties would generally be sentenced to imprisonment of not less than three years or more than seven years and a fine by the discretion of the People's Court based on the circumstances of the above crimes. If the amount of fraudulent commerce is substantial or there are any severe extenuating circumstances, defendants found guilty can be sentenced to imprisonment of not less than seven years, life imprisonment, a fine, or the forfeiture of their property. Where a unit commits the crime, as mentioned above, a fine shall be imposed, and the persons directly responsible for the offense shall be punished according to the preceding paragraph. Like many other crimes stipulated under Chinese Criminal Law, conviction is a fundamental issue in criminal adjudications concerning the cybercrime of cultural relics, which needs to be interpreted.

Determining the imaginative joinder in Cases 2–3 (involving the online resale of cultural relics) presents a further interpretive issue: it reveals situations where a single criminal act may simultaneously violate multiple criminal provisions, partly or wholly endangering protected legal interests. Although Chinese Criminal Law lacks express provisions for imaginative joinders, doctrines of "concurrence of offenses" and "merger of crimes"are well-established in legal theory and judicial practice. Case 2 punished the conduct solely as illegal relic reselling (Article 326) while Case 3 required distinguishing the imaginative joinder from separate offenses at sentencing. While multiple offenses may arise from one act, only the most severe applicable punishment is imposed, in contrast to common law approaches found in the U.S. "separate offense" doctrine (Chemerinsky, 2009), which permits cumulative penalties. In other words, if the same suspected offenders committed two or more offenses before receiving an arrest warrant, they might be identified as codefendants. They may be tried under one accusatory instrument, with each offense stated in a separate count, or their offenses may be combined for trial following the recommendation of the prosecuting attorney or defense.

In contrast, the civil law system was headed by China. When one crime concerning tangible cultural relics is similar to any other crime concerning tangible cultural relics, issues regarding the imaginative joiner of the offense need to be addressed. If criminal activities simultaneously constitute multiple crimes, they could also constitute the imaginative joiner of offenses. However, the legal nature of the different crimes is essential, as they all fall under a single article and are punished as a single crime. When the act of reselling cultural relics (Chinese Criminal Law Art. 326) overlaps with the act of robbing a cultural heritage site of its historical, artistic, or scientific value (Chinese Criminal Law Art. 328)—specifically, where a theft is committed with the intent of reselling the looted relics—the offense shall be subject to the heavier penalty applicable to either crime. Otherwise, if the illegal excavation and the resale constitute distinct criminal acts—such as where (i) the cultural relics sold are not the proceeds of the specific illegal excavation in question, or (ii) the resale occurs subsequently to the illegal excavation and the circumstances of the resale are serious—then the offender shall be punished concurrently for separate crimes.

Finally, although Criminal Law identifies general and financial fraud, judicial practice should interpret these crimes differently. In Case 1, the codefendants used fraudulent techniques to induce investors to make frequent transactions by allowing them to earn high commissions on fraudulent gains. Compared with traditional fraud, this method causes substantial confusion, and the scope of harm to the victims is enormous. Interpretations of this case should focus on platform manipulation, online platform profit sources, and the flow of victims' funds, which can also accurately identify which platform is being used for the illegal possession of investment money and which group members can be prosecuted. However, the crime of illegal fundraising does not exist in the Chinese criminal context. Illegal fundraising is not separate from illegal activity in general.

The illegal activities in question in these cases primarily comprise illegal fundraising for different purposes and of different consequences. The extent of the fundraising determines whether financial crime is applicable under Chinese Criminal Law. It is generally necessary to deconstruct each constituent element, such as illegality, publicity, sociality, and inducement to participate, as in Case 5. This illegality in Case 5 indicates that those who bought the online platform purchased digital collectibles for resale to obtain the expected income. Buyers constitute investment and financial management activities by buying and selling digital collectibles and withdrawing funds from Tonggu's online platform. The codefendants used Tonggu to collect and deposit funds, forming a liquidity pool to absorb public funds through commodity repurchases and secondary market transactions. In terms of the NFTs themselves, their rate of appreciation and collection value, and the lack of similar scenarios occurring previously on Tonggu, the codefendants not only did not provide substantial commodities as a consideration for the payment of funds by buyers but also violated relevant financial management regulations by setting up a secondary market for trading without obtaining permission to establish a trading venue for cultural and artistic interests.

Regarding the public and social aspects of the cybercrime, the codefendants instructed others to publicize their available digital collectibles on Tonggu to unspecified individuals via social networking platforms such as QQ and WeChat. This embodied the fact that the codefendants fictionalized facts and concealed the truth, causing others to be misled and invest in digital collectibles issued by Tonggu, inventing their sources, falsely promising rebates and ensuring their NFTs would appreciate, and making false transactions to create the illusion of appreciation. Although the illegal absorption of public deposits was not mentioned in the above cases, judicial practices struggle to differentiate between such a particularly Chinese crime and the crime of financial fraud in general, a distinction hinging on the purpose of the illegal appropriation. The latter comprises illegal fundraising through fictitious fraud, with the strict purpose of acquiring investors' money; the collected funds are not used mainly for production and business activities. The series of activities involved in Case 5 shows that the codefendants secretly withdrew funds and hid assets to evade debt repayment, which can also be recognized as financial fraud.

Criminal Motives: Why and How?

This section now examines the criminal motives behind the cybercrime of cultural relics in China. In general, the following subjective and objective factors have influenced the presence and structure of this category of cybercrime.

In the wake of the development of blockchain technology and the promotion of the digital economy, different forms of internet technology are gradually being applied to the Chinese art market as a growth area of the Chinese economy, fueled by the various online platforms established by art traders and organized criminal syndicates trafficking in cultural relics. Objectively speaking, the internet technology revolution inevitably promotes a new form of cybercrime concerning cultural relics and the fraudulent trade in digital collectibles. The cybercrime of cultural relics in China has expanded rapidly, primarily because of the virtual and hidden nature of the criminality involved and the intelligent and professional approaches taken to commit such cybercrimes. Criminals trafficking in cultural relics can take advantage of the convenience and dissemination benefits of the internet to carry out cross-administrative organized crime and resell cultural relics through online platforms.

Seeking benefits and avoiding harm are fundamental to the existence and development of participants in Chinese art markets. There are countless profitable people with whom criminals want to transact for higher economic benefits with lower transaction costs to achieve profits. Such reasoning can also be applied to the five cases discussed above. In other words, the cybercrime of cultural relics is subjectively viewed as economically profit driven. New technology has made it easier to traffic cultural relics, at least at present, attracting more people to cybercrimes. From the perspective of legal economics, the weighing of costs and benefits is directly related to the decisions made by sellers (generally regarded as criminals) involved in the supply-demand relationship. Legal costs include external expenses sellers incur in exercising their rights, fulfilling their obligations, assuming their responsibilities, and covering the costs of human, material, and financial resources and time that sellers waste. Thus, sellers choose to act, and their costs and benefits are closely related. In other words, the level of potential benefit directly affects sellers' decision-making. Abundant and considerable profit and a simple operational model drive potential criminal sellers. Social, market, and legal factors should be examined regarding this question. In addition, China has a vast expanse of land and the world's largest population, representing a tremendous amount and enormous variety of cultural relics (Liu 2023). Such congenital conditions have stimulated low-income criminals driven by lucrative businesses in poverty-stricken areas (like Gansu, Yunnan, and Guizhou Provinces), which has led to illegal excavation of heritage sites and looting of cultural relics on a large scale (Gallagher 2017), as well as choosing to traffic cultural relics through online platforms to meet the endless demands of both the Chinese art market and online customers, accompanied by increasingly high prices and the diversification of looting into different categories of cultural relics in the Chinese context.

Another key factor is the ongoing evolution of organized cybercrime, which is becoming increasingly sophisticated and commercial. While the transparency of most online platforms generally promotes orderly transactions, online heritage crime syndicates skillfully exploit information gaps and phishing tactics, leading to market inefficiencies that facilitate cybercrime and undermine regulatory efforts. Additionally, the complexities of online trading environments and transaction models exceed those of traditional physical commerce, making it significantly more challenging and costly for buyers or investors with weaker positions to gather accurate transaction information and evaluate risks than it would for syndicates. This dynamic development only deepens the information asymmetry and unfair distribution of benefits between investors (the buyers) and criminals. As mentioned in Cases 1 and 4, it is not difficult to see why criminals choose to fabricate online platforms to manage their financial affairs and invest in implementing online fraud schemes by deliberately concealing accurate transaction information or organizing and leading pyramid schemes to sell cultural relics.

Many cultural relics or other cultural heritage stolen from archaeological or historical sites generate relatively high profits when sold online. Thus, criminal networks have transformed physical art markets into online markets to more quickly dispose of stolen cultural relics, avoid legal and market regulations, and fuel new criminal opportunities such as online fraud, illicit trafficking, and money laundering. Although Chinese legislation often aims to suppress illegal excavations through heavy penalties, strict criminal proceedings, and seizure of stolen cultural relics (Polner 2019), the Chinese administrative regime regulating this area remains weak and faces substantial defects that it must overcome.

In addition, the traditional offline art market has gradually but significantly changed, and the online art market has replaced the traditional art market since at least the end of the 1990s (Lidington 2002). At that time, state-owned auction houses, art galleries, and antique shops were legally opened in parallel with online art markets, hosted by online trading platforms, to buy and sell cultural relics, including contemporary Chinese artifacts, in a way allowed by the LPCR. Given the above, several actors coexist within and underpin the Chinese art market and its online platforms, with grave robbers, collectors, and art dealers existing within the supply chain. This supply chain exploits specific systemic weaknesses: the anonymity given to online platform users; the uncertainty regarding the legal interest in prosecuting such crimes; and the legal challenges involved in examining the provenance and provenience of cultural relics (Brodie, 2004). Collectively, these weaknesses allow the free online transaction of cultural heritage relics with unestablished provenance, authenticity, and provenience. Consequently, from a criminological perspective, online platforms have become an effective channel for criminals to dispose of looted or stolen cultural relics. This ecosystem creates a feedback loop: online platforms facilitate cyber-enabled organized cultural relics crime, while the scale and profitability of such crime further incentivize the expansion and sophistication of these platforms.

Firstly, organized criminal groups have gradually recognized the strength of leveraging information and new technology to facilitate control sales and orderly promotion of supply chains via online transactions to close the deal. As the suppliers in such traditionally organized online cultural relics crime networks, grave robbers initially excavate illegally or steal cultural relics from heritage sites. Then, they need to collaborate with art dealers in the supply chain. However, what follows after the initial theft differs from the offline trafficking of cultural relics in China. In case 4, suppliers of cultural relics do not need to seek art dealers to expand sales opportunities or evade the related administrative regulations and legal risks for transporting cultural relics to transit ports or falsifying export documents to whitewash the introduction of illegal cultural relics into the legitimate art market. Therefore, the efficiency and simplicity of online platforms attract dealers, leading to cybercrime. Given the significant economic and cultural value of cultural relics, unscrupulous people are attracted to the sale of cultural relics and are willing to engage in illicit or fraudulent online transactions to reap the rewards. Due to the lack of self-regulation and external supervision, online platforms are not required to prove their legitimacy and trustworthiness; therefore, criminals prefer to knowingly transact illegally acquired goods without provenance and legal title.

Secondly, online platforms provide a hidden space for illicit trade in cultural relics, with criminals utilizing the aforementioned social media and e-commerce websites to carry out illicit transactions. At the same time, online platforms facilitate the dissemination of both authentic and unverified (or fake) information about cultural relics. Criminals, therefore, make use of amplifying the presence of cultural relics with questionable provenance and cultural relic forgeries. This makes it difficult for ordinary consumers to identify whether or not they are genuine, leading to confusion in the online cultural relics market. In addition, due to their dominant, established, commercially focused, and profit-driven nature, online platforms prioritize demand and profit maximization. This focus leads to the degradation of their own essential functions (such as preventing illicit trade or verifying provenance). Consequently, the regulatory oversight of cultural relics traded online becomes disorganized as platforms adopt a laissez-faire approach. This environment reduces cultural relics to the status of ordinary commodities, stripping them of their inherent cultural, scientific, and artistic value.

Two Major Legal Challenges

Although physical art and online transaction markets are not subject to a comprehensive and unified regulatory regime, the consequences of two art market transactions are subject to domestic law and administrative regulation in China, not merely under Criminal Law but also civil and administrative law. Given this, the legal approaches to regulating cybercrimes of cultural relics should be examined first and foremost along the following two dimensions: legislation and administrative supervision. However, current online trading platforms have normative deficiencies and regulatory loopholes, as well as a lack of due legislation, resulting in the inability to effectively protect the legal interests of ficticious stolen and trafficked cultural relics and the involved victims, thus providing convenience for the criminals involved in the cybercrime of cultural relics in the above five cases.

The Lack of Appropriate Legislation to Compliance Governance

Criminal legislation is the process by which the sovereign nation, through legal procedures, formulates specialized laws on criminal relations. This legislation not only establishes a clear legal framework and codes of conduct for regulating criminal activity, but also imposes specific criminal liability on natural persons, legal persons, and other entities that commit criminal offenses. Additionally, it empowers courts to order offenders to provide restitution to the victims within the context of criminal proceedings. Although there is no denying that civil trials which address copyright infringements and tort claims related to ownership are undoubtedly crucial, criminal issues permeate almost every stage of online transactions. This necessitates critical reflection on current legislative challenges in combating cybercrimes involving cultural relics.

As far as criminal legislation is concerned, Chinese criminal legislation relevant to cybercrime began with the 1997 Criminal Law of the PRC and its subsequent two amendments (the seventh and the ninth in 2009 and 2015, respectively) within the latest (2020) version of Chinese Criminal Law. Judicial interpretation stemming from this law can be seen as the basis for prosecuting and regulating cybercrime. Although the existing body of Chinese Criminal Law has been amended twelve times, commentary on the latest version regarding its achievements and weaknesses is beyond the scope of this chapter. This latest version of the Criminal Law code deals with two main aspects of the two distinct forms of cybercrime discussed above. One form defines computer-related crimes as the use of computer technology, with the help of the network, to attack a system or information, and to damage or use the network to carry out other crimes; the other form defines crimes involving unauthorized access, modification, impairment, and malware.

However, some Chinese criminal scholars have focused on the weaknesses of current Criminal Law and criticized its provisions regarding cybercrimes. For example, the current version has a narrower scope of protection for legal interests (Chong 2015) and lacks specific provisions and regulations for other categories of cybercrime (Ke 2024). However, it should be recognized that the provisions for cybercrimes of cultural relics under Chinese Criminal Law have undergone a developmental process, from an initial absence to a comprehensive enactment of a statutory regime. With the increasing development of new types of cybercriminal activities, there are no legal provisions detailing how to regulate the cybercrimes of cultural relics or provisions to combine and revise the six categories of crime discussed above that affect the administration of cultural relics. Although the NPCSC and the State Council have enacted various regulations within Cybersecurity Law (ratified in 2016) and crafted normative legal documents, such as the Regulations on Protecting the Safety of Computer Information Systems, to assist the criminal legal system in prosecuting cybercrime, these legislations primarily regulate cybersecurity rather than organized cybercrime. Therefore, it is challenging to systematically regulate cybercrime without the practical guidance of an unambiguous legislative foundation and overarching purpose.

Given the status quo of Chinese legislation and the unique characteristics of and forms that cybercrimes associated with cultural relics and fraud involving digital collectibles can take, the necessity and urgency to strengthen Chinese criminal legislation can be summarized by three key points:

(1) Incidents of cybercrimes involving cultural relics have gradually increased and can be done independently. They are characterized by unique features and motives, creating significant differences between how cybercrimes involving cultural relics and traditional forms of cybercrime are prevented and regulated.

(2) The approaches and processes involved in committing cybercrimes against cultural relics involve special terminology unique to criminal networks. Existing

laws and regulations have not been sufficiently defined to encompass this terminology, causing vagueness and ambiguity in the application of existing laws within the Chinese legal system.

(3) As cybercrime of cultural relics is a new category of cybercrime, the consequences fundamentally differ from traditional cybercrime and financial crime in China. Therefore, criminal judicial practices must acknowledge that the online art market is rapidly evolving and the line between financial and legal regulations is not always easy to draw. Hence, the standard application of cybercrime law to cybercrimes of cultural relics far from achieves substantial justice. Reforming existing law will inevitably require the continual monitoring of online art market development and taking further legislative action.

Based on the above, the most common approach to prosecuting cybercrimes of cultural relics within Chinese criminal courts cannot easily draw on precedent from traditional cybercrime, nor can traditional financial crime legislation be readily used. Although the NPCSC and the State Council may have realized the difference between cybercrimes of cultural relics and general cybercrime, the existing criminal legal framework may not fully apply. Given this, there is legislative space to consider whether Chinese legislators should adopt new names for cybercrimes involving tangible cultural relics and/or digital collectibles fraud or whether an appropriate criminal legal framework to deal with these specific cases becomes critical. Owing to the highly technical and significantly harmful nature of cybercrime in general, criminal penalties for cybercrime are relatively light under current criminal legislation. Punishment usually involves being sentenced to prison for not less than three years or more than seven, and a fine by the People's Court's discretion based on the crime's circumstances. Such sentencing contradicts the principle that the punishment should fit the crime.

However, cybercrime of cultural relics has gradually shown itself to be economically and scientifically destructive, socially hazardous, and highly technical. Suppose the essential legal function of Criminal Law is to protect the legal interests of victims and subject matter. In that case, it is necessary to adopt harsher penalties to regulate the cybercrime of cultural relics, but not in contradiction to the original intention of the principle of restraint. When the social harm of the behavior has reached such a degree that trial and punishment under Criminal Law is warranted, and existing laws can no longer regulate the criminal activities, it is necessary to adopt relatively strict criminal legislation. This is also a favorable embodiment of the last relief measure under Chinese Criminal Law. Owing to the lack of due legislation concerning the cybercrime of cultural relics, there are no provisions for tangible cultural relics or digital collectibles as new categories of tradable objects under broad definitions of cybercrime, so criminal adjudication can only be made according to subjective motivations, the subjects of cybercrime, and the objects of cybercrime as the essential elements of the cybercrime of cultural relics.

Fragile Administrative Supervision

Administrative supervision concerning the cross-border movement of cultural relics via online platforms mainly relates to issues on the overlapping application of the Civil Code and Administrative Law rather than the single realm and scope of Criminal Law, which can cope with it in the Chinese legal system. When the judges delimit the legal scope of cybercrime, it should be noted that different (civil and criminal) legal approaches of remedies are available, and coincidences exist within a parallel hierarchy under the Chinese legal system.

Although the cases discussed above did not directly disclose the realities of legal administrative supervision over online platforms, there is a significant proliferation of counterfeit works of art, forged and fictitious cultural relics, and other varieties of illicit items illegally traded online. It is challenging for market supervision departments to effectively monitor online platforms because the people involved in the above cases are often not residents of the same regions of China, making it difficult for the authorities to manage complaints. Similarly, the issues of unlicensed operations, unauthorized advertising, and false propaganda in the Chinese offline art market also exist on online platforms, which makes it difficult for market supervisors to hold online perpetrators accountable.

In addition, online transactions concerning cultural relics cannot be conducted without meeting the requirements of Chinese State regulations of electronic commerce. According to Article 6 of the E-Commerce Law, 2019, the relevant departments of the State Council shall promote the development, supervision, and administration of online transactions according to divisions of labor based on assigned duties. The central bodies overseeing the supervision of online trading platforms include the market supervision department, tax department, intellectual property administrative department, and other competent departments. However, an unclear division of responsibilities and authorization between the relevant departments has resulted in a fragile administrative supervisory structure. The first reason for this is explainable in three steps:

(1) Chinese supervision of online platforms remains mostly a category of special supervision. There is a lack of comprehensive and coordinated supervision across online trading platforms, underlying the fragmented nature of administrative supervision regarding cybercrime of cultural relics.

(2) Overlapping responsibilities between competent administrative departments has led to overregulation, loopholes, and buck passing. This inevitably results in inefficient supervision, intensifying conflicts between departments.

(3) At present, the departments in charge of supervising online commerce work separately and are not jointly regulated, which results in low supervision efficiency, wasted resources, and a failure to enforce joint oversight in a concerted manner.

The second reason can be attributed to the lack of comprehensiveness in regulatory matters, explainable in two steps:

(1) Considering the inherent advantages of online platforms in terms of information acquisition and the use of algorithmic technology, regulatory capacities for their oversight are significantly constrained. Competent supervisory departments lack the authority to oversee the rules of online platforms. The legal nature of these rules can be described as belonging to soft law. However, they differ in their legal effects from domestic law. The terms of service of online platforms are legally enforceable for all platform users. Currently used platforms have been increasingly important to the art market, forcing participants to accept the rules that govern content and how online platforms are designed or altered. This coerced control of users by platform administrators has consolidated the dominance of online platform use.

(2) Competent supervisory departments lack the technical capacity to manage current online platforms. The algorithmic technology of online platforms is a threat to digital human rights in this networked era, manifested in the ability of platform regulators using data, algorithms, or other technical means to influence the choices of participants, hijack traffic, disrupt the operation of their or others' online platforms, and inflict big data–enabled price discrimination against existing customers. Regarding the ability to oversee online platform technology, competent administrators cannot monitor the use of a platform's hidden algorithmic technology, which leads to algorithmic infringement becoming a routine activity. This has generated systematic infringement consequences and poses a significant challenge in supervising new online platforms.

Future Criminal Legislation and Regulations

The legal issues mentioned above should allow readers to reflect on the Chinese criminal court's response to the cause-and-effect logic applied to the traditional legal discourse discussed above. Although existing criminal legislation and administrative regulations within Chinese jurisdictions are far from satisfactory to cope with the legality or not of online commerce involving cultural relics, the legal regulations governing cybercrime in China remain subject to definitions in criminal case law and the stipulations of administrative supervision. However, it can be presumed that the speed with which the cybercrime of cultural relics can be committed will make it obligatory for Chinese legislators to develop new legal mechanisms to specifically control this emerging form of cybercrime. Ironically, it can be taken as a positive that cybercrime cases have occurred almost every year since 2020, providing criminal case law with further references to how existing laws have been applied within the regulatory landscape for the cybercrime of cultural relics. Moreover, the five cases discussed above differ in the category of cybercrime committed. This section will recommend which new legislative approaches are needed to better situate the cybercrime of cultural relics within Chinese criminal legislation and suggest a practical mechanism of administrative supervision.

The enactment of domestic legislation is a fundamental prerequisite for the effective functioning of law enforcement and maintenance of the legal system, which requires adopting an appropriate legislative model for the efficient and orderly implementation of domestic legislation within a given country. China is no exception. Although the types of cybercrime discussed above essentially limit the resolution of the criminal legal framework, no current provision or law can be treated as the legal basis to regulate the cybercrime of cultural relics. The following legislative approaches can instead be considered.

First, legislation and terminology on the cybercrime of cultural relics should be specific and clear in response to the degree of technological specialization needed to commit organized cybercrime of cultural relics. In addition, judicial interpretations should clarify the meanings of specific terminology within legislative provisions and further explain how the interpretation addresses one or more of the six already-defined crimes regarding the administration of cultural relics offline, traditional financial crime, or the five abovementioned categories of computer-mediated crime. Doing so would enhance the abilities of courts to try these crimes and provide a legal distinction between them and the cybercrime of cultural relics.

Second, the NPCSC should be considered not only to establish the effective articulation of a criminal legal system headed by the Criminal Law and other domestic laws concerning the protection of cultural relics to regulate the cybercrimes of cultural relics but also to balance the interests of the participants (buyer and seller, users, creators) in the online art market. This recommendation would allow courts to take advantage of the edict *lex superior derogat legi inferiori* (if there is a conflict between high and low laws and regulations, the high one must take precedence) for the cybercrime of cultural relics.

Third, in light of the expanding scope of legal interests in the protection of cyberspace for new situations not covered by existing Criminal Law, it is recommended that the NPCSC individually stipulate the cybercrime of cultural relics, accompanied by provisions to clarify which penalties apply in order to redress currently insufficient penalties under criminal legislation and the absence of specific criminal charges for the cybercrime of cultural relics. In the case of the cybercrime of cultural relics with significant legal consequences, it would be advisable to increase the upper limit of statutory penalties from a legislative perspective and consider adding property and disqualification penalties, which could be applied simultaneously with other penalties under the existing criminal framework.

Concerning the administrative supervision of the cybercrime of cultural relics, the following practical suggestions can be proposed.

First, it is recommended that multiple administrative authorities carry out joint law enforcement or supervisory activities to better protect cultural relics and fight against cybercrime of cultural relics. Based on this, strengthened administrative mechanisms would bolster information and resource sharing among different administrative authorities, integrate administrative supervisory powers, formulate unified standards, strengthen interagency coordination, and establish a comprehensive and multidimensional management structure for all online trading platforms. Doing so would eliminate the shirking of responsibilities among certain administrative authorities from the onset and allow the multifaceted supervisory work of each administrative authority to continue.

Second, the specific ways in which third-party supervision (that taken by independent institutes recognized by the Chinese government) plays its most significant role should be encouraged under the guidance of administrative supervision. In addition, administrative authorities should be encouraged to cooperate with professional organizations to conduct credit investigations, evaluations, and technical reviews of online platforms. Third-party and industry expertise in protecting the cultural heritage items in question will enable it to strengthen third-party oversight and detect relevant violations, increase the exposure of illegal transactions through online platforms, and facilitate multiparty participation in maintaining an environmentally conscious and honest online trading landscape.

Third, it is necessary to divide the rules governing online platforms into general and specific rules in terms of online transactions. General rules, such as those applicable to the platform itself, may be formulated by the representative parties (creators and users) alone. In contrast, special rules, such as those concerning the sharing of responsibilities and risks and data privacy, require the participation of a broader range of stakeholders to ensure the participation of users, industry associations, and other relevant parties in the e-commerce network. In addition, it is recommended that a diverse range of experts be included in formulating new rules for the online platforms, ensuring a balanced and informed approach and avoiding the homogenization of knowledge. Experts from various fields, including law, technology, cultural relics, economics, and society, are encouraged. Additionally, online platforms are encouraged to engage a certain number of experts in the rule-making process, thus facilitating the establishment of open communication channels between experts, online platforms, industry associations, and users.

Fourth, establishing and promoting alternative dispute-resolution mechanisms would help resolve disputes flexibly, distribute judicial resources reasonably, and reduce dispute-resolution costs. Online dispute resolution is a new approach combining alternative dispute-resolution and technology development to resolve disputes conveniently, efficiently, and cheaply. Therefore, in the context of e-commerce, dispute-resolution technologies should be developed to facilitate the resolution of disputes arising from online platforms and given due attention.

Conclusion

From examining the status quo and involved legal issues to proposing new, practical criminal legislation and administrative regulations, this chapter has not only reviewed the historical development of cybercrime of Chinese cultural relics but also systematically revealed a series of cybercriminal matters concerning cultural relics through the discussed case studies in China for the first time. In addition, it has attempted to elaborate on relevant legal problems and solutions involving cybercrime of cultural relics. It could be concluded that cybercrime of cultural relics will continue to coexist with other forms of organized crime and will extend to harm the scope of the interests of different kinds of property and persons with the update and upgrade of these digital technologies to enable the emergence of cybercrime groups and new cybercrime types. Therefore, two ways of resolving cybercrimes emerge from the adoption of case-by-case solutions from judicial and legislative approaches that provide long-term legal remedies from administrative regulations and law enforcement. In essential, the successful regulations on cybercrime of cultural relics can be divided into the proposed three-pronged approach: (i) Prevention: Mitigating business and legal risks arising from the routine use of new digital technologies, facilitated by a robust domestic legal framework and practical, enforceable criminal legislation implemented proactively before cybercrime occurs. (ii) Law enforcement: Effectively combating cybercrime targeting cultural relics through enhanced coordination mechanisms between administrative law enforcement and criminal justice authorities. (iii) Legal remedy: Providing diverse remedies to affected parties following cybercrime incidents, irrespective of the stage of criminal proceedings against perpetrators.

Acknowledgment

Many thanks are due to Dr. Damien Huffer, Dr. Eveline Handby, and the anonymous referees for their constructive comments and pertinent suggestions on earlier versions of this chapter. I would like to express my sincere gratitude to the project of China's National Administration of Cultural Heritage (Grant: No. 2024-56) and the Humanities and Social Sciences Project of the Ministry of Education (Grant: No. 24YJCZH169) for their support and assistance with this research study. Any errors or omissions are, of course, the author's own.

Dr. Hao Liu is an associate professor of international cultural heritage law at the Law School at Shandong University, PRC. His work focuses on law and ethics approaches to the restitution and cross-disciplinary research on the protection of cultural heritage. He not only has worked as a postdoctoral research fellow at the National Museum of China and contributed to the national policy of restitution, the revising of the Law on the Protection of Cultural Relics of the PRC, and the drafting of Hainan legislation but also was appointed as an individual partner of the 1995 UNIDROIT Convention since 2021.

NOTES

1. If there is no special interpretation or announcement, the PRC mentioned in this chapter covers mainland China and both Special Administrative Regions. Hong Kong will always be treated as an essential transit location in the PRC because traditional illegal antiquities dealers often ship the subject matter via transit regions or nations to avoid detection and create false provenance and thereby good faith, providing opportunities for smugglers.
2. See Art Basel and UBS, "Art Market Report 2025," https://theartmarket.artbasel.com/download/The-Art-Basel-and-UBS-Art-Market-Report-2025.pdf.
3. See People's Bank of China, "Notice on Further Preventing and Resolving the Risks of Virtual Currency Trading and Speculation," http://www.pbc.gov.cn/en/3688110/3688172/4157443/4353814/index.html.
4. See Supreme People's Procuratorate. "The First Batch of Five Typical Cases of Punishing Crimes Involving Cultural Relics in 2023," https://www.spp.gov.cn//xwfbh/dxal/202310/t20231030_632402.shtml.
5. See (2019) Jiangsu 06, the Second Instance of Criminal Case, No. 318; (2020) Zhejiang, the Second Instance of Criminal Case, No. 123, which are selected by the Guiding Cases from the Supreme People's Procuratorate. (2014) Liaoning 01, the First Instance of Criminal Case, No. 325; (2015) Shanghai 0109, the First Instance of Criminal Case, No. 1040; (2016) Shaanxi 01, the First Instance of Criminal Case, No. 233, are selected by the Guiding Cases from the Supreme People's Court.
6. See (2010) Guangdong, the Second Instance of Criminal Case, No. 326; (2010) Hubei, the Second Instance of Criminal Case, No. 56; (2010) Tianjin 01, the First Instance of Criminal Case, No. 182; (2015) Beijing 0108, the Second Instance of Criminal Case, No. 513; (2016) Beijing, the Second Instance of Criminal Case, No. 592; (2018) Zhejiang 01, the First Instance of Criminal Case, No. 5; (2020) Shandong, the Second Instance of Criminal Case, No. 663; (2021) Shanghai 02, the First Instance of Criminal Case, No. 1152. The above cases are selected by Model Cases from the Supreme People' s Court.
7. See (2017) Shandong 13, the First Instance of Criminal Case, No. 26; (2019) Shanghai 0104, the First Instance of Criminal Case, No. 345.
8. See (2021) Guangdong 0304, the First Instance of Criminal Case, No. 789; (2022) Beijing 0102, the First Instance of Criminal Case, No. 123.
9. See Interpretation of the Supreme People's Court and the Supreme People's Procuratorate on Several Issues Concerning the Application of Law in the Handling of Criminal Cases Concerning Hampering the Administration of Cultural Relics (2016); Opinions of the Supreme People's Court, the Supreme People's Procuratorate, the Ministry of Public Security, and the National Administration of Cultural Heritage on Several Issues Concerning the Handling of Criminal Cases of Hampering the Administration of Cultural Relics (2022). See Opinions of the Supreme People's Court, the Supreme People's Procuratorate, and the Ministry of Public Security on Several Issues Concerning the Application of Criminal Procedures in the Handling of Cases Concerning Information Network-Related Crime (2022). See Interpretations of the Supreme People's Court and the Supreme People's Procuratorate on Several Issues Concerning the Application of Law in Handling Criminal Cases Involving Crimes of Illegally Using an Information Network or Providing Aid for Criminal Activities in Relation to Information Network (2019).
10. See (2002) Henan, the Second Instance of Criminal Case, No. 178.
11. See the Special Report of 2012 from the *Chinese Newspaper of Cultural Relics*.

12. See "Microblog Auction Pitfalls: Sellers Disappear After Paying Deposits," *Beijing Evening News*, 18 July 2012.
13. See National Administration of Cultural Relics. "Special Action to Crack Down on Illegal Short Videos and Live Broadcasting Activities," http://www.ncha.gov.cn/art/2024/10/28/art_722_192003.html.
14. See Convention on Cybercrime (ETS No. 185) 2001, https://rm.coe.int/1680081561.
15. See United Nations Convention against Cybercrime 2024, https://www.unodc.org/unodc/en/cybercrime/convention/home.html.
16. See the Italy Legge sul Cybercrime No. 48/2008, https://rm.coe.int/octocom-legal-profile-italy/16809e59c9.
17. See The Australian Cybercrime Act 2001, https://rm.coe.int/cybercrime-act-2001/16808e70b4.
18. See The Philippines Cybercrime Prevention Act 2012, https://www.officialgazette.gov.ph/2012/09/12/republic-act-no-10175/.
19. See the Nigeria Cybercrime (Prohibition and Prevention) Act 2015, https://www.nfiu.gov.ng/images/Downloads/downloads/cybercrime.pdf.
20. See South Africa Cybercrimes Act 2020, https://www.gov.za/documents/acts/cybercrimes-act-19-2020-english-afrikaans-01-jun-2021.
21. See "Dunhuang Murals Inspire Digital Art," *China Daily*, 2021, https://www.chinadaily.com.cn/a/202111/24/WS619d9928a310cdd39bc77321.html.
22. See "Tencent Launches NFT Trading Platform Huanhe," *PINGWEST*, 2021. https://en.pingwest.com/w/9042. See "Alibaba Launches Its NFT Marketplace to Trade Intellectual Property," *The Tokenizer*, 2021. https://thetokenizer.io/2021/08/18/alibaba-launches-its-nft-marketplace-to-trade-intellectual-property/.
23. See "China's Push to Lead Global Web3 Development: The First National NFT Marketplace in 2023," *NFTICALLY*, 2023, https://www.nftically.com/blog/chinas-push-to-lead-global-web3-development-the-first-national-nft-marketplace-in-2023/.
24. See the 1954 Hague Convention for the Protection of Cultural Property in the Event of Armed Conflict, http://portal.unesco.org/en/ev.php-URL_ID=13637&URL_DO=DO_TOPIC&URL_SECTION=201.html.
25. See the adoption by the 1970 UNESCO Convention on the Means of Prohibiting and Preventing the Illicit Import, Export, and Transfer of Ownership of Cultural Property of the term *cultural property*, https://www.unesco.org/en/legal-affairs/convention-means-prohibiting-and-preventing-illicit-import-export-and-transfer-ownership-cultural.
26. See The 1995 UNIDROIT Convention on Stolen or Illegally Exported Cultural Objects, https://www.unidroit.org/instruments/cultural-property/1995-convention/.
27. See Law of the PRC on the Protection of Cultural Relics, 2024, https://flk.npc.gov.cn/detail2.html?ZmY4MDgxODE5MjdiMDgzYjAxOTMwYzk0ZGU5NzZjNjY percent3D.
28. See China Judgments Online: https://wenshu.court.gov.cn/.
29. See the Cases Database of the People's Court: https://anli.court.gov.cn/.
30. The crime of fraudulent fundraising in the Chinese legal context, which refers to the use of fraudulent methods to illegally collect funds (fictitious projects, forged approvals, false propaganda, inducing the public to contribute funds) in a large amount for illegal possession.
31. The crime of unlawfully raising funds in the Chinese legal context, which refers to absorbing funds from unspecified social objects without legal approval, on the condition of repayment of principal and interest or payment of return, and disrupting the financial order.
32. A typical case brief consists of five parts: the summary of facts, issues, holding or ruling, rationale, or reasoning.

33. See (2019) Yue 03, the First Instance of Criminal Case, No. 2749; (2020) Yue, the Second Instance of Criminal Case, No. 469.
34. The current Chinese Rating Standards for Cultural Relic Collections sets the rating standards for grade 3 cultural relics as follows: (1) relatively important cultural relics that reflect the productive forces and the production relations, the economic systems and political systems of various historical phases of China, and the relevant development of the society and history; (2) cultural relics that have relatively important values and reflect a region, a nationality, or an era; (3) cultural relics that reflect some historical events or persons, and have relatively important values in the research of some historical issues; (4) cultural relics that reflect some kinds of archeology culture types or culture characteristics, and have relatively important values; (5) cultural relics of nationalities and folk-customs that have relatively important values; (6) works of some historical phases that are of relatively high artistic levels and craft levels, but are somehow damaged; (7) good editions of ancient books that have relatively important values; (8) cultural relics that have relatively important values and reflect the important events, prominent persons, famous martyrs and famous heroes and models in the modern history (1840–1949) of China; (9) cultural relics that have relatively important values and reflect the historical events, important construction achievements, prominent leaders, famous martyrs and famous heroes and models since the foundation of the People's Republic of China; (10) cultural relics that have relatively important values and reflect the important events, prominent persons, patriotic overseas Chinese, and other eminent persons of society of the Communist Party of China and other parties and organizations in the modern history; (11) other cultural relics that have relatively important historical, artistic, and scientific values.
35. See (2020) Su0706, the First Instance of Criminal Case, No. 162.
36. See (2020) Gui0327, the First Instance of Criminal Case, No. 97.
37. See (2022) Zhe 01Hangzhou, the Second Instance of Civil Case, No. 5272.

REFERENCES

Adler, Amy. 2023. "Artificial Authenticity: Art, NFTs, and the Death of Copyright." *New York University Law Review* 98(3): 706–69.

Artzt, Matthias, and Thomas Richter. 2020. *Handbook of Blockchain Law: A Guide to Understanding and Resolving the Legal Challenges of Blockchain Technology*. Alphen aan den Rijn, Netherlands: Kluwer Law International.

Arora, Beenu. 2020. "Council Post: Five Key Reasons Dark Web Markets Are Booming." *Forbes*, 23 June.

Bull, Toby. 2009. "Lack of Due Diligence and Unregulated Markets: Trade in Illicit Antiquities and Fakes in Hong Kong." In *Art and Crime: Exploring the Dark Side of the Art World*, edited by Noah Charney, 26–38. Santa Barbara: Praeger.

Cai, Tianji, Du Li, Xin Yanyu, and Chang Lennon Y. C. 2018. "Characteristics of Cybercrimes: Evidence from Chinese Judgment Documents." *Police Practice and Research* 19(6): 582–95. (In Chinese.)

Carback, Joshua T. 2018. "Cybersex Trafficking: Toward a More Effective Prosecutorial Response." *Criminal Law Bulletin* 54(1): 64–183.

Chambers-Jones, Clare. 2022. "How Cybercriminal Communities Grow and Change: An Investigation of Ad-Fraud Communities." *Technological Forecasting and Social Change* 174: 121–282.

Chatterjee, Bidisha B. 2001. "Last of the Rainmacs: Thinking About Pornography in Cyberspace." In *Crime and the Internet*, edited by D. S. Wall, 74–99. New York: Routledge.
Chemerinsky, Jeffrey M. "Counting Offenses." *Duke Law Journal* 58, no. 4 (January 2009): 709–46.
Crang, Michael, Philip Crang, and Jon May, eds. 2001. *Virtual Geographies*. London: Routledge.
Deng, Jianpeng, and Li Jianing. 2022. "Authority Certificate of the Digital Artworks: NFT's Value Source, Right Dilemma and Countermeasures." *Journal of Exploration and Free Views* (6): 87–95. (In Chinese.)
ECDB. 2021. "China's NFT Market Is Surging—New Potential for E-Commerce?" https://ecommercedb.com/insights/chinas-nft-market-is-surging-new-potential-for-ecommerce/4536.
Egan, Mo. 2018. "A Bit(Coin) of a Problem for the EU AML Framework." In *The Palgrave Handbook of Criminal and Terrorism Financing Law*, edited by Colin King, Clive Walker, and Jimmy Gurulé, 161–80. London: Palgrave Macmillan.
EveryCRSReport. 2008. "Botnets, Cybercrime, and Cyberterrorism: Vulnerabilities and Policy Issues for Congress". Retrieved June 2025 from https://www.everycrsreport.com/reports/RL32114.html.
Gallagher, Steven. 2017. "Purchased in Hong Kong: Is Hong Kong the Best Place to Buy Stolen or Looted Antiquities?" *International Journal of Cultural Property* 24(4): 479–96.
Gordon, Sarah. 2006. "On the Definition and Classification of Cybercrime." *Journal in Computer Virology* 2: 13–20.
Grabosky, Peter. 2007. *Electronic Crime*. Upper Saddle River, NJ: Pearson.
Grose, Thomas K. 2006. "Stealing History." *US News and World Report* 140(23): 40–41.
He, Tianxiang, and Zhang Huam. 2024. "Copyright, Platforms and NFT Digital Collections: Exploring the Proper Regulatory Mode in China." *Journal of Intellectual Property Law & Practice* 19(1): 18–31.
Hufnagel, Saskia, and Colin King. 2023. "Non-Fungible Tokens: Art and Crime in a Virtual World." SSRN, 21 February. https://ssrn.com/abstract=4370145.
Kafteranis, Dimitrios, and Umut Turksen. 2022. "Art of Money Laundering with Non-Fungible Tokens: A Myth or Reality?" *European Law Enforcement Research Bulletin* 22(6): 23–31.
Kshetri, Nir. 2022. "Scams, Frauds, and Crimes in the Nonfungible Token Market." *Computer* 55(4): 60–64.
Lehman, Jeffrey, and Shirelle Phelps. 2005. *West's Encyclopedia of American Law*. 2nd ed. Vol. 3. Detroit: Thomson/Gale.
Lepofsky, Ron. 2006. "Cyberextortion by Denial-of-Service Attack." *Risk Magazine*, Retrieved June 2025 from https://www.ere-security.ca/PDF/Cyberextortion%20by%20DoS,%20Risk%20Magazine%20June%202006.pdf.
Lidington, Helen. 2002. "The Role of the Internet in Removing the Shackles of the Saleroom: Anytime, Anyplace, Anything, Anywhere." *Public Archaeology* 2(2): 67–84.
Liu, Hao. 2017. "Take the Long Way Home: The Recovery of 32 Chinese Gold Foils from France." *International Journal of Cultural Property* 24(3): 377–400.
———. 2023. "Whose culture is it? Recovering illegally excavated Chinese bronze wares from Japan." *International Journal of Cultural Policy* 29, no. 5: 576–91.
Ma, Xiujuan. 2008. "Application Study on Penalty of Cultural Relics Crimes." *Journal of Shanxi Police Academy* 16(1): 10–12. (In Chinese.)
Merryman, John Henry. 1986. "Two Ways of Thinking about Cultural Property." *American Journal of International Law* 80(4): 831–53.
Palo Alto Networks. 2022. "The Growing Ransomware Threat: 4 Trends and Insights." 25 March.

Polk, Kenneth. 2000. "The Antiquities Market Viewed as a Criminal Market." *Hong Kong Lawyer* (September): 82–91.

Polner, Mariya. 2019. "Preventing Illicit Trafficking of Cultural Objects: A Supply Chain Perspective." In *The Palgrave Handbook on Art Crime*, edited by Saskia Hufnagel and Duncan Chappell, 775–92. London: Palgrave Macmillan.

Pulgarin, Xènia Egea. 2022. "Can NFTs Be Stolen?" SSRN, 12 November. https://ssrn.com/abstract=4275490.

Richet, Jean-Loup. 2022. "How Cybercriminal Communities Grow and Change: An Investigation of Ad-Fraud Communities." *Technological Forecasting and Social Change* 174: 121–282.

Seitz, Lyndon. 2024. "All the Latest Cyberbullying Statistics and What They Mean In 2024." BroadbandSearch.net.

Smith, Russell, Peter Grabosky, and Gregor Urbas. 2004. *Cyber Criminals on Trial*. Cambridge: Cambridge University Press.

Sun, Changxiang. 2011. "Countermeasures for the Detection and Prevention of Crimes of Smuggling of Cultural Relics on the Internet." *Journal of Hubei University of Police* 120(3): 84–86. (In Chinese.)

Tao, Qian. 2022. "The Legal Connotation of NFT Transactions." *Journal of Oriental Law* (2): 70–80. (In Chinese.)

U.S. Congressional Research Service. 2023. "Botnets, Cybercrime, and Cyberterrorism: Vulnerabilities and Policy Issues for Congress." 8 September. https://www.everycrsreport.com.

Wall, David S. 2007. *Cybercrime: The Transformation of Crime in the Information Age*. Cambridge: Polity Press.

Wang, Bin. 2018. "An Empirical Study on the Present Situation of Cultural Relics Crime in China and Prevention Countermeasures." *Journal of Shanxi Police College* 26(4): 61–65. (In Chinese.)

Williams, Matthew. 2001. "The Language of Cybercrime." In *Crime and the Internet*, edited by D. S. Wall, 152–66. New York: Routledge.

Yang, Yan. 2015. "Research on Some Difficult Problems about the Crime of Cultural Relics." *Journal of Huanghe University of Science and Technology* 17(3): 119–23. (In Chinese.)

Yu, Haisong. 2016. "Legal Analysis of Issues Relating to Crimes against Cultural Relics." *Journal of Law Application*, no. 6: 90–96. (In Chinese.)

Yu, Junyuan. 2022. "The Nature, Rules and Legal Risks of NFT Transactions." *Journal of Science-Technology & Publication* (10): 103–13. (In Chinese.)

Zeamari, I., and W. Laurier. 2025. "Defining Digital Platforms: A Systematic Literature Review." In *Digital Economy. Emerging Technologies and Business Innovation*, edited by M. A. Bach Tobji, R. Jallouli, H. Sadok, K. Lajfari, D. Mafamane, and H. Mahboub, 45–67. Cham: Springer.

Zhang, Huibin, and Zhang Qi. 2022. "NFT Artworks: New Forms of Digital Art and Copyright Rules Response." *Science Technology and Law* (3): 42–50. (In Chinese-English Version.)

Zhang, Lanxiao. 2024. "Legal Regulation of Reselling NFT Digital Works." *Science Technology and Law* (1): 111–21. (In Chinese-English Version.)

Zhuge, Jianwei, Thorsten Holz, Guo Chengyu Song, Jinpeng Han, Xinhui Zou, and Zou Wei. 2009. "Studying Malicious Websites and the Underground Economy on the Chinese Web." In *Managing Information Risk and the Economics of Security*, edited by M. Eric Johnson, 225–44. New York: Springer.

CHAPTER

6

The Auction of Human Remains

Challenges, Case Studies, and Reflections

Amy E. Rattenbury and Paige Tynan

Introduction

The trade in human remains is a multifaceted issue that touches on deep ethical, legal, and cultural concerns. From historical practices to contemporary challenges, the commercialization of human remains raises critical questions about respect for the deceased, consent, and the potential exploitation of individuals whose remains are commodified. This chapter aims to provide a thorough examination of the issues surrounding the trade in human remains, exploring both the legal and illegal dimensions, the ethical implications, and the role of various stakeholders in this complex landscape with a focus on a United Kingdom (UK) perspective.

The commercialization of human remains has been a contentious topic for centuries, rooted in historical practices of anatomical study and medical education. Today, the trade has evolved, encompassing a range of activities from legitimate scientific use to questionable auctions and online sales. The issue is compounded by the existence of a gray market where legal and illegal activities often intersect, making regulation and ethical oversight challenging. The sale of human remains, whether through traditional auction houses or online platforms, raises significant ethical concerns about the objectification of human bodies, the potential for exploitation, and the violation of cultural and personal dignity.

Understanding the legal trade in human remains is crucial for comprehending the broader context of illegal activities. Legal sales, often justified for educational or scientific purposes, can inadvertently fuel illegal markets by creating demand and providing a cover for illicit transactions. This interconnectedness complicates efforts to regulate the trade and protect human rights. Examining how legal avenues can facilitate illegal activities provides a nuanced understanding of the challenges faced by law enforcement and regulatory bodies. It also highlights the need for comprehensive legal frameworks and robust ethical guidelines to mitigate these issues.

The primary purpose of this chapter is to illuminate the ethical, legal, and societal dimensions of the trade in human remains. By tracing the historical evolution of the trade, from early medical and anatomical uses to contemporary practices, the chapter will offer insights into how past practices inform present-day challenges. A significant focus will be on the ethical dilemmas posed by the commercialization of human remains, including real-world examples drawn from personal experience. This includes discussions on consent, respect for the deceased, and the implications of treating human bodies as commodities. Through these case studies, the chapter will illustrate how these ethical concerns manifest in practice, particularly in the context of modern auctions. The chapter will review existing laws and regulations governing the trade in human remains, highlighting both strengths and gaps. This includes key legislation such as the Human Tissue Act of 2004 and its impact on current practices. Auction houses and online platforms play a pivotal role in the trade of human remains. This chapter will scrutinize their responsibilities, the challenges they face, and the criticisms levied against them. Through detailed case studies, the chapter will illustrate the real-world complexities and ethical dilemmas associated with the trade in human remains. These case studies will provide a grounded understanding of the theoretical discussions. The role of new technologies, such as computer vision and machine learning, in monitoring and regulating the trade will be explored. While these technologies offer significant benefits, they also raise new ethical concerns. Finally, the chapter will propose pathways toward more ethical and regulated practices. This includes recommendations for stricter regulations, better enforcement, and more responsible handling and display of human remains.

By addressing these objectives, the chapter aims to contribute to a more informed and ethical approach to the trade in human remains. It seeks to foster a dialogue among stakeholders, including policymakers, academics, auction houses, social media companies, and the general public, about the importance of respecting human dignity and preventing exploitation in the trade of human remains. Through a comprehensive exploration of historical context, ethical considerations, legal frameworks, and modern practices, this chapter will provide a robust foundation for understanding and addressing the complex issues surrounding the commercialization of human remains.

The Legal Sale of Human Remains

The commercialization of human remains has evolved significantly from historical practices to contemporary challenges, shaped by various legislative milestones and ethical considerations. Understanding this evolution is crucial to appreciating the current regulatory and ethical landscape that governs the handling and sale of human remains.

Timeline

Throughout the sixteenth to eighteenth centuries, the sale of human remains was prevalent, often associated with anatomical dissections for medical education and research purposes. The lack of regulations led to the unauthorized procurement and sale of bodies for anatomical studies (Ghosh 2015). Moving into the nineteenth century, the Anatomy Act of 1832 in the UK was a significant legislative development aimed at regulating the supply of bodies for anatomical purposes. This act sought to address the illicit trade in human bodies and introduced measures for the legal procurement of cadavers (UK Parliament 2014). By the mid-twentieth century, the Human Tissue Act of 1961 in the UK further refined regulations concerning the use and storage of human tissue for medical and scientific purposes. This legislation aimed to ensure ethical practices in handling human remains (Human Tissue Act 1961). Following a major scandal across several hospitals who retained human tissue without consent, significant legislative changes were required. The Human Tissue Act of 2004 in the UK was a pivotal moment in the legal framework surrounding the sale of human remains. This Act introduced stringent regulations governing the removal, storage, and use of human bodies, organs, and tissue, including provisions to prevent unauthorized trading (Human Tissue Act 2004).

Between 2012 and 2013, researchers analyzed data from 454 sales of human skulls on eBay, shedding light on sales trends. This review highlighted the challenges of regulating the online trade of human remains (Halling and Seidemann 2016). Although focused on a US rather than a UK perspective, Halling and Seidemann's review discussed the effectiveness of state laws in deterring such transactions. Especially as in 2015 the sale of a human skull at an auction in Sussex raised ethical concerns, emphasizing the need for continued discussions on the commercialization of human remains and the implications of such transactions (della Dora 2009; McCorristine 2015). From 2017 onward, preexisting technology, such as computer vision and machine learning, were used to investigate human remains trafficking online. These technological developments aimed to enhance understanding of the online trade in human remains and address ethical dilemmas associated with such activities (Huffer and Graham 2017; Huffer et al. 2019).

The timeline in figure 6.1 depicts the evolution of the sale of human remains from historical practices to contemporary challenges, highlighting key legislative milestones and changing ethics surrounding the commercialization of human remains.

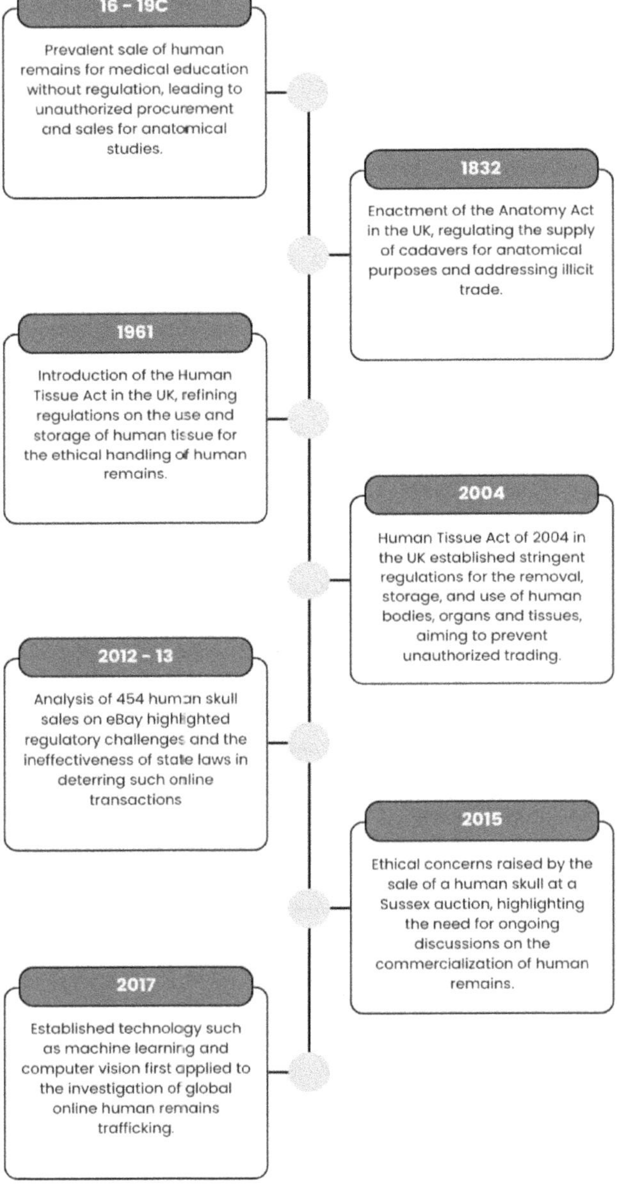

Figure 6.1. A timeline spanning from the sixteenth century to 2017, highlighting key events and the introduction of legislation. © Amy Rattenbury and Paige Tynan.

Legal Frameworks

In the UK the handling and commercialization of human remains are governed by strict consent requirements as outlined in the Human Tissue Act (2004). The Act emphasizes the necessity of obtaining informed consent for the removal, storage, and use of human tissue. It also stipulates that consent must be explicit and documented, ensuring that the wishes of the deceased and their families are respected. These ethical guidelines are critical in preventing the commodification of human remains and maintaining public trust.

Ethical considerations in the handling and commercialization of human remains are rigorously addressed by the Human Tissue Authority's (HTA) guidelines. According to the public guide, consent is fundamental to the lawful removal, storage, and use of body parts, organs, and tissue. The Human Tissue Act (2004) specifies that appropriate consent must be obtained for different purposes, whether from living or deceased persons. This ensures that the dignity of the deceased is respected and that activities involving human tissue are conducted ethically (Human Tissue Authority 2024).

The Act outlines "scheduled purposes" for which human tissue can be used, including anatomical examination, determining the cause of death, public display, research, and transplantation. For these activities, consent is required to ensure legal compliance and ethical integrity. However, the Act does not cover human remains over one hundred years old or certain human materials such as hair and nails, which may not require the same level of regulation but should still be handled with care and respect.

The ethical handling and commercialization of human remains are rigorously overseen by the HTA. The framework agreement with the Department of Health and Social Care underscores the HTA's responsibility to ensure that all activities involving human tissues are performed ethically, with proper consent, and under stringent regulatory oversight (Department of Health and Social Care and Human Tissue Authority 2022). This framework not only protects individual rights but also addresses broader ethical concerns, ensuring that the commercialization of human remains does not compromise ethical standards and public trust.

The HTA's commitment to ethical standards and public accountability is evident in its rigorous inspection and licensing processes. The Annual Report 2022/2023 highlights that the HTA conducted 210 inspections, focusing on high-risk areas while using innovative inspection models to enhance efficiency and effectiveness (Human Tissue Authority 2023). High-risk areas identified by the HTA include the postmortem sector, due to the need for careful handling of recently deceased individuals, and the anatomy sector, involving the use of human bodies for medical education and research. While the report does not explicitly list the sale of human remains as a high-risk area, it emphasizes the importance of consent and proper documentation for any activities involving human tissue. This includes ensuring that human remains are more than one hundred years old if they are to be exempt from certain regulations under the Human Tissue Act (2004). This approach underscores the importance of maintaining high ethical standards in the handling and commercialization of human remains (Department for Culture 2005).

Ethical considerations in the public display of human remains are meticulously addressed by the HTA's standards. The guidance emphasizes the importance of obtaining informed consent and maintaining the dignity of the deceased. It outlines procedures for ensuring that human remains are treated with respect, including specific requirements for the documentation and verification of consent, governance frameworks, and traceability measures. These protocols are essential for maintaining public trust and ethical integrity in the display and potential commercialization of human remains. The ethical considerations in the public display of human remains are meticulously addressed by the HTA's Code of Practice. It also provides guidance on handling sensitive material, which includes ensuring that human remains are treated with the utmost respect and that their display serves an educational or commemorative purpose rather than mere spectacle (Human Tissue Authority 2024).

The British Association for Biological Anthropology and Osteoarchaeology (BABAO) Code of Ethics (British Association for Biological Anthropology and Osteoarchaeology 2019a) provides a comprehensive framework for the respectful and lawful handling of human remains. The code emphasizes that human remains should never be considered private property and must always be treated with dignity and respect. It explicitly prohibits the buying, selling, or illegal appropriation of these remains, ensuring that any transactions involving human remains are transparent and ethically justified. Proper handling, packing, and transportation protocols are essential to prevent damage and ensure the respectful treatment of remains during auctions (British Association for Biological Anthropology and Osteoarchaeology 2019a).

Ethical Considerations

The commercialization of human remains raises profound ethical considerations regarding respect for the deceased, consent, and the potential exploitation of human skeletal material. Auctioning human remains can lead to the objectification of individuals and their remains, sparking debates on the ethical implications of treating human bodies as commodities. An example of a sale of a human skull at an auction in Sussex serves as a poignant example that underscores the ethical concerns surrounding the commercialization of human remains (McCorristine 2015).

Consent

A paper by McCorristine (2015) looks into the ethical considerations surrounding the sale of human remains, specifically focusing on the auction of John Parker's skull, who was executed in 1813 for robbing Henbury Church and De Boudrie's School. The sale of Parker's skull raises significant ethical concerns due to the likelihood of it being illicitly obtained by medical professionals, leading to a discussion on consent and the implication of objectifying human remains without proper context. McCorristine (2015) underscores the need to address issues of context and consent when dealing with the sale and display of human remains, urging for a more intimate and informative approach, especially in museum settings.

In museum settings, the ethical considerations surrounding the sale and commodification of human remains involve educating the public while respecting the dignity of the deceased. This requires providing comprehensive contextual information to explain the historical, cultural, and scientific significance of the remains, avoiding their objectification as mere curiosities. Museums must also navigate the complex issue of consent, increasingly seeking and honoring the wishes of descendant communities in decisions about the display and interpretation of remains.

The issue of consent in relation to historical medical collections presents a significant ethical challenge. Often, consent was either not obtained at the time of collection or, if it was, the documentation has not been preserved. This situation prompts critical questions regarding the continued use of such remains: does their historical use for teaching purposes justify their ongoing utilization? Additionally, the concept of an expiration date on consent must be considered, especially in cases where no living relatives can be contacted. Moreover, there is a need to determine the appropriate course of action for remains that are no longer used for educational or research purposes. Addressing these complex issues requires a thorough reevaluation of the ethical guidelines governing the handling and use of historical human remains.

In the context of educational use, Coman et al. (2022) stress the ethical principle of autonomy, which requires explicit consent for using human remains in education. They argue that without such consent, the use of these bones cannot be ethically justified, especially when high-quality replicas are available. The authors call for a nationally consistent process to manage the legacy of human bone sets in education, underscoring the need for respectful disposal and handling of human remains.

Jarus (2020) highlights the ethical implications of the online trade of human remains, noting that the sale of looted skulls and other remains often occurs without proper consent or provenance. This lack of transparency not only violates ethical principles that mandate respect and dignity for the deceased but also facilitates the exploitation of vulnerable communities. Jarus's insights reinforce the ethical concerns raised by other researchers about the commodification and objectification of human remains in digital marketplaces.

Furthermore, the paper written by McCorristine (2015) draws attention to the historical injustices related to the movement and display of human skulls, particularly those of executed criminals, emphasizing the risks of theft and objectification by collectors. It also touches upon the broader issue of the global marketplace in objectified body parts, shedding light on the disturbing nature of such practices. The author advocates for a nuanced understanding of the complexities surrounding the display and sale of human remains, urging for a more thoughtful and ethical approach that considers the wishes of the deceased individuals.

The ethical considerations surrounding the commercialization of human remains are further complicated by the advent of new technologies. Huffer, Wood, and Graham (2019) explore the ethical questions posed using computer vision and machine learning in this context. They argue that while these technologies can significantly enhance the monitoring and regulation of online human remains trafficking, they also raise concerns about privacy, consent, and the potential for surveillance overreach. These ethical issues must be addressed to ensure that the use of technology in this field is both effective and respectful of individual rights.

Commodification

The commodification of human remains raises profound ethical dilemmas, particularly concerning the dehumanization of individuals through commercial practices. The ethical concerns extend beyond simple legality, involving deep-seated moral questions about respect and dignity (Volper 2023). Breda (2023) critically examines the commodification of human skeletal remains in online marketplaces, highlighting the transition from personhood to objecthood. This transformation often occurs without considering the provenance of or obtaining consent from the deceased, raising significant ethical concerns about the respect and dignity accorded to human remains. Breda argues that when remains are transformed into art or collectibles, they are stripped of their human identity and reduced to mere objects, posing profound ethical dilemmas.

This issue of commodification is further elaborated by Mahoney (2000), who discusses the ethical tension between commodification and altruism in the market for human tissue. Mahoney emphasizes that while the commercialization of human biological materials is widespread, it raises significant ethical concerns about treating human body parts as commodities. She advocates for ethical guidelines that balance commercial interests with respect for human dignity, echoing Breda's concerns about the objectification of human remains. Similarly, Huxley and Finnegan (2004) address the ethical dilemmas posed by the online sale of human remains. They emphasize the commodification of human bones without proper consent or provenance, which leads to the exploitation and objectification of human remains. The lack of transparency and documentation in online sales exacerbates these ethical concerns, aligning with the critiques raised by Breda (2023) and Mahoney (2000).

The ethical implications of trading human remains on social media platforms are profound. According to Graham and Huffer (2020), the visibility and accessibility of human remains for sale on the social networking site Instagram also raises significant ethical concerns. These include the commodification of human bodies, the potential for exploitation, and the disrespect toward the deceased. The authors argue that the ease with which these remains can be bought and sold online necessitates stricter ethical guidelines and a more vigilant approach to monitoring and reporting such activities. Considerations often hinge on the question of ownership and property rights. Wall (2011) argues that while control rights over body parts can be justified based on personal autonomy and self-ownership, income rights, where individuals can profit from the sale of body parts, are harder to justify ethically. This distinction is vital in the context of auctions, where the ethical implication of treating human remains as commodities must be carefully examined.

The ethical considerations surrounding the commercialization of human remains are deeply intertwined with the concept of body ownership and property. Phillips (2011) argues that treating bodies as property commodifies them, which can obscure the power relations and inequalities inherent in such transactions. She highlights the importance of recognizing bodies as integral to personal identity, not just as objects for trade. This perspective questions the ethical acceptability of markets in human remains and calls for a reevaluation of our approach to bodily integrity and autonomy.

However, even with the advent of new technologies through imaging and modeling capabilities, it is important to consider that the creation and use of 2D and 3D digital images of human remains must be justified with a valid educational or research purpose and carried out with the utmost respect for the dignity of the deceased (British Association for Biological Anthropology and Osteoarchaeology 2019b). Digital imaging offers significant preservation benefits by reducing the need for physical handling, thus preventing damage and degradation. This is particularly relevant in auctions, where the remains might be handled multiple times. Moreover, the sharing and display of digital images should be conducted transparently and ethically, ensuring that all necessary permissions are obtained, and that the images are contextualized appropriately to avoid sensationalism (British Association for Biological Anthropology and Osteoarchaeology 2023). These guidelines help ensure that the auction of human remains adheres to high ethical standards, protecting both the integrity of the remains and the sensitivities of associated communities.

Lavoie (1989) considers the ethical dilemmas of treating human tissue as property, particularly concerning consent and the potential for exploitation. Lavoie argues that a property-based approach to human tissue can undermine ethical principles, leading to commodification that conflicts with public trust and ethical standards. This perspective aligns with Herring and Chau (2014), who emphasize the ethical complexities of treating human bodies as property. They argue that such an approach fails to respect the dignity and interconnected nature of human bodies, advocating for a view that emphasizes the social and ethical dimensions rather than reducing them to mere property.

Cultural Sensitivity

The ethical implications of collecting and commercializing human remains are deeply rooted in historical practices. Govor and Howes (2020) illustrate how the acquisition of remains, such as the ornamented skulls from Nuku Hiva collected during Russian expeditions, often disregarded the sanctity of Indigenous cultures and burial practices. This historical context underscores the ethical issues we face today, where the commercialization of human remains must be carefully weighed against the need for respect and reparative justice for affected communities. These implications are starkly illustrated by the historical skeleton trade in India. During the Bengal famine of 1943, entrepreneurs profited by exporting skeletons of famine victims, a practice that continued for decades. This trade not only commodified human remains but also involved unethical sourcing practices, such as body snatching and exploitation of the impoverished Dom community, who traditionally handled the dead (Banerjie 2014). These historical practices highlight problems with the commercialization of human remains, stressing the importance of ethical guidelines and respect for human dignity as the commercialization is deeply intertwined with their historical acquisition. Agarwal (2024) discusses how skeletal remains from India, often obtained through dubious means during colonial times, continue to be used in educational institutions without sufficient ethical scrutiny. The commodification of these remains, stripped of their personhood and historical context, raises significant ethical questions about consent and the dehumanization of individuals (Agarwal 2024). Addressing these issues requires a reevaluation of current practices and the development of ethical guidelines that respect the dignity of the deceased.

The ethical considerations of commercializing human remains are further complicated by the illicit trade, as detailed by Huffer and Chappell (2014). The authors discuss how the trade often involves remains that are "nameless and faceless," lacking proper provenance and often obtained through unethical means such as looting and grave robbing. These practices not only violate the dignity of the deceased but also disrupt the cultural and historical heritage of communities. Addressing these ethical concerns requires a multifaceted approach, including stricter regulations, ethical guidelines, and public awareness.

In the context of cultural heritage, Klesert and Powell (1993) argue for respecting the cultural values and rights of descendant communities in the treatment of human remains. They emphasize that archaeologists have no inherent right to access or retain human remains and that respecting diverse cultural views does not undermine academic freedom. This view is supported by Jones and Harris (1998), who stress the importance of considering the cultural and spiritual significance of human remains in archaeological and anthropological research. They highlight the guidelines provided by the Human Tissue Authority in the UK, which ensure that human remains are handled with cultural sensitivity and respect, preventing their commodification.

Kaufmann and Rühli (2010) and Jones and Whitaker (2013), explore the ethical challenges posed by the public display and study of ancient remains. Kaufmann and Rühli argue that modern biomedical ethics, which emphasize informed consent and respect for individual autonomy, are often not applicable to ancient remains. Similarly, Jones and Whitaker highlight the lack of consent and potential disrespect toward the deceased in the public display of human bodies, raising significant ethical concerns about dignity and respect.

Goold et al. (2014) discuss the ethical complexities involved in the use of human body parts, particularly balancing scientific advancement with respect for human dignity. Goold and colleagues argue that while the property model provides a means to regulate tissue use, it may not adequately capture the emotional and psychological significance of human bodies. Foster (2014), on the other hand, emphasizes human dignity as a comprehensive ethical framework, supporting the view that human tissue should not merely be treated as property but respected as part of a relational and thriving human being.

Dias (2015) extends the concept of human dignity to include the treatment of human remains, arguing that ethical frameworks must address the sanctity of human remains to ensure that they are treated with respect and not commodified. This is particularly relevant in the context of public displays, as seen in the BODY WORLDS exhibition, which underscores the importance of obtaining informed consent and maintaining the dignity of human remains.

Halperin (2007), and Cassman and Odegaard (2004) highlight the historical and ethical issues associated with the use of cadavers and the preservation of human remains. Halperin documents the disproportionate targeting of marginalized and vulnerable populations for dissection in medical schools, emphasizing the importance of historical awareness in shaping contemporary ethical practices. Cassman and Odegaard (2004) argue for cultural sensitivity and respect for Indigenous communities in the preservation of human remains, ensuring they are not commodified.

Balachandran (2009) and Licata et al. (2020) discuss the ethical complexities in the preservation and exhibition of human remains. Balachandran emphasizes the role of conservators in rehumanizing remains by preserving their associated narratives, arguing for a balance between technical preservation and moral obligations. Licata and colleagues argue for handling human remains with respect and dignity, considering the cultural values of the community and the preservation of intangible heritage.

McCorristine (2015) and Huffer (2024) highlight the ethical dilemmas in the sale and gifting of human remains. McCorristine (2015) argues that the sale of human remains, such as the skull of John Parker, ignores the historical and ethical contexts, advocating against their commodification. Huffer (2024) highlights the exploitation of legal loopholes in the gifting of remains as part of online sales in Australia, underscoring the need for comprehensive guidelines to address these ethical issues and prevent the exploitation of human remains in online markets.

Public opinion is significantly shaped by media portrayals and the visibility of auctioned remains on social media platforms. How these platforms frame the trade influences public perception, and can either mitigate or exacerbate ethical concerns (Huffer and Graham 2018). Alternatives to current commercial practices suggest pathways toward ethical acquisitions and the use of remains in scientific research. These alternatives emphasize respect for the deceased and aim to restore dignity to the remains and their communities (Huffer and Graham 2018).

As this review demonstrates, the ethical considerations surrounding the commercialization of human remains are multifaceted and complex. It is crucial to develop and adhere to ethical guidelines that respect the dignity of the deceased, ensure informed consent, and protect cultural heritage. By implementing best practices and fostering public awareness, bioanthropologists can address these ethical challenges and promote a more respectful and informed approach to the treatment of human remains.

The Role of Auction Houses

Auction houses have a crucial responsibility in the authentication of items, including human remains. This process involves verifying that the remains are genuine human body parts, determining their origin, and assessing their antiquity to ensure accurate representation. Auction houses must adopt rigorous authentication procedures and seek expert advice when dealing with human remains to uphold ethical standards and legal requirements.

One major criticism is the lack of stringent regulations and oversight. While auction premises may need to register with local councils, requirements vary by location. For instance, auction houses in London must register when selling certain items, but outside London, the necessity of a license depends on local council regulations. This inconsistency can lead to gaps in regulatory compliance and ethical oversight (UK Government 2025). Moreover, the penalties for noncompliance, such as fines up to £5,000, may not be a sufficient deterrent for auction houses prioritizing profits. The exemptions for charitable auctions or items not brought onto the premises can also create loopholes that undermine regulatory efforts.

There are a few key professional bodies associated with the auction process, and they can play a key role. The Royal Institution of Chartered Surveyors (RICS) is a globally recognized professional body that sets and enforces high standards in the valuation, management, and sale of property, including art and antiques. The RICS

Consumer Guide to Buying and Selling Art and Antiques at Auction provides essential guidance on best practices for auction processes, emphasizing transparency, proper documentation, and consumer protection (Royal Institution of Chartered Surveyors 2013). In addition, NAVA Propertymark (the professional body representing valuers and auctioneers under the broader Propertymark umbrella) plays a significant role in setting professional standards within the broader auctioneering and valuing professions, particularly in areas such as fine art, chattels, and property. Originally established in 1988 as the National Association of Valuers and Auctioneers (NAVA), it now forms part of a collective body that supports various sectors of the property and auction industry. NAVA Propertymark unites professionals from valuing, auctioneering, and insolvency to create ethical industry standards based on expertise, integrity, and honesty. By emphasizing continued professional development (CPD), it ensures that members remain informed about the latest legislation and best practices, equipping them to handle a range of items. Moreover, members follow a strict code of practice, which includes due diligence in all transactions (GAUK Auctions 2024). While NAVA Propertymark's remit does not currently extend to the auction of human remains, its established framework for ethical conduct and professional accountability could offer a valuable model for creating clearer standards in this complex area. Collaboration with specialist organizations such as BABAO could facilitate the development of sector-specific guidelines and play a key role in shaping the future of auctioning human remains.

The process of organizing auctions, whether for fundraising or commercial purposes, involves several critical steps. Establishing terms and conditions in advance is crucial, and auctioneers must ensure that potential bidders have clear and accurate information on the items, allowing them to make informed decisions (Chartered Institute of Fundraising 2024). Providing opportunities for inspection prior to the auction and having detailed information available in printed brochures or digital formats are best practices. However, this raises further ethical considerations, particularly in the production and circulation of images of human remains. Auction houses often focus on generating appealing images to facilitate sales, rather than considering the ethical implications. BABAO (2019) emphasizes that photographs of human remains should respect the dignity of the deceased and avoid sensationalism. Proper contextualization within their archaeological or historical framework is crucial, alongside securing consent and considering the impact on descendant communities. Ensuring that images are stored securely and access is restricted to prevent misuse maintains professional integrity and contributes to the respectful treatment of human remains. However, this approach can conflict with the promotion of remains for sale, which requires wide-reaching dissemination and often online promotion.

The Auctions (Bidding Agreements) Act 1969 outlines specific legal frameworks regarding auction practices. This Act amends previous laws and extends the penalties and conditions under which auction agreements must operate, emphasizing the importance of fair-trading practices and imposing penalties on those who engage in bidding agreements to manipulate auction outcomes. Key aspects of the Act ensure the structured regulation of auction practices and the prevention of fraudulent activities. Offenses under the Act can be prosecuted either summarily or on indictment, with penalties including imprisonment for up to two years, fines, or both. Additionally, individuals convicted under the Act may be prohibited from attending or participating in auctions for up to three years, which aims to deter unethical behavior. The Act also grants sellers the right to void contracts if collusion is discovered, protecting them from fraudulent bidding practices and ensuring a fair competitive environment. To further promote transparency, auction houses are required to exhibit a copy of the Act at sales, ensuring that all participants are aware of the legal frameworks governing auction practices.

These legislative measures aim to enhance the ethical conduct of auction houses and ensure transparency and fairness in auction practices. However, the effectiveness of these regulations depends on rigorous enforcement and compliance by auction houses. They are also focused on the rights of sellers and buyers, not on the rights of the deceased who may be auctioned.

The auction process involves competitive bidding, which can significantly affect the value and sale price of human remains. While competitive auctions are designed to attract multiple bids and drive up prices, this environment can raise serious ethical and legal concerns, particularly when dealing with human remains. The higher prices resulting from competitive bidding can incentivize the trade and commodification of human remains, leading to potential ethical breaches. Auction houses must navigate these challenges carefully, ensuring that all transactions comply with legal standards and uphold ethical practices to avoid further commodifying these sensitive items (Davies and Chubbock 2017).

Auction houses sometimes inadvertently facilitate the sale of culturally sensitive items due to inadequate verification processes. This can lead to auction houses facing significant public scrutiny of their ethical responsibilities when items of questionable provenance are offered. A pertinent example (emerging at the time of writing) is the case in Dorset where an auction house withdrew eighteen ancient Egyptian human skulls from sale after significant public backlash and ethical concerns. MP Bell Ribeiro-Addy, chair of the all-party parliamentary group on Afrikan reparations, condemned the sale as perpetuating the atrocities of colonialism and a gross violation of human dignity. The skulls, originally collected by Victorian British soldier Augustus Henry Lane Fox Pitt-Rivers, were part of his second collection displayed privately (Batty 2024). The criticisms levied at these institutions often stem from their role in perpetuating historical injustices and their failure to adequately address ethical concerns (Volper 2023). The ethical and legal considerations surrounding the auction of human remains are paramount in the fight against digital heritage crime. As outlined in the updated guidelines by Boylston et al. (2004), maintaining high ethical standards and adhering to established codes of practice are essential for professionals handling human remains. These guidelines emphasize the importance of thorough documentation and the use of advanced technologies, such as CT scanning and digital databases, to record and analyze skeletal remains meticulously. This meticulous documentation is crucial in establishing the provenance of human remains, ensuring they are legally obtained and ethically handled. By implementing these practices, the archaeological community can help prevent the illicit trade and auction of human remains, thereby protecting cultural heritage and respecting the dignity of the deceased. The integration of digital data and metadata also enhances the traceability and transparency of human remains in digital and physical marketplaces, further combating heritage crime and unethical auctions.

Auction houses, including online platforms like eBay, are known to play a significant role in the trade of human remains (Halling and Seidemann 2016). Despite some controls in place, such as making it explicit in the policy that the sale of human body parts is prohibited, removing listings, issuing warnings, restricting activity and suspending accounts (eBay 2025), the sale of human remains on eBay has persisted over the years. Instances of human remains, such as skulls, being sold have been identified, underscoring the actual trade of such items through these auction sites (Seidemann et al. 2009). Previous research has shed light on the buying and selling of human skeletal remains on eBay, with some sellers attempting to justify these sales for instructional purposes (Huxley and Finnegan 2004).

The trade of human remains through auction houses raises ethical concerns, particularly regarding the loss of historical context and the absence of consent from the individuals whose remains are being traded (McCorristine 2015). The sale of human remains at auctions should spark discussions on the ethical implications and the necessity for stricter regulations to prevent such transactions. Auction houses can learn valuable lessons from the Department for Culture, Media and Sport (DCMS) guidance (Department for Culture, Media and Sport 2005), which currently applies to museums but provides a robust framework for handling human remains. The DCMS guidelines emphasize the importance of careful documentation of provenance, secure storage, and responsible access management to prevent misuse and ensure the dignity of the deceased. By adopting these practices, auction houses can enhance their legal and ethical standards. For instance, maintaining detailed records of the origins and histories of human remains ensures transparency and accountability, which can build trust with buyers and descendant communities. Implementing secure storage solutions protects the remains from damage and unauthorized access, thereby preventing potential ethical and legal violations. Moreover, managing access responsibly, particularly concerning the sale and dissemination of images of human remains, ensures that these images are used respectfully and contextually. By learning from the DCMS guidelines, auction houses can align their practices with best practices in the field, thereby safeguarding the integrity of human remains and respecting the sensitivities of all stakeholders involved.

Furthermore, advancements in technology, such as computer vision and machine learning, have been explored to investigate human remains trafficking online, indicating a growing effort to comprehend the extent and nature of this trade on social media platforms (Huffer and Graham 2018; Huffer et al. 2019). This underscores the evolving methods being utilized to monitor and address the trade of human remains through online channels. Continued research and technological advancements are crucial to combat this trade and ensure the respectful treatment of human remains.

The sale of human remains can also significantly affect forensic investigations, especially when the remains are obtained illicitly or mishandled. Removing human remains from forensic contexts for sale can disrupt investigations by potentially depriving forensic experts of crucial evidence needed to determine the cause and manner of death, establish the identity of the deceased, or reconstruct the circumstances surrounding the death. Improperly handled remains can impede the accurate estimation of the postmortem interval, cause of death, and other critical aspects of an investigation (Woess et al. 2017).

Furthermore, the commercialization of human remains through online platforms like eBay raises ethical concerns and legal issues, underscoring the importance of regulating the trade of such items to prevent interference with forensic cases (Halling and Seidemann 2016). The unauthorized sale of human skulls or other body parts can potentially result in the loss of valuable evidence that forensic investigators rely on to solve crimes or identify individuals. In a case study involving the recovery of a human skull from an eBay sale, it was argued that curated human skeletal remains are indispensable for the purpose of teaching future investigators forensic identification techniques (Seidemann et al. 2009).

Moreover, the alteration of forensically relevant human remains obtained through auctions and online sales can significantly impede forensic investigations by complicating the analysis of skeletal remains and potentially obscuring evidence crucial for determining the cause of death or facilitating identification (Berger et al. 2018).

Modern Case Studies

In this section, we present two case studies drawn from the personal experiences of one of the chapter authors, Amy Rattenbury, senior lecturer in forensic science. Adopting an autoethnographic approach, these case studies illustrate the complexities and ethical dilemmas associated with the sale of human remains. By sharing these personal experiences, we seek to underscore the urgent need for comprehensive oversight and adherence to established ethical standards in the sale and handling of human remains. These case studies also highlight the broader implications for the field of forensic science and anthropology, emphasizing the importance of ethical practices in our professional community.

Case Study 1: A Question of "Composition"

In the summer of 2022, a concerning incident arose where human remains were listed for sale online by a UK auction house, raising serious ethical, legal, and regulatory questions. This case study illuminates the sequence of events and the challenges encountered during this unsettling episode.

A recent graduate from the BSc (Hons) Forensic Science program at Wrexham University (formerly Wrexham Glyndŵr University) in North Wales, UK, discovered an online listing entitled "Vintage composite partial human skeleton" with an estimated price of £30–40. Having previously studied a module in Anatomy, Pathology, and the Forensic Examination of Human Remains, the student believed the lot would interest the university and promptly shared a screenshot with staff in the Applied Science Department. Upon closer examination of the image, I was shocked that something like this was for sale nearby. I became deeply concerned that the items were not composite as advertised but were, in fact, real human bones, likely belonging to more than one individual. I was curious about where the remains had come from and why the auction house believed they were composite. I was also glad that the graduate had come across them and brought them to my attention.

In response to these concerns, I decided to act, contacting the auction house to discuss the lot. Due to the limited timeframe to act, with less than twenty-four hours before the planned auction, I felt the need to act quickly. I consulted with some colleagues who are also members of the British Association for Biological Anthropology and Osteoarchaeology (BABAO), sharing the photos and checking if they also felt they were real human bones. I also checked what the process for reporting these remains to BABAO was. I was conscious that the auction house might not believe I was an expert in the identification of human remains or trust my analysis, so I felt it important to be able to provide supporting evidence and reference material. An appointment was scheduled later the same day for me to visit the auction house personally and assess the authenticity of the remains. Accompanied by samples of real and composite bone for reference and armed with a copy of the guidance produced by BABAO on the sale of human remains, I aimed to confirm the nature of the items in question and engage in discussion with auction house staff.

Upon reaching the auction house, I was sad to see the way the remains were placed. The remains were found split between a cardboard vegetable box and an old suitcase, on the floor of the auction room. Regrettably, I was quickly able to confirm that the items were indeed real human bone, as suspected. I was not permitted to take any photographs of the remains and was only able to view them briefly before being escorted away from other auction attendees to a private office. My preliminary inventory (figure 6.2) of the contents of both containers showed that there was a minimum of three individuals present, determined by the presence of multiple elements of the same skeletal portions. There appeared to be parts of three separate crania, one of which also had a mandible, and then one side of a set of postcranial elements, some of which had been strung together for display.

Despite facing what I felt was resistance and hostility from auction house staff, I attempted to communicate the ethical standpoint and best practices observed in the field. I requested that the remains be immediately removed from sale, at least until further research into the provenance could be undertaken. The alarming aspect of this case was that the auction house failed to conduct any preliminary checks to determine the authenticity of the remains before my intervention. This lack of due diligence could have far-reaching consequences in the trade of human remains. Without any checks, they could have even been forensically relevant.

I raised my concerns directly with the auction house, emphasizing that the items were not composites but real skeletal remains. I explained the importance of treating human remains with dignity and respect and referenced the relevant guidelines from the HTA and BABAO. I advised the auction house to remove the items from display and consider donating them to a suitable teaching and research facility where they could be properly curated. At this point, it was suggested by the auction staff that this was a way to take the remains away myself. They did agree to speak with the "owner" about the sale; however, it is unclear if this ever occurred. Later that day, in a follow-up call, the auctioneer defended their position, asserting that the disputed item was merely a small part of a much larger consignment. They

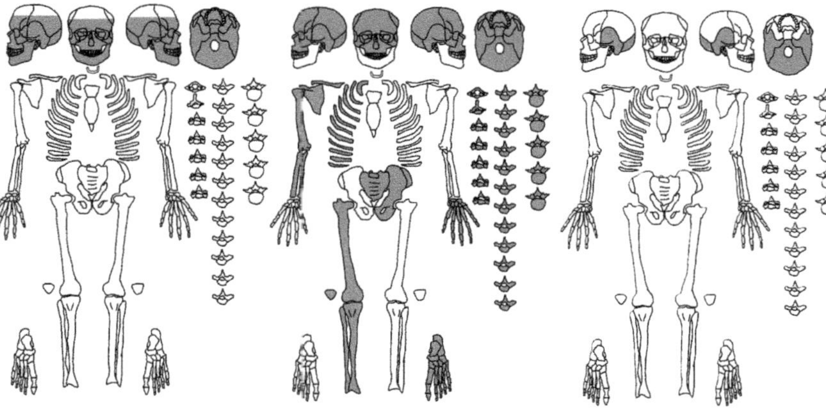

Figure 6.2. A basic skeletal inventory produced from author's initial observations and the images published with the online listing. © Amy Rattenbury and Paige Tynan.

repeatedly attempted to compare the sale to that of animal taxidermy, asking if I would buy animal remains, questioning if I thought people should not be interested in these things. When the auctioneer asked me "Where do we draw the line?," they seemed unhappy with my response of "At people."

Recognizing the gravity of the situation, I reported the matter to the local coroner and BABAO in a proactive attempt to address the potential legal and ethical violations associated with the sale of human remains. However, at this stage, it was late in the day, the evening before the auction was scheduled, with little time for anyone to take further action. I hoped that BABAO or HM Coroner might have more power to act, and that the auction house might respect and listen to them more than they did me.

Post-auction Aftermath

Despite my efforts, the auction proceeded as scheduled, culminating in the sale of the human remains for a sum of £160, significantly more than the estimate given when the remains were not believed to be real bone. This outcome left me feeling as though I had let the individuals down. I was worried that my response, which may have come across as too emotional or confrontational, had caused the auction house to feel attacked and become defensive. I felt like I had failed as a professional by being unable to convince them to stop the sale.

Furthermore, the auction house disputed the sale on social media, claiming that the bones were removed from sale, despite staff at the university and concerned BABAO members following the live auction online. I found their social media posts particularly interesting and somewhat disheartening. Although I had posted about the incident on my own social media, I was careful not to identify them and focused on expressing my disappointment rather than criticizing their actions. Their response not only identified themselves but also felt like a personal attack. I felt they were accusing me of interfering or having nothing better to do, undermining my professional and ethical concerns.

To date, it is still unclear where these remains came from and what their fate was following the auction. The auction house did not provide any further information on where the remains went after the auction. Although it was likely that they originated from an old medical teaching collection, based on my brief observations of the preparation and preservation and experience of having worked with similar collections previously, the auction house never made any effort to ensure that the remains were more than one hundred years old. They put them on display in their shopfront window like an oddity or morbid curiosity, which could have potentially contravened the Human Tissues Act or required an HTA license. Although I had hoped that the sale did not go ahead and that the remains were not reduced to a commodity for financial gain, I do not know who is currently in possession of them. I still regularly check local auction listings to see if they come up again anywhere. I can only hope that they are being carefully and respectfully curated and have not been disposed of, sold on (through legal or illegal modes), or otherwise objectified, turned into "art," or mutilated.

This incident underscores the critical need for transparency and accountability in the sale of human remains. Auction houses must conduct thorough preliminary checks to verify the authenticity and provenance of remains to prevent potential ethical and legal violations. The possibility that these remains could have been forensically relevant or less than one hundred years old further highlights the importance of stringent regulations.

Reflections and Ethical Considerations

This case study serves as a stark illustration of the ethical, legal, and regulatory challenges associated with the sale of human remains by auction houses. It underscores the need for comprehensive oversight and adherence to established ethical standards within this contentious domain. The sale of human remains at auctions poses significant ethical and legal challenges, as highlighted by this case. The auction house did not conduct any preliminary checks to authenticate the remains, leading to potential ethical and legal violations. The seller's failure to provide proper documentation regarding the origin of the remains raises serious concerns about their ethical handling and legality. Despite clear evidence and ethical arguments presented, the auction house's reluctance to withdraw the remains from sale reflects a disregard for ethical standards in the trade of human remains and the prioritization of profits. The public dispute on social media between the university representative and the auction house underscores the importance of transparency and accountability in handling sensitive issues. This incident highlights the necessity for stricter regulations and enforcement mechanisms to ensure that the sale and display of human remains are conducted ethically and legally, if at all.

Reflecting on this incident, I personally grapple with a deep sense of guilt for not being able to protect these remains. Despite my best efforts, the remains were sold, and I remain uncertain about their current status. I also feel guilty about the likely damage to the relationship with the auction house, which may now be reluctant to seek future support or consultation due to this event. Additionally, I regret that by confirming these remains were real bone, I may have inadvertently increased their value, ultimately resulting in greater financial gain from their sale. In hindsight, I have questioned whether I should have simply purchased them myself at the lower estimated price to ensure they were treated with dignity.

However, this raises deeper ethical concerns about the role of researchers in the human remains market. By purchasing human remains, even with good intentions, academics risk perpetuating the very market they critique. The demand created by collectors, museums, and researchers has historically contributed to the commodification of human remains, often without consent or regard for cultural sensitivities. This incident forced me to reflect on how researchers can navigate these moral dilemmas, balancing a duty to protect human remains with the risk of inadvertently legitimizing their sale. The tension between intervention and complicity is one that scholars in anthropology, bioarchaeology, and related fields must continuously contend with, particularly as auction houses and online marketplaces remain largely unregulated.

This experience has reinforced my belief in the urgent need for stricter policies governing the sale of human remains, alongside a deeper reflection on the ethical implications of academic engagement in such markets. Rather than relying on individual interventions, such as mine, the academic and professional communities must commit to a broader disciplinary response: one that challenges the systems enabling this trade and advocates for legal and ethical reform. This incident has profoundly reshaped my perspective on the auction industry. I remain firmly of the belief that the sale of human remains, regardless of their antiquity or origin, is fundamentally wrong. These individuals should not be treated as possessions to be used transactionally, and certainly not to make a profit. I often think about them and wonder what more I could have done. The frustration with the auction house lingers, as I feel they failed to appreciate the ethical implications of their actions. Professionally, this incident has reinforced my commitment to driving change. I now actively monitor auction listings and engage with regulatory bodies to prevent similar incidents in the future. The potential consequence of selling unverified human remains, which could be forensically relevant or less than one hundred years old, highlights the critical need for stringent oversight.

Moving forward, it is essential to establish more robust regulations that require thorough preliminary checks and proper documentation for a sale to occur. Auction houses must be held accountable for their role in ensuring that human remains are treated with the dignity and respect they deserve. I plan to continue advocating for these changes by working with professional organizations, with regulatory bodies, and through public awareness initiatives. This case has shown me the importance of balancing professional persistence with sensitivity in communication. The way we approach these situations can significantly affect the outcomes, and it is crucial to maintain a respectful and evidence-based approach even when faced with resistance. Reflecting on this incident, I remain dedicated to protecting the dignity of human remains and ensuring they are treated with the utmost respect and care.

Case Study 2: A "Foot" in the Door

Upon discovering in October 2023 an online listing for human remains described as "An anatomical human tibia, fibula and skeletal foot, late 19th/early 20th century," I decided to act. Unlike previous instances, I was not surprised to see such a listing, as I had become more aware that this practice was still occurring. I felt it was crucial to approach the situation thoughtfully, aiming to gather more information about the provenance rather than simply opposing the sale outright.

I initially reached out to the auction house via phone and left a voicemail expressing my concerns and requesting a conversation about the remains. In the voicemail, I sought to understand how they assessed the item to determine if it was real bone and how they dated it to the late nineteenth/early twentieth century. After leaving the voicemail, I felt a mix of hope and anxiety, anticipating that my message might be ignored. Following up later that day, I sent the auction house an email, copying in the head of the BABAO sale of human remains group and attaching their guidance on the sale of human remains. I framed my concerns professionally, explaining that I was part of a wider group of professionals who shared these concerns. I hoped that this would add weight to my request and demonstrate that my views were supported by a professional body. In the email, I requested further details about the provenance and authentication of the listed human remains. I also offered to discuss the ethical implications of their sale based on BABAO guidelines and suggested considering alternative, ethical options for the remains. I provided my contact information and expressed my hope that the auction house would be receptive to discussing these concerns. Copying BABAO in the email was strategic. I wanted to show that I was not a lone individual with a strong opinion but part of a larger professional community concerned with ethical practices. I also hoped that if the auction house did not respond to me, BABAO might follow up or reach out independently.

Due to the distance, I was unable to meet the staff in person or view the remains physically. This limitation was challenging, as I would have liked to see the remains and speak with the auction house directly. However, unlike in the previous case, it was less critical for me to physically see the bones as they had not been incorrectly identified as composite. My primary focus was on understanding the provenance and ensuring the remains were treated ethically.

Engagement and Outcome

The following day, the auction house called me back. I was surprised and pleased by their prompt response. They were engaged in the conversation and seemed keen to hear my perspectives. They confirmed that they rarely get human remains listed for sale and were not experienced in this area. They admitted that they had not performed any checks other than seeing that the remains "looked" old. This openness and willingness to discuss the matter put me at ease. During our conversation, I suggested several alternatives to selling the remains. I recommended that they engage directly with BABAO for guidance or speak with a local university that might have an archaeology or anthropology department. The auction house staff appeared receptive to these suggestions and agreed to discuss the remains with the "owner" to explore these options further. I was relieved that my actions were leading to positive change and potentially protecting these, and future, remains from unethical sale.

A few days later, the auction house followed up to explain that the owner had agreed to remove the lot from sale. Additionally, they had contacted a local university that was willing to take the item into their collection. This outcome was particularly gratifying, as it meant that the remains would be respectfully curated in an academic setting rather than commodified. The auction house also expressed interest in working with the university in the future should similar listings arise. This willingness to collaborate with academic institutions indicated a significant shift in their perspective on handling human remains. I felt optimistic about the potential for ongoing collaboration between auction houses and academic institutions, which could help to ensure ethical practices in the future.

Reflections and Ethical Considerations

This case shows the stark contrast and much more positive outcomes that can result from constructive interactions between auction houses, institutions, and individuals dedicated to protecting the dignity of human remains. Reflecting on my approach, I tried not to get too emotional or frustrated in my discussions. Instead, I provided the auction house staff with an opportunity to explain their practices and ask me questions in a professional and supportive environment rather than an accusatory one. This strategy seemed effective, as the auction house could have easily ignored my phone call and email but chose to engage constructively.

The auction house's willingness to engage in conversation and seek advice demonstrated a proactive approach to addressing ethical concerns. Even after our initial conversation, they could have chosen not to take any action. I certainly did not expect them to follow up with me to explain the outcome. Their transparency and proactiveness in this case were reassuring, highlighting several key issues and positive aspects. The auction house demonstrated willingness to engage in discussion and seek expert advice, reflecting a proactive approach to addressing ethical concerns. Although they had not initially conducted any preliminary checks beyond visual assessment, their openness to guidance and willingness to correct this oversight was commendable. Their decision to remove the remains from sale and collaborate with a local university exemplified a positive resolution through ethical considerations and respect for human remains. Furthermore, their willingness to adhere to the guidance from BABAO underscored the importance of clear ethical guidelines and demonstrated the benefits of following established best practices.

Reflecting on this incident, I feel optimistic about the potential for ethical resolutions when auction houses and academic institutions work together. This experience reassured me that not all auctioneers have the same attitude toward the commodification of human remains and that just because a sale is legal does not mean it is ethical. The successful outcome in this case underscores the importance of communication, collaboration, and adherence to ethical standards in the handling and sale of human remains. Professionally, this positive outcome has contributed significantly to my development and confidence in handling similar situations. I feel better equipped and experienced now to approach auction houses that may be selling human remains, especially as I can refer to this positive example. It reassured me that there are people in the industry who are receptive to information and advice and willing to question and adjust their practices, even when they are not legally obligated to do so.

This case illustrates the broader importance of proactive engagement and collaboration in ensuring ethical practices. The potential benefits of auction houses working closely with academic institutions and professional organizations are substantial. Such collaborations can help ensure that human remains are treated with the dignity and respect they deserve, while also fostering a culture of transparency and accountability within the industry. Moving forward, it is essential to encourage more auction houses to adopt similar ethical practices. Steps should be taken to promote awareness and education about the ethical implications of selling human remains. I plan to use this experience to advocate for better regulations and guidelines within the industry, working with professional organizations and regulatory bodies to ensure that ethical standards are upheld.

Summary

The two case studies illustrate contrasting outcomes in the sale of human remains by auction houses, underscoring the importance of ethical considerations and proactive engagement. In the first case, despite efforts to communicate concerns and provide ethical guidance, the auction house proceeded with the sale of the human remains. This incident highlighted several critical issues: a lack of preliminary checks to authenticate the remains, inadequate documentation and provenance, resistance to ethical guidelines, and a disregard for public accountability.

In stark contrast, the second case demonstrated a positive outcome through proactive engagement and collaboration. Upon discovering the listing, I reached out to the auction house to discuss the provenance and ethical implications of selling the remains. The auction house was receptive and took immediate steps to address the concerns. They consulted with the "owner," agreed to remove the lot from sale, and arranged for the remains to be transferred to a local university for proper curation. This case exemplified the potential for constructive interactions and ethical resolutions when auction houses and academic institutions work together.

These experiences underscore the need for stricter regulations and robust enforcement to ensure that the sale and display of human remains are conducted ethically and legally. They highlight the importance of communication, collaboration, and adherence to established ethical standards to protect the dignity of human remains and respect their cultural and historical significance. Reflecting on these incidents, I feel a deep sense of responsibility to continue advocating for ethical practices and fostering positive relationships with auction houses to ensure that human remains are treated with the utmost respect and care.

From Legal to Illegal Markets

The intersection between legal and illegal markets in the trade of human remains, particularly skeletal material, presents a multifaceted issue encompassing ethical, legal, and enforcement dimensions. Online platforms have emerged as significant venues for the sale of human skeletal remains, blurring the boundaries between lawful and unlawful transactions (Halling and Seidemann 2016). Despite regulatory measures in place to curb such activities, the anonymity and ease of listing skeletal material online has fostered a gray area where legal and illegal markets converge.

Legal avenues for the sale of human remains could inadvertently support and perpetuate illegal markets. For instance, auction houses and online platforms often provide a veneer of legitimacy that can be exploited by unscrupulous sellers to offload illegally sourced remains. This occurs when items with questionable provenance are mixed with legally obtained remains, making it difficult for buyers and regulators to discern their origins. Sellers may be aware that checks on provenance are often minimal, and they rely on the likelihood that any illegally sourced remains will not be detected. This lack of stringent verification processes allows sellers to exploit legal channels to legitimize their illicit activities.

Online platforms, including auction house websites and independent sales sites, as well as social media platforms, have become significant conduits for the illegal sale of human remains. The ease of creating listings, coupled with the broad reach of these platforms, allows sellers to operate with relative impunity (Graham et al. 2022). Even when listings are removed, sellers often relist the items, sometimes within minutes, exploiting the platforms' lenient oversight mechanisms. Additionally, sellers can set up multiple accounts, circumventing bans and blocks to continue their activities (Myers West 2018). This issue is compounded by the sheer number of platforms available for listing such items, from well-known social media and online stores to numerous niche collector forums.

Law enforcement agencies face considerable challenges in monitoring and regulating these activities due to the sheer volume of transactions and the anonymity provided by these platforms (Huffer 2020). Often, the responsibility of flagging or reporting listings falls on other platform users. However, given the high volume of reports these platforms receive daily, many of which may pertain to more pressing issues such as firearms, abuse, or exploitation, the time allocated to reviewing reports of human remains is minimal (Wang et al. 2024). Consequently, illegal listings can remain active for extended periods before being addressed, if at all.

In some cases, the review time for these flagged listings can be very quick, suggesting a lack of proper consideration and care in the review process. This rapid review can be attributed to other workload pressures faced by moderators, who may be overwhelmed by the sheer number of reports and the need to prioritize cases deemed more urgent or severe. The expedited review process could lead to superficial assessments that fail to properly identify or authenticate human remains, allowing many illegal listings to slip through the cracks (Gilbertson 2020). Additionally, even when listings are removed or sellers are blocked, this does not necessarily mean that any legal action, such as reporting to the police, occurs. The removal of listings is often seen as an end in itself rather than a step in a broader legal enforcement process. This lack of follow-up action can enable sellers to continue their activities with minimal interruption, simply by creating new accounts or using different platforms.

The effectiveness of the review process depends heavily on the proficiency and training of the personnel or algorithms used to examine the flagged listings. Identifying human remains from listing photos and descriptions requires specialized knowledge, which many platform moderators may lack. Inadequate training and reliance on automated systems that are not tailored to detect the nuances of human remains further exacerbate the problem. This gap in expertise means that many illegal listings may go undetected or unaddressed, allowing the trade in human remains to persist relatively unchecked. Gongane et al. (2022) highlight that even sophisticated algorithms and Artificial Instelligence (AI) systems struggle with the nuanced identification required online, often leading to false negatives or false positives. Furthermore, it would be unrealistic to expect moderators working for sites with international reach to be aware of the laws regarding the sale of human remains in all countries where they have users. The legal frameworks governing the sale of human remains vary widely between jurisdictions, adding another layer of complexity to the issue. This lack of uniformity in laws and regulations can lead to inconsistent enforcement and varying levels of protection against the illegal trade of human remains.

The global demand for human remains, driven by collectors, researchers, and cultural institutions, significantly affects the illegal trade. High demand from wealthy countries can lead to exploitation in regions where human remains are sourced, often under dubious or unethical circumstances. This international demand perpetuates a cycle of exploitation and desecration, complicating efforts towards repatriation and reconciliation, highlighting the need for international cooperation and stricter regulations (Volper 2023). The illicit trade is further fueled by the high prices that human remains can fetch in the global market, incentivizing illegal activities.

The ease with which transactions can be masked under the guise of legality on digital platforms illustrates a pathway to potential ethical decline from legal to illegal markets. This transition complicates the enforcement of laws and the protection of human rights (Huffer and Graham 2018). Law enforcement agencies encounter challenges in discerning between legitimate and unlawful sales of human skeletal remains. The determination of population affinity, a critical component in forensic investigations involving human remains, becomes intricate in scenarios where the origins and legality of the skeletal material are dubious (Seidemann et al. 2009).

While there are significant concerns regarding the sale of human remains through legal avenues such as auction houses, imposing further restrictions may inadvertently exacerbate unethical and illegal practices. The demand for human remains persists, and individuals who encounter medical collections may be uncertain about proper handling. In the absence of auction houses or similar systems for legitimate transfer, the risk of illicit sales or improper disposal and destruction of remains is likely to increase. Auction houses offer a semi-regulated environment where intervention, education, and discussion can occur, thereby facilitating the removal of remains from commercial circulation and ensuring careful curation. These institutions are accessible and may be willing to engage with ethical considerations, in contrast to private transactions or those seeking to dispose of remains, who are less likely to seek guidance or consider ethical alternatives.

The intersection of legal and illegal markets in the trade of human remains underscores the need for robust regulatory frameworks and international cooperation. By addressing the ethical, legal, and enforcement challenges associated with this trade, stakeholders can work toward a more ethical and transparent market. Auction houses, online platforms, and regulatory bodies must collaborate to ensure that human remains are treated with the dignity and respect they deserve, thereby preventing their commodification and the perpetuation of historical injustices.

Conclusion

This chapter has explored the complex and multifaceted issue of the trade in human remains, offering a comprehensive overview of its historical context, ethical considerations, and regulatory frameworks with a UK focus. Through detailed analysis and personal case studies, the profound ethical dilemmas and legal challenges associated with the commercialization of human remains have been highlighted. By tracing the historical evolution of the trade, from its roots in medical and anatomical studies to its current manifestations in auctions and online sales, this historical perspective has illuminated how past practices continue to influence contemporary challenges, particularly in the regulation and ethical oversight of human remains.

A central theme of this chapter has been the ethical implication of treating human remains as commodities. The lack of consent, the objectification of individuals, and the potential for exploitation raise significant moral questions. The chapter has underscored the need for stringent ethical guidelines and respect for the dignity of the deceased in all transactions involving human remains.

The role of auction houses and online platforms has been scrutinized, revealing their pivotal position in the trade of human remains. The responsibilities of these entities in authenticating items and ensuring ethical practices are paramount, and so too are the criticisms and challenges they face, which are increasingly acknowledged in the field. The analysis has shown that inconsistent regulations and a lack of stringent oversight often leads to ethical lapses and potential legal violations.

Case studies have provided real-world illustrations of the complexities involved in the sale of human remains. These narratives have underscored the critical need for transparency, accountability, and ethical consideration in handling such sensitive items. They have also highlighted the importance of proactive engagement and collaboration between auction houses, regulatory bodies, and academic institutions.

The chapter has also explored the potential of new technologies, such as computer vision and machine learning, in monitoring and regulating the trade in human remains. While these technologies offer significant benefits in enhancing regulatory capabilities, they also introduce new ethical concerns that must be carefully managed.

This chapter has charted the evolution of the trade in human remains, highlighting how historical practices have informed contemporary issues. The historical perspective is essential for understanding the current state of the market and the challenges faced in regulating it. As the trade in human remains has moved from physical auction houses to online platforms, new directions in investigative and regulatory approaches are required. These shifts underscore the necessity for interdisciplinary research and collaboration among historians, ethicists, legal experts, and technologists to develop comprehensive strategies to combat heritage crime effectively.

A significant aspect of this chapter is its exploration of the role of technology in monitoring and regulating the trade in human remains. Technologies such as computer vision and machine learning are revolutionizing how illicit activities online are detected and tracked (Huffer et al. 2019). These tools can enhance the capability of law enforcement and regulatory bodies to identify and prevent the sale of human remains on digital platforms. However, the ethical considerations of using such technologies, including privacy concerns and the potential for surveillance overreach, must be carefully managed to ensure that they are deployed responsibly and ethically.

The chapter's discussion of online platforms as venues for the sale of human remains highlights the emergence of new markets facilitated by digital technology. The anonymity and global reach of online marketplaces complicate efforts to regulate the trade and protect cultural heritage (Halling and Seidemann 2016). By analyzing case studies and current practices, this chapter underscores the importance of robust legal frameworks and international cooperation in addressing these challenges. It also calls for a reevaluation of existing regulations to better accommodate the realities of digital commerce.

The ethical dilemmas associated with the commercialization of human remains are emblematic of broader issues in heritage crime, where the commodification of cultural and historical artefacts can lead to significant harm. The chapter advocates for more stringent ethical guidelines and better enforcement mechanisms to ensure that human remains, and by extension all heritage items, are treated with the dignity and respect they deserve.

Looking forward, the insights from this chapter suggest several avenues for future research and policy development. The integration of advanced technologies in the detection and regulation of heritage crime is a promising area, but it requires careful ethical consideration and robust legal support. Moreover, the chapter highlights the need for continued interdisciplinary dialogue to address the multifaceted nature of both the sale of human remains and wider issues in heritage crime effectively.

Amy E. Rattenbury is a senior lecturer in forensic science at Wrexham University, North Wales. Holding a BSc Forensic Biology and an MSc Forensic Archaeology, she leads on the BSc Forensic Science and MRes Forensic Anthropology & Bioarchaeology programs. Amy's expertise covers search, recovery, and identification of human remains in forensic and historical contexts. A fellow of the Royal Anthropological Institute, member of the British Association of Biological Anthropology and Osteoarchaeology, and former committee member of the British Association for Forensic Anthropology, Amy is committed to upholding ethical standards in the utilization of human remains for teaching and research.

Dr. Paige Tynan is a senior lecturer in biosciences at Wrexham University, North Wales, where she teaches across a number of undergraduate Applied Science courses and supports PhD students. She earned her PhD in forensic taphonomy through the University of Chester, titled "Building Decompanion: A Step Towards Standardisation and the Enhancement of Inter- and Trans-disciplinary Research in Forensic Taphonomy." Her expertise includes human body decomposition, decomposition dynamics, and 3D technologies. As a member of the university's Research Ethics Committee and a fellow of AdvanceHE, Paige plays a key role within the department, leading initiatives on ethically informed research and teaching.

REFERENCES

Agarwal, Sabrina C. 2024. "The Bioethics of Skeletal Anatomy Collections from India." *Nature Communications* 15(1): 1692.

Auctions (Bidding Agreements) Act. 1969. C. 56.

Balachandran, Sanchita. 2009. "Among the Dead and Their Possessions: A Conservator's Role in the Death, Life, and Afterlife of Human Remains and Their Associated Objects." *Journal of the American Institute for Conservation* 48(3): 199–222.
Banerjie, Indranil. 2014. "Government Bans Export of Human Skeletons." *India Today*.
Batty, David. 2024. "Dorset Auction House Withdraws Egyptian Human Skulls from Sale." *The Guardian*.
Berger, Jacqueline M., et al. 2018. "Analysis of Class Characteristics of Reciprocating Saws." *Journal of Forensic Sciences* 63(6): 1661–72.
Boylston, Anthea, et al. 2004. *Guidelines to the Standards for Recording Human Remains*. Southhampton: Chartered Institute for Archaeologists.
Breda, Evelyn. 2023. "Bone Collectors: Personhood and Appeal in the Sale and Trade of Human Skeletal Remains on Facebook." Master's thesis, Florida Atlantic University.
British Association for Biological Anthropology and Osteoarchaeology. 2019a. *BABAO Code of Practice*. https://babao.org.uk/wp-content/uploads/2023/08/BABAO-Digital-imaging-code-2019.pdf.
British Association for Biological Anthropology and Osteoarchaeology. 2019b. *BABAO Recommendations on the Ethical Issues Surrounding 2D and 3D Digital Imaging of Human Remains*. https://babao.org.uk/wp-content/uploads/2023/08/BABAO-Digital-imaging-code-2019.pdf.
British Association for Biological Anthropology and Osteoarchaeology. 2023. *Photographs of Human Remains on Personal Devices*. https://babao.org.uk/wp-content/uploads/2023/08/Photographing-Human-Remains-FINAL.pdf.
Cassman, Vicki, and Nancy Odegaard. 2004. "Human Remains and the Conservator's Role." *Studies in Conservation* 49(4): 271–82.
Chartered Institute of Fundraising. 2024. "Auctions." Retrieved 26 February 2025 from https://ciof.org.uk/events-and-training/resources/auctions.
Coman, Jonathan, et al. 2022. "Skeletons in the Closet: Time to Give Human Bones Acquired by Health Practitioners for Educational Purposes the Respect They Deserve." *Medical Journal of Australia* 216(8): 392–96.
Davies, Mark, and Trinh Chubbock. 2017. "The Auction Process: Advantages and Disadvantages and the Key Steps." *EMPEA Legal & Regulatory Bulletin*.
Department for Culture, Media and Sport. 2005. *Guidance for the Care of Human Remains in Museums*. London.
Department of Health and Social Care, and Human Tissue Authority. 2022. *Framework Agreement between DHSC and the Human Tissue Authority*.
Dias, M. 2015. "Dignity after Death and Protecting the Sanctity of Human Remains." *Voices in Bioethics* 1.
della Dora, Veronica. 2009. "Travelling Landscape-Objects." *Progress in Human Geography* 33(3): 334–54.
eBay. 2025. "Human Body Parts Policy". Retrieved 26 February 2025 from https://www.ebay.co.uk/help/policies/prohibited-restricted-items/human-remains-body-parts-policy?id=4325#:~:text=We percent20don percent27t percent20allow percent20the percent20sale percent20of percent20human percent20bodies percent2C,well percent20as percent20respect percent20the percent20rights percent20of percent20third percent20parties.&msockid=056ff28a536f6b283530e78e52696add.
Foster, Charles. 2014. "Dignity and the Use of Body Parts." *Journal of Medical Ethics* 40(1): 44–47. doi:10.1136/medethics-2012-100763.

GAUK Auctions. 2024. "*NAVA National Association of Valuers and Auctioneers*". https://www.gaukauctions.com/auctioneer/nava-national-association-of-valuers-and-auctioneers.

Ghosh, Sanjib Kumar. 2015. "Human Cadaveric Dissection: A Historical Account from Ancient Greece to the Modern Era." *Anatomy & Cell Biology* 48(3): 153.

Gilbertson, Annie. 2020. "Unlike Other Tech Giants, Amazon Won't Say How Many Workers Review Posts." *The Markup*, 9 July.

Gongane, Vaishali U., et al. 2022. "Detection and Moderation of Detrimental Content on Social Media Platforms: Current Status and Future Directions." *Social Network Analysis and Mining* 12(1): 129.

Goold, Imogen, et al. 2014. "The Human Body as Property? Possession, Control and Commodification." *Journal of Medical Ethics* 40(1): 1–2.

Govor, Elena, and Hilary Howes. 2020. "Physical Anthropology in the Field." In *The Routledge Companion to Indigenous Repatriation*, edited by Nikolai Miklouho-Maclay. Routledge. 799–826.

Graham, Shawn, et al. 2022. "When TikTok Discovered the Human Remains Trade: A Case Study." *Open Archaeology* 8(1): 196–219.

Graham, Shawn, and Damien Huffer. 2020. "Reproducibility, Replicability, and Revisiting the Insta-Dead and the Human Remains Trade." *Internet Archaeology*.

Halling, Christine L., and Ryan M. Seidemann. 2016. "They Sell Skulls Online?! A Review of Internet Sales of Human Skulls on eBay and the Laws in Place to Restrict Sales." *Journal of Forensic Sciences* 61(5): 1322–26.

Halperin, Edward C. 2007. "The Poor, the Black, and the Marginalized as the Source of Cadavers in United States Anatomical Education." *Clinical Anatomy* 20(5): 489–95.

Herring, Jonathan, and P-L Chau. 2014. "Interconnected, Inhabited and Insecure: Why Bodies Should Not Be Property." *Journal of Medical Ethics* 40(1): 39–43.

Huffer, Damien. 2020. "Mummy Dearest? Including Human Remains in Facebook's Community Standards Is Meaningless without Enforcement." *Medium*, 2 July.

Huffer, Damien. 2024. "Buy One Get One: The Legal and Socio-cultural Context of 'Gifting' within the Australian Human Remains Trade." *Journal of Computer Applications in Archaeology* 7(1): 115–25.

Huffer, Damien, et al. 2019. "What the Machine Saw: Some Questions on the Ethics of Computer Vision and Machine Learning to Investigate Human Remains Trafficking." *Internet Archaeology*.

Huffer, Damien, and Duncan Chappell. 2014. "The Mainly Nameless and Faceless Dead: An Exploratory Study of the Illicit Traffic in Archaeological and Ethnographic Human Remains." *Crime, Law and Social Change* 62(2): 131–53.

Huffer, Damien, and Shawn Graham. 2017. "The Insta-Dead: The rhetoric of the human remains trade on Instagram." *Internet Archaeology* 45(5).

———. 2018. "Fleshing Out the Bones: Studying the Human Remains Trade with Tensorflow and Inception." *Journal of Computer Applications in Archaeology* 1(1): 55–63.

Human Tissue Act. 1961. C. 54.

Human Tissue Act. 2004. *C. 30*.

Human Tissue Authority. 2024. "Public Guides to the HTA Codes of Practice." *Guidance for the Public*, 27 September.

Human Tissue Authority. 2023. *Human Tissue Authority Annual Report and Accounts 2022/23*. London: HH Associates Ltd. Retrieved February 2025 from https://assets.publishing.se

rvice.gov.uk/media/64db5dc6c8dee400127f1c6d/human-tissue-authority-annual-report-2022-2023-web-accessible.pdf.

Huxley, A. K., and M. Finnegan. 2004. "Human Remains Sold to the Highest Bidder! A Snapshot of the Buying and Selling of Human Skeletal Remains on EBay®, an Internet Auction Site." *Journal of Forensic Sciences* 49(1): 1–4.

Jarus, Owen. 2020. "Looted Skulls and Human Remains Are Being Sold in Black Markets on Facebook." *Live Science*, 2 July.

Jones, D. Gareth, and Robyn J. Harris. 1998. "Archeological Human Remains: Scientific, Cultural, and Ethical Considerations." *Current Anthropology* 39(2): 253–64.

Jones, D. Gareth, and Maja I. Whitaker. 2013. "The Contested Realm of Displaying Dead Bodies." *Journal of Medical Ethics* 39(10): 652–53.

Kaufmann, I. M., and F. J. Rühli. 2010. "Without 'Informed Consent'? Ethics and Ancient Mummy Research." *Journal of Medical Ethics* 36(10): 608–13.

Klesert, Anthony L., and Shirley Powell. 1993. "A Perspective on Ethics and the Reburial Controversy." *American Antiquity* 58(2): 348–54.

Lavoie, Jennifer. 1989. "Ownership of Human Tissue: Life after Moore v Regents of the University of California." *Virginia Law Review* 75(7): 1363.

Licata, Marta, et al. 2020. "Study, Conservation and Exhibition of Human Remains: The Need of a Bioethical Perspective." *Acta Bio-Medica: Atenei Parmensis* 91(4): e2020110.

Mahoney, Julia D. 2000. "The Market for Human Tissue." *Virginia Law Review* 86(2): 163.

McCorristine, Shane. 2015. "The Dark Value of Criminal Bodies: Context, Consent, and the Disturbing Sale of John Parker's Skull." *Journal of Conservation and Museum Studies* 13(1).

Myers West, Sarah. 2018. "Censored, Suspended, Shadowbanned: User Interpretations of Content Moderation on Social Media Platforms." *New Media & Society* 20(11): 4366–83.

Phillips, Anne. 2011. "It's My Body and I'll Do What I Like with It." *Political Theory* 39(6): 724–48.

Royal Institution of Chartered Surveyors. 2013. *A Clear, Impartial Guide to Buying and Selling Art and Antiques at Auction*. London.

Seidemann, Ryan M., et al. 2009. "The Identification of a Human Skull Recovered from an EBay Sale." *Journal of Forensic Sciences* 54(6): 1247–53.

UK Government. 2025. "Auction Premises Registration." Retrieved 26 February 2025 from https://www.gov.uk/find-licences/auction-premises-registration.

UK Parliament. 2014. "Body Snatching." 1 May. Retrieved 26 February 2025 from https://webtest.parliament.uk/about/living-heritage/transformingsociety/private-lives/death-dying/dying-and-death/bodysnatching/.

Volper, Julien. 2023. "Bones in Auction—A History of Creating, Acquiring, and Selling Human Relics." *Culture: Policy, Management, and Entrepreneurship* 2(1): 97–107.

Wall, J. 2011. "The Legal Status of Body Parts: A Framework." *Oxford Journal of Legal Studies* 31(4): 783–804.

Wang, Hongyu, et al. 2024. "Detecting and Understanding the Promotion of Illicit Goods and Services on Twitter."

Woess, Claudia et al. 2017. "Assessing Various Infrared (IR) Microscopic Imaging Techniques for Post-Mortem Interval Evaluation of Human Skeletal Remains." *PLOS One* 12(3): e0174552.

CHAPTER 7

Culture of Oddities
The Appeal of the Human Remains Market on Facebook

Evelyn Breda

Introduction

Discussion surrounding the ethics of human remains being bought and sold has swirled among academics in recent years, bringing up arguments related to both general consent and cultural views surrounding death. In this chapter I will explore the cultural perceptions surrounding death and the human body within the United States in relation to the desire to buy and sell human remains in Facebook oddities groups. These desires often relate to rejecting societal norms, embracing the taboo and morbid, and aligning with the uncomfortable.

Human skeletal remains can be found for sale across several online marketplaces and social media websites including Facebook, Instagram, eBay, Amazon, TikTok, and Etsy (Huffer and Charlton 2016; Halling and Seidemann 2016). This market is visibly in demand for both professional buyers and sellers as well as amateur collectors. Collectors choose to purchase human skeletal remains for several reasons; within this research it became clear that the most prominent reason people purchase remains is for oddity collections. For many sellers and buyers, this collecting has become a hobby or passion. The taboo nature of these morbid and macabre objects is what attracts them. Facebook is a prominent place for these sales and therefore significant to understanding this market.

The bulk of the data within this research comes from my observations of human remains sales in six Facebook groups from January to December 2021. This research variously draws from the date of listing, price, the group it was sold in, elements present, and the intended purpose of remains for 319 separate listings. These listings range from fully articulated skeletons to singular elements in various contexts, including weapons, jewelry, and even soap. This chapter will also use documented posts and interactions between members of the groups discussing collections, sales, desires, and general views of death culture to further understand the desires held by buyers and sellers. The primary research goals presented here are as follows: first, to understand why individuals desire owning, selling, and buying human skeletal remains, and second, to create a snapshot of this ever-growing market on Facebook to further understand it.

Perspectives on Human Remains

A large aspect of this research revolves around the concept of personhood, the concept of being an individual. Understanding when personhood ends and when the body becomes an object is the crux of one ethical debate surrounding the ownership of human skeletal remains. Cross-culturally, some people see human skeletal remains as objects, others see them as people, and still yet others see them as a mix of both (Sofaer 2006). To understand the nuances of the sale of human remains on Facebook, it is important to explore the differing perspectives of the notion of personhood. For the purposes of this research, there are three primary perspectives associated with what is considered the ethical treatment of remains. Those three perspectives are as follows: the public perspective, the descendent perspective, and the anthropologist's perspective.

The public perspective can be exemplified by a controversy surrounding human remains sales on TikTok in the summer and fall of 2021. During this time, TikTok user Jon Ferry became a major flash point. This user's content on TikTok garnered heavy attention because much of his content featured human skeletal remains, such as his personal collection of human spines (Anders 2021). Among this video content, which he provided for his over five hundred thousand followers, human remains are often used as props to advertise his online store that specialized in the sale of human skeletal remains. This includes videos of him using femurs as batons, allowing his pets to play with skeletal remains (alleged replicas), transporting skeletal remains in precarious situations, and overall treating these remains with little regard to their safekeeping or to any idea that those items once belonged to a person. As of 2025, his content mainly surrounds his museum of skeletal remains.

Despite these videos being easily accessible online, Ferry has also explained to *The Washington Post* the importance of treating remains "with the utmost respect" (Anders 2021). During this time, Ferry's comment section became flooded with commenters who claimed anthropological and osteological knowledge and who then attempted to educate him on these issues. He often responded by blocking these users. This situation was covered by several outlets, including *The Washington Post*, ABC News, Yahoo!, and *The New York Post*, indicating a controversy that attracted mainstream media attention. This viral discussion came at the same time the data collection for this project was being conducted. Due to this discussion, the controversy works as a representation of both the importance of this topic in the current climate as well as an indication of the necessary expansion of public understanding on this issue.

The descendent perspective primarily focuses on the opinions of those who are descended from the individuals whose skeletal remains are being commodified or collected. A poignant example of this perspective came to light in May of 2021, during which it was revealed that the remains of several individuals who died in the MOVE bombing of 1985 were being used as teaching specimens by the University of Pennsylvania (Levenson 2021). The MOVE bombing was an event in which the US government bombed a neighborhood in Philadelphia where the MOVE group (an African American activist organization) was meeting, killing six adults and five children. It caused immense uproar in the Black community in the 1980s (Levenson 2021).

MOVE was founded in 1973 by John Africa as a movement directed toward the rejection of societal norms contributing to systemic racism. This movement was viewed as disruptive by police and led to significant tensions, eventually culminating in the 1985 bombing in Philadelphia. This bombing left eleven individuals dead and destroyed sixty-one homes. The trauma of that experience was brought back to light when it was revealed in 2021 by the surviving family members that remains of two of the children killed in the bombing were being used as teaching specimens without their permission. The use of these bones in an academic institution without the family's consent was not the only issue for victims' family members, however. The possession of these remains had changed several times, going from forensic anthropologists to medical examiners and academic institutions. The remains were also used in publicly available online courses and as tools in informative videos for students. Though this case is one of academic use, the overarching theme of descendant views on the (mis)treatment of human remains is an important perspective to consider.

This leads into the final perspective that is important to explore: the perspective of anthropologists and archaeologists. Though it would be negligent to assume all anthropologists have the same viewpoint on this topic, many have written on the trade of human skeletal remains in the broader sense (Huffer and Charlton 2019; Huffer and Chappell 2014; Halling and Seidemann 2016; Huxley and Finnegan 2004). In the field of anthropology, theoretical perspectives take an important role in the discussion of ethics, however, and theoretical perspectives of the transformation of death have been explored in archaeologist Joanne Sofaer's (2006) book *The Body as Material Culture*. In her work Sofaer (2006) examines the divide between the social body and the physical body. According to Sofaer, once death occurs, personhood is replaced with status as an object, even though the body itself remains the same. Sofaer also points out the paradox that is identifying a human body as both sentient and inanimate in tandem. Sofaer argues that this is not a black-and-white sentiment; rather, she suggests that the body can be both material and symbolic at the same time due to the meanings society places upon it. As a fixture of humanity that can be altered by human intervention to become symbolic in a multitude of ways in both life and death, Sofaer sees the human body as an example of material culture (2006).

The perspectives of anthropologists are important to consider in a nontheoretical way that is more tangible in its applications through codes of ethics, which are established in academic institutions and organizations, including the American Association of Biological Anthropologists (AABA). Within the AABA code of ethics, there is no distinct statement on human remains treatment. However, the language leaves an opening for this discussion. Under section III, it is stated that "anthropological researchers have primary ethical obligations to the people, species, and materials they study and to the people with whom they work"; additionally, "while anthropologists may gain personally from their work, they must not exploit individuals, groups, animals, or cultural or biological materials" (American Association of Biological Anthropologists 2003). The Society for American Archaeology also has a similar code of ethics, updated in 2018, stating, in Principle No. 7: "Archaeologists should work actively for the preservation of, and long-term access to, archaeological collections, records, and reports. To this end, they should encourage colleagues, students, and others to make responsible use of collections, records, and reports in their research as one means of preserving the in situ archaeological record, and of increasing the care and attention given to that portion of the archaeological record which has been removed and incorporated into archaeological collections, records, and reports".

As well, the Society for American Archaeology (SAA) board established an updated Statement Concerning the Treatment of Human Remains in 2021 and an Acknowledgment of Harm in 2022. The Acknowledgment of Harm statement addresses the negative impact and harm inflicted upon Indigenous individuals within the United States by archaeologists of the past (Society for American Archaeology 2022). The SAA's Statement Concerning the Treatment of Human Remains establishes five principles, including that working with human remains is a privilege and not a right, as well as the importance of treating remains with "dignity and respect" (Society for American Archaeology 2021). When, and if, human remains are seen as persons or as materials, as defined in these codes of ethics, is up for interpretation, as is clearly expressed throughout this chapter. When human bodies are examined through an anthropological lens, the argument surrounding the buying and selling of human remains can be elaborated upon further.

For example, the sentiment that many sellers and buyers share—that by displaying these remains they are providing a second life to these individuals—falls within Sofaer's idea of the body being material culture. One may think this would support the ownership of human remains with this sentiment; however, it is quite the opposite. Sofaer expresses that viewing the body as both an object and a person helps to instead connect the two rather than separate them, encouraging an emphasis on the personhood of the object and treating it in respect to cultural and ethical beliefs by ensuring that the symbolic nature of human bodies is represented.

As is evident, these three perspectives have differing reasonings behind them as well as similarities. The public perspective, which includes sellers, buyers, and the public, is that of relative ambivalence toward applying personhood to human skeletal remains. These items are objects, pieces of art for display. Descendants see it quite differently; their perspective is one that heavily lies within the concept of personhood. These remains represent more than bones: they are family, and therefore the lens of personhood is strongest in their eyes. The anthropologist's perspective has overlapping features with both perspectives: understanding that these remains are objects to many, while also understanding the personhood the remains may still represent.

Understanding Facebook Groups

Facebook has many groups dedicated to the sale of oddities, including animal bones, antiques, taxidermy, and human skeletal remains. These groups are easily accessible and easy to find for any Facebook user with an interest in oddities. These groups garner a large membership base, some of which include between three and five thousand members. Others have up to thirty thousand members with new additions every day. Within these Facebook groups, many maintain a group mentality in which people assist one another in sales and trades. These activities include frequent "in search of" (ISO) posts and weekly posts to share favorite pieces. Although it varies among Facebook groups, the frequency of listings ranges anywhere from single posts per week to multiple posts per day.

Many members in these groups understand that "buying or selling of human body parts" (Facebook 2021) is prohibited in the Facebook Commerce Terms of Service in rule 5 (see figure 7.1). Due to this rule, many members of these groups will use tactics to avoid detection by the Facebook algorithm, which works through categorization and prioritization of terms used by Facebook users (Diakopoulos 2014). This algorithm often works by presenting ads related to what an individual has interacted with on Facebook and other areas of the internet; however, algorithms do more work that may not be as easily visible to a user. In this usage, the algorithm refers to Facebook's ability to categorize specific terms that should be avoided due to their prohibition in the Facebook terms of service. For example, if one were to make a post with the statement "Human remains for sale," theoretically the Facebook algorithm would detect such a post and remove it.

To avoid this detection, many users write their posts using specific language. Examples of such posts include using emojis instead of numbers to indicate price, indicating what states prohibit sale, spelling *human* incorrectly (most often "hooman" or "h00man"), using words like "noggin" instead of skull, censoring one

3. Prohibited Content

Buying or selling of the following is prohibited on Facebook, Instagram, and WhatsApp commerce surfaces and features:

1. Community Standards

Commerce listings must not violate our Community Standards.

2. Adult Products

Listings may not promote the buying, selling, or use of adult products.
Learn More

3. Alcohol

Listings may not promote the buying or selling of alcohol.
Learn More

4. Animals

Listings may not promote the buying or selling of animals.
Learn More

5. Body Parts and Fluids

Listings may not promote the buying or selling of human body parts or fluids.

Figure 7.1. Facebook Terms of Service "Prohibited Content." © Facebook.

or more letters of a word with asterisks, and refraining from using terms like "For sale" in the listing itself (see figure 7.2). Several of the groups studied here include these as part of the rules for the group itself and require the obfuscating language for any post marketing human skeletal remains to avoid detection.

Understanding Oddities

The collection of oddities finds its origin within the cabinets of curiosities of the past. The origin of these cabinets of curiosity derives from the common seventeenth-century desire to show opulence and intrigue among aristocrats (Zytaruk 2011). Individuals came into possession of items within their collection through travel to distant lands, and they presented objects found along the way as curiosities of faraway cultures (Zytaruk 2011). Today, oddities serve a similar purpose by representing what may be considered odd to present an air of intrigue. Throughout this research, items that fall within oddity categories include taxidermy of both animals and insects, medical antiques, animal bones, wet specimens, and memorabilia from serial killers, true crime, and even psychiatric asylums. The rarer and more in-demand items within these collections are often human bodies or body parts, especially human skulls.

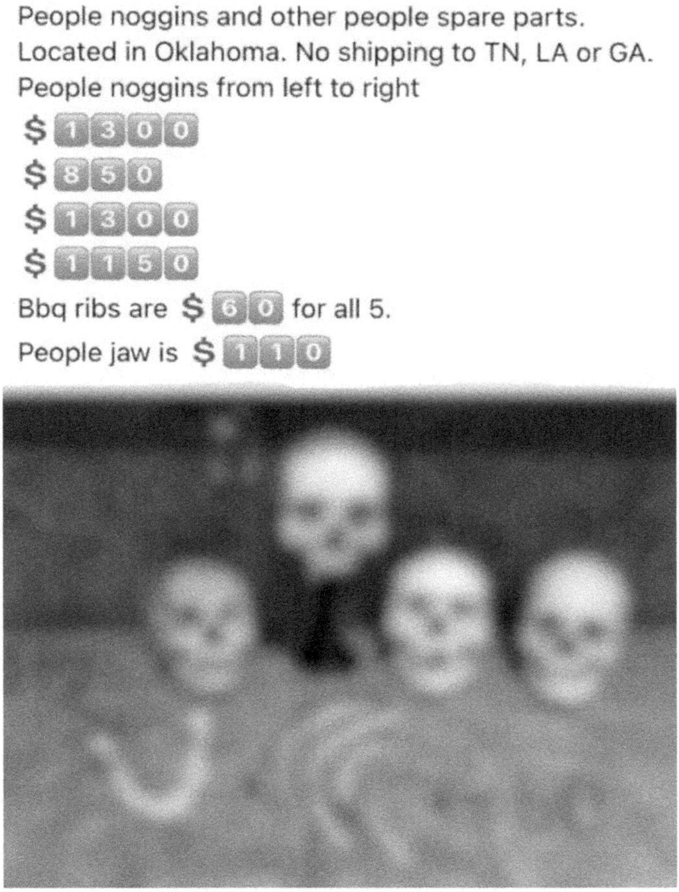

Figure 7.2. Example of a listing with evasive language. © Facebook.

It is necessary to understand the origin of human skeletal remains to understand ethical pitfalls that arise within this market. Though from an objective perspective everyone understands that a human skeleton was once a fully fleshed human being, discussion within these groups of the individual in life, of personhood, is virtually nonexistent. Common sources of human skeletal remains include medical institutions, dentists, and pathologists. These institutions often "retire" and sell their retired antique teaching and medical specimens (Jarus 2020). A large aspect of the debate about buying and selling human skeletal remains relates to the idea of consent: did the person consent to be bought and sold for decoration and collection? Did they even consent to being used for medical purposes before they were "retired"? Often, retired medical teaching specimens come from dubious origins, including both grave robbing (Coman et al. 2019; Highet 2006) as well as the appropriating of the remains of individuals experiencing poverty, often due to remains being unclaimed (Muller et al. 2016).

Though determination of exact origins cannot be established for the remains present within this research due to lack of access to originating paperwork, one can infer that some sets of remains represented here were likely sourced from one of these origins. If an individual's cultural beliefs and preferences are not being considered when interacting with their remains, can it be ethical to buy and sell them? This is the cornerstone of the debate between collectors on the one side and anthropologists and descendants on the other. Across the world, vastly distinct cultural beliefs surrounding death and treatment of human remains can be found. Within this research, the remains are exclusively bought and sold within the United States; however, many of the remains originate from other countries, such as India (bone trade), Japanese and Vietnamese trophy skulls from WWII and the Vietnam War, or China (Carney 2011; Hsu and Lincoln 2007; Harrison 2006; Harrison 2014; Sledzik and Ousley 1991; Yucha et al. 2017).

Very little scholarship exists on the Indian bone trade. Much of the attention to this issue comes from Scott Carney, an anthropologist who worked with both Wired and NPR in 2007 to explain this market and how it works. According to Carney, many of the remains that come from the Indian bone trade are products of grave robbing. Though this market was made illegal in 1985, India is still the largest supplier of human skeletal remains, as the market has instead gone underground instead of disappearing (Carney 2007; Agarwal 2024).

In 1985 much of the scholarly discussion around the companies in India selling human remains focused on grave robbing and the theft of cadavers; the companies were accused of grave robbing and stealing cadavers from hospitals (Banerjie 1985). Many rumors at the time discussed child murder as well. One of the largest critics of the Indian bone trade at the time was Sanker Narayan Sen, who ironically worked as an exporter of anatomical specimens for well over forty years (Banerjie 1985). Once holding a monopoly over the export of human skeletal remains, Sen became a vocal critic following his retirement. His critiques included his views regarding how various cost-cutting techniques that drove him to retire result in the grave robbing in question (Banerjie 1985). Though the exact details of the language used within the law are difficult to find, the overarching result was a total ban on the export of human skeletal remains out of India.

The 1985 Indian export ban in turn caused other countries, such as China and many parts of Europe, to begin exporting human remains in higher numbers, though not to the quality or extent of India (Carney 2011). Carney went on to author a book discussing this market in 2011, titled *The Red Market,* wherein he interviewed locals who witnessed firsthand this market in Calcutta, a city considered a hub for the sale and trade of human skeletal remains in India. According to these interviews, most cemeteries are now barren of remains due to extensive grave robbing to satisfy market demand. Once these remains have been procured, they are processed and shipped to medical institutions, personal collectors, and academic institutions in other countries. One individual expressed his fear that when he dies, his remains will be stolen much like many of the remains that were once in local cemeteries (Carney 2011).

The ethics associated with this specific aspect of the market are undeniable: remains that have been procured through grave robbing cannot be ethically sourced. Carney also describes a situation in 2001, sixteen years after the ban, in which a company associated with these sales, Young Brothers, was raided due to complaints of a stench coming from their facility. During this raid, one hundred human skeletons were found and taken by the local constables, all believed to be products of grave robbing (Carney 2011). These remains were intended to be exported and sold to other countries. Another source of international remains is China. The largest example of the Chinese market is that of Bodies . . . The Exhibition, which originates in China. Though these remains are not known to end up in private collections, such exhibitions raise important questions about the procurement of remains. The exhibition claims that the remains they plastinate and display originated from unclaimed remains that became property of the Chinese government (Hsu and Lincoln 2007). However, concern has been raised due to claims that the remains may belong to executed prisoners, a claim that Hsu and Lincoln see as "plausible but unproven" (2007). Though these remains are not those of private collections, it works as another example of ignored personhood for the sake of displaying remains.

One of the lesser-known origins of human skeletal remains is that of trophy skulls. Trophy skulls are the skeletal remains, primarily skulls, of individuals taken as trophies or mementoes by US servicemembers during conflicts such as World War II and the Vietnam War (Harrison 2006; Harrison 2014; Sledzik and Ousley 1991; Yucha et al. 2017). A 2017 case study of twenty-four trophy skulls found within the United States attempts to produce taphonomic profiles to determine their geographical origin as well as explore the issue of trophy skulls. One of the most concerning aspects of trophy skulls is that family members who find them often "lack sufficient knowledge of their provenience," leading to significant issues for disposal or treatment (Yucha et al. 2017). The taking of trophy skulls has been documented throughout history and prehistory, as well as in some Indigenous groups around the world; for trophy skulls found in the United States, the two largest sources are from World War II and the Vietnam War (Yucha et al. 2017). Despite the title of *trophy skull*, these items, as emphasized by Yucha et al., were not frequently war trophies of a kill but rather "souvenirs" taken at opportunistic times (2017).

One other potential source of trophy skulls comes from Indigenous populations of the Americas (Colwell 2017). In his book *Plundered Skulls and Stolen Spirits*, Chip Colwell details his work helping to identify and return Indigenous remains in compliance with NAGPRA; several cases he mentions involved trophy skulls taken during battles between colonizers and Indigenous populations and the difficulties involved with the repatriation process (Colwell 2017). Through this work, Colwell repeatedly emphasizes just how important the returning of these remains is, most importantly for the sake of cultural respect toward Indigenous beliefs and atonement for their treatment within the United States. Throughout this research, individuals within the Facebook groups on several occasions made posts attempting to sell off trophy skulls from World War II and the Vietnam War found among their grandparents' belongings, raising concern for how rampant of a problem this may be. It is, however, important to note that despite these posts now being deleted, many of the commenters at the time were group members expressing that the individuals should contact police instead to ensure owning the skull would not be illegal.

Methodologies and Data Source

The selection of the groups came about through the ease of access presented by a Facebook search. When one searches "oddities" on Facebook, a multitude of groups dedicated to collecting, sharing, and selling are easily accessible. The six groups discussed in this research were selected due to ease of accessibility. Though many require answering a few questions to join, these questions are simple in nature, ranging from "Why do you want to join?," "What oddities do you enjoy?," and "Do you plan on buying and selling within these groups?" Aside from those brief questions, these groups are both easy to enter and become active within. Throughout my time in these groups, I refrained from any interactions with members or their posts or any form of participation.

It is important to note that according to 2010 research produced by Lauren B. Solberg for *The Illinois Journal of Law, Technology, and Policy*, "Facebook likely does not constitute research with human subjects, and therefore does not require IRB review, because a researcher who collects data from Facebook pages does not interact, as the term is used in the regulatory definition of human subject, with the individual users" (2010: 316–17). Additionally, the data collected for this research from private Facebook groups, the nature of Facebook, and social media as a whole are all considered public in nature. While the ethical considerations of private versus public Facebook groups is outside of the scope of this research, the author refrains from using the names of these groups or their members to maintain their confidentiality.

In an anthropological sense, I was a nonparticipant observer in these groups. My role was to log all listings within the United States for human skeletal remains and observe the public interactions of group members. Of the six groups, four were dedicated to regular oddity selling, one was dedicated to high-end oddities (no items priced below $200), and one was dedicated to human remains. Once in the groups, I discovered considerable overlap in membership, especially of sellers. Many sellers are members of several groups to broaden their customer base.

Sellers will also frequently cross-list their sale postings in one or more groups, which was accounted for within the data analysis based upon which group was given priority (i.e., where an item was posted first). Within the world of antiquities, Lauren Dundler (2021) has established four specific types of "seller personas," a concept she introduced that establishes specific types of personas that antiquities dealers adopt for their selling platforms. One of these four personas occurs frequently in the posts reviewed in this research. This persona is described as "the performance of trust and discretion through use of authenticity guarantees and collecting advice" (Dundler 2021). This idea of trust, discretion, and authenticity can be exemplified by many of the interactions found within the groups reviewed. Examples include many sellers who will not only emphasize the authenticity of their own product but who will also go as far as to call out potential "scammers" within the groups as a means of heightening their own level of trust in the group.

This level of trust and discretion from sellers, combined with a level of friendship among members within these groups, presents an obvious group dynamic based upon a level of trust and comradery among members. Though, when one examines the origins of the sold and traded human remains, the idea of authenticity can be blurred due to the dubious nature of their procurement. By leaving out information about the procurement as well as excluding personhood from these remains, sellers within these groups can maintain the curtain of trust with their buyers without compromising the details of their behaviors for acquisition. Such behavior leads into important discussion relating to illegal procurement of remains within these groups.

In August of 2022, CBS Philadelphia announced that a man had been arrested in Pennsylvania in July for attempting to buy human remains on Facebook that were illegally acquired. The human remains in question were stolen by a woman in between their transfer from a mortuary facility to the University of Arkansas for Medical Sciences. Once the remains were stolen, an individual then attempted to purchase the remains online from the woman who stole them. This case holds specific importance to this research due to the purchaser's presence within three of the groups used for this research, as well as several of his listings being present within the statistical data. Many of his listings involved using the remains to create sculptures and other art using human skeletal remains as well as human skin. This presents evidence of a long-theorized aspect of this research: is there illegal activity (beyond any buying, selling, or possessing of remains) present within these groups? The apparent answer is "yes," but how frequent this activity may be within these groups is unclear from the collected data. With a definitive connection between the analyzed group and a publicly visible crime now shown, there exists a pitfall in the air of trust given to these sellers by the members of which they may be unaware.

Laws

As previously stated, the United States does not currently have federal laws in place prohibiting the sale and trade of non-Native American human remains. The only current federal law related to the distribution of human remains is the Native American Graves Protection and Repatriation Act (NAGPRA) which prohibits the sale of human remains deemed to be of Native American origin (Beisaw 2010; Halling and Seidemann 2016). NAGPRA, established in 1990, created a procedure for possessing Native American remains and cultural items. It also established procedures for returning Native American remains and items to their descendants and/or tribes of origin. This law largely focuses on remains within academic institutions, museums, and other federal agencies. Chapter 53 of Title 18 establishes the illegality of buying, selling, or transporting Native American human remains and objects for sale (NAGPRA 1990).

Despite NAGPRA, remains that are Native American in origin are still often found for sale. This is exemplified by a published case of a biological profile of a skull bought on eBay in 2009, which was determined to be of Native American origin using several methods, including a biological profile, analysis of cultural modification to remains, and analysis of sediment present in the remains (Seidemann et al. 2009). Due to a lack of federal legislation for the sale and trade of non-native human skeletal remains, several states—Georgia, Tennessee, and Louisiana—have opted to create their own legislation to curb the market (Georgia State Legislature 2010; Tennessee State Legislature 2010; Louisiana State Legislature 2016) (see figure 7.3).

Statistical Analysis

Throughout 2021, both qualitative and quantitative data was recorded for all listings including human remains found within the six aforementioned Facebook groups dedicated to the sale of oddities. Within this data, where available, the geographical location of the listing, the element(s) present, the price, the date, and the group within which it was posted were all recorded for each listing. Though these groups are set as private, they are easily accessible to any Facebook user who indicates any desire to view, buy, or sell oddities on Facebook. Over the course of 2021, 319 listings for human remains were found and recorded. These listings came from thirty states within the United States and accounted for most elements found within the human skeletal system. The most frequently sold element within these groups was human skulls, accounting for 116 of the listings, which is 36.4 percent of the total listings available. This finding is consistent with previous research conducted by Shawn Graham and Damien Huffer, who, in their research, found that skulls accounted for 40 percent of sales in their own datasets (Graham and Huffer 2019). The second most common element sold was vertebrae, which accounted for fifteen listings, or 4.7 percent of the total recorded listings (see figure 7.3).

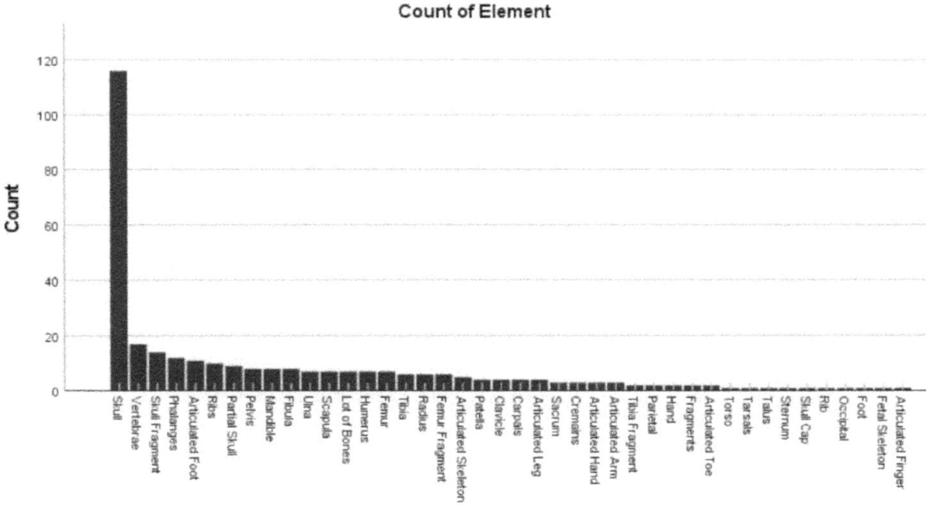

Figure 7.3. Count of skeletal elements represented in the data. © Evelyn Breda.

Analysis then looked at the dates in which posts were made to see if there are seasonal upticks within this market (figure 7.4). Sales of human remains within these groups rose in January and December, as well as in October, although at a lower rate. December had the highest rate of listings with forty-six, or 14.7 percent of listings for human remains. Following that was January, which had forty-three

Figure 7.4. Listings per month. © Evelyn Breda.

listings, accounting for 13.5 percent. The third leading month is October, which had thirty-six listings, accounting for 11.6 percent. Together these three months account for 39.8 percent of all listings in 2021. Potential explanations for this could be seasonal holidays, as in December many collectors may be attempting to sell more inventory to coincide with the winter holidays. January's high rate of listings could potentially be residual effects of the holidays, or perhaps it could be explained by sellers wanting to offset their collections for the new year. Lastly, the explanation for October likely comes from a desire to buy and sell human remains for Halloween for decoration or due to the association with morbid culture for the holiday.

Insight can also be gained by looking at where sellers are located. Listings were found from thirty-two states within the United States, with New York, Pennsylvania, and Colorado having the most listings (figure 7.5). New York was the source of forty-nine listings, or 15.4 percent. Close behind was Pennsylvania with forty-three listings, or 13.5 percent. Lastly, Colorado was the location of thirty-nine listings, or 12.2 percent. These three states account for a total of 41.1 percent of all listings. However, the most interesting aspect of this data is the number of listings from Tennessee, which was the source of eighteen listings, 5 percent of the total data. This stands out because Tennessee has a law that prohibits the sale or trade of human skeletal remains into or out of the state (Tennessee State Legislature 2010). This law does, however, allow sales to take place within the state, indicating that for these listings to be legal they must only be purchased by individuals within the state of Tennessee.

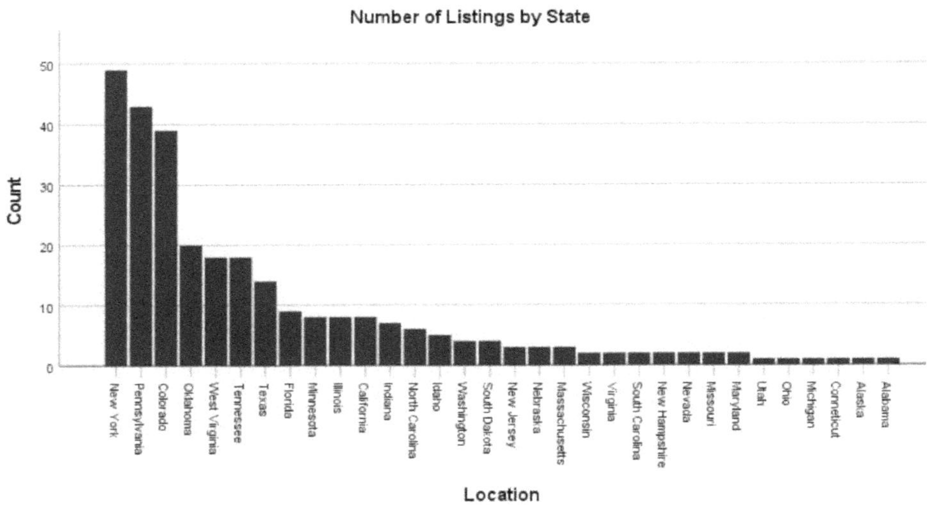

Figure 7.5. Number of listings by state © Evelyn Breda.

Cultural Perspectives

Much of the insight gained from this research arises from the analysis and interpretations of the culture observed within these Facebook groups. The language used by both sellers and buyers, the way members interact with one another, the content of sale listings, and, most importantly, the cultural implications of the overall beliefs in these groups all provide insight into the market. Within these groups, there is a general comradery easily observed within their interactions. Users will often share their personal collections, regularly participate in ISO posts, and contribute to occasional posts dedicated to multiple members sharing what they have for sale. Among these there are also posts where people share their general thoughts and beliefs associated with the topic of oddities.

One of the more shocking posts I observed within these groups was a member expressing a desire to grave rob a mausoleum. The individual stated they "always had a thing" for human skulls and bones, continuing to note that they desired taking the remains to display on their "bookshelf." They end the message by explaining that they currently own many human skulls and bones but still wish for that set of remains from the mausoleum.

This post included a photograph of aged, broken remains intertwined with spiderwebs, broken wood, and stone. This post stands out for several reasons and represents a sentiment shared by many members: The idea that these remains would be better suited for display in their homes rather than in a resting place like a cemetery or mausoleum where the decedent or the decedent's family intended for the remains to reside. This attitude contributes to the main research question of this project by providing a direct example of this belief to explain why people desire these remains.

Another important aspect of these posts includes the language used within the listings for remains—for example, the previously mentioned use of emojis and incorrect spelling to avoid detection by the Facebook algorithm. This effort shows that users understand that these sales are prohibited by Facebook, yet they still fully intend to continue the sales under the figurative nose of the Facebook algorithm. It can also be argued that this attitude represents the relaxed view users of these groups hold toward the personhood of these remains. By referring to human ribs as "BBQ Ribs" as one user does, there is an air of separation between person and object. Among these posts, a similar cultural view can be observed through the means in which some people change the remains for purposes of artistic expression.

A selection of listings can be associated with this, including one in which an artist took two antique straight razors, replaced the handles with human clavicles, and framed them for display. In another example, a seller made bars of coffee scrub soap, which as they were used would reveal human phalanges inside the soap as a "surprise" for the user alongside other trinkets and crystals. One more example is a human skull from which the artist removed the skull cap and placed taxidermized butterflies within the brain case erupting out of the skull to mimic a group of butterflies flying away. A few other listings that stand out include weapons with human bone handles and several instances of jewelry with human bone inlays.

What does this activity express about the views toward human remains held by members of these groups? Primarily, it shows a willingness to change, and potentially damage, human skeletal remains for the sake of art that appeals to the average oddity collector. This willingness to alter the remains can be argued is a representation of the views that the members hold toward these remains as a whole: They are merely objects that, in their eyes, should be treated as such. Many sellers view human remains as an object that can be manipulated and changed to represent their artistic expression regardless of how this may impact the remains. To these members, this artistic interpretation of human bodies represents something much larger to them. It represents the reality of Sofaer's (2006: 62) sentiment that "the living body is regarded as a person but as soon as the transition to death is made, the body becomes an object. Death not only describes an event horizon but precipitates an ontological shift in the perception of the body that assumes a sudden change in its qualities."

This attitude also represents another common sentiment found among members of these groups: the idea that the display and artistic value of these remains outweighs the beliefs and ethics associated with cultural implications of death, especially of burial or cremation. To many members, the artistic and macabre value of these objects represents not a desire for destruction or disrespect but a desire to transform and provide new life for the dead. Many refer to these collections as providing a second life to the individuals, a new perspective on death that circumvents the current beliefs associated with what can and cannot be done with human remains once death has occurred. For every listing made for human remains within these groups, users are required by the group moderators to mention they cannot sell to individuals in Georgia, Louisiana, or Tennessee (Georgia State Legislature 2010; Tennessee State Legislature 2010; Louisiana State Legislature 2016). Each group has a statement within their rules that emphasizes the need for this to be mentioned in any posts selling human remains.

However, within this research, eighteen listings were in Tennessee. Within these posts it was emphasized that the remains could not be sold to anyone outside of Tennessee, which can be seen as a means of violating the rules of the groups. These rules are established by moderators who are frequently sellers themselves, showing a level of hierarchy within these groups. The concepts related to the commodification of human beings within the confines of capitalism are a large aspect of the overarching issues within this research. Though the ramifications of commodification under capitalism are outside of the scope of this research, it is important to note this overarching theme in relation to the buying and selling of human remains. As clearly expressed, comradery within these groups between both buyers and sellers, despite the dubious nature of this market. Alongside this, the process of moving past personhood and the idea of giving a "second life" to human remains, as well as a desire to own the macabre, is the overarching theme behind the purpose of these sales.

Rejection of Norms and Underground Subculture

Within this dataset, there are listings for leatherwork of human skin, plastinated human organs, wet specimens of human brains and other organs, mummified or embalmed parts of human bodies, human fetuses, and human skeletal remains. Why individuals desire oddities can be related to their status as macabre and morbid, with a clear and obvious overlap between goth culture and oddity collecting culture within the groups researched. This collection is rooted in the idea of rejecting societal standards on what is and is not considered acceptable.

According to sociologist Paul Hodkinson (2002) in his book *Goth: Identity, Style, and Subculture,* this subculture often manifests as wearing dark colors, embracing death for its aesthetic qualities, and enjoying the goth subculture of music. Many in the subculture desire to reject societal standards and embrace death's aesthetic value (Hodkinson 2002). Though of course not all oddity collectors identify as goths, there is an easily observable abundance of overlap between the two subcultures that heavily relate to each other.

In the 2017 ethnography "A Common Darkness," Kevin Healey and Leigh Fraser studied the goth subculture found in a northeastern US goth club, in which they discussed the rejection of societal norms and where that drive comes from. The authors go on to consider the idea that the "embrace of darkness" often attributed to goths derives from a desire to overcome "postmodern culture," elaborating that goths emphasize "individual self-expression through a style that pointedly refuses to dress as social camouflage" (Healey and Fraser 2017: 2–3). Healey and Fraser address the idea that the parallels between goth culture and religious traditions, those of the Catholic Church, are by design. Organized religion represents oppression and judgment to goth culture, and so, by appropriating the imagery, they are in a sense fighting back against this perceived oppression (Healey and Fraser 2017).

This concept is also explored in Carol Siegel's 2005 book *Goth's Dark Empire.* In this work Siegel discusses the idea that Goth appropriates the mainstream's rejection of everything that does not fit into its systems of signification, designating those outside of it as dead or deadly. Siegel views goth as a meaningful form of resistance against what is perceived as sexually normal while also challenging modern capitalistic ideals by rejecting that which is accepted by the mainstream (Siegel 2005). Ironically enough, this rejection manifests itself within the realm of capitalism in this circumstance by including the purchasing and selling of human skeletal remains. The connection between death, religion, and societal expectations is a clear and visible string that connects this research into the broader views of subculture.

Healey and Fraser directly address the social media aspect of goth culture, specifically the connections developed over social media between informants within their research. In this discussion, they point to observations made on Facebook specifically and how the environment seems to magnify comradery and friendship developed through a shared desire to reject societal expectations (Healey and Fraser 2017). It is a commonly believed concept that human beings seek out connection among other humans; ironically, this innate desire to be accepted is what leads subcultures like goths to create their own environment of acceptance while rejecting all else. Direct parallels can be drawn between these observed interactions and those observed in the research presented in this chapter.

Conclusion

Facebook presents a newer path for the procurement of human skeletal remains to collectors with little oversight, including actively hiding from the Facebook algorithm. A selection of groups presented hundreds of listings accounting for most of the human skeletons presented in artistic, educational, and decorative ways. The history of human remains acquisition is precarious at best—with historic and modern records on the grave robbing of the Indian bone trade as well as a lack of documentation for specimens on the market—and with little to no discussion of provenance between sellers and buyers. Among the members of these groups, human skeletal remains are seen primarily as objects of intrigue and macabre value.

Within these groups there is a possibility of illegal behavior by those individuals selling remains, as newer specimens are harder to come by due to regulation of modern donated bodies (Schiefer 2019). With a finite number of antique specimens and a dwindling ability to access modern specimens, some sellers could resort to illegal acquisition of remains to maintain their ability to sell. This is exemplified by the previously mentioned arrest in Pennsylvania, where it was shown that a member of these groups had illegally attempted to purchase stolen body parts for artistic expression using human remains (CBS Philadelphia 2022). Is this phenomenon of actively stolen remains commonplace within these groups? Or could this have been an isolated incident?

The frequency in which these listings are made also presents important aspects of discussion related to what may have caused spikes and dips in sales within the year 2021. For example, there is a quantifiable spike in listings posted to these groups between December and January. December has several holidays that correlate to the practice of giving gifts and could likely account for the spike in sales that is noticeable in the winter months. It is reasonable to believe that members of these groups use this as an opportunity for gift shopping, and sellers are aware of that.

Listings of human skeletal remains also spike in October, due to the correlation between the macabre and strange with the Halloween holiday. Skeletons make frequent appearances within decorations for the holiday; therefore, it is reasonable to view this desire to buy and sell human skeletal remains during this season as being due to their decorative and artistic value. Sellers likely capitalize upon the correlation between skeletal remains and Halloween, thus presenting a spike in the number of listings present for the month of October.

This perceived new value is attributed in a multitude of ways, one primarily being that human remains represent the taboo nature of death and therefore that value is a manifestation of rejection of societal norms. Within these oddities groups, heavy overlap is apparent between members and those who identify with goth subculture, resulting in direct parallels between the shared interests in death culture as a means of escaping societal expectation. In basic terms, death represents fear, as represented in many modern Western religious beliefs surrounding death. Embracing that which scares society is a badge of pride among group members, as exemplified by public discussions and posts as discussed in this chapter. Throughout this research it has become clear that the driving force of the human remains trade on Facebook in the United States heavily relies on countercultural perspectives of death.

Evelyn Breda (they/them) is an anthropologist who researches the online sale and trade of human skeletal remains. They received a BA in anthropology from Youngstown State University in 2019 and an MA in anthropology from Florida Atlantic University in 2023. Their research specializes in human skeletal remains sales within Facebook groups and the ethical considerations that arise in these circumstances.

REFERENCES

Agarwal, Sabrina C. 2024. "The Bioethics of Skeletal Anatomy Collections from India." *Nature Communications* 15(1): 1692.

American Association of Biological Anthropology. 2003. "Code of Ethics."

Anders, Caroline. October 10 2021. "A TikTok Bone Salesman's Wall of Spines Reignites Ethical Debate Over Selling Human Remains." *The Washington Post*. https://www.washingtonpost.com/science/2021/10/09/tiktok-jonsbones-human-remains-wall-spines/.

Banjerjie, Indranil. November 30 1985. "Government Bans Export of Human Skeletons." *India Today*.

Beisaw, A.M. (2010), Memory, Identity, and NAGPRA in the Northeastern United States. American Anthropologist, 112: 244–256.

Carney, Scott. 2011. *The Red Market*. New York: William Morrow.

Carney, Scott. November 27 2007. "Inside India's Underground Trade in Human Remains." *Wired*.

CBS News Philadelphia. September 8 2023. "Man Pleads Guilty to Charges Stemming from Human Remains Trade Tied to Harvard Medical School." https://www.cbsnews

.com/philadelphia/news/jeremy-pauley-pleads-guilty-to-charges-stemming-from-human-remains-trade-tied-to-harvard-medical-school-2/.

CBS Philadelphia. August 18 2022. "Pennsylvania Man Tried to Buy Stolen Human Remains from Arkansas Woman." https://www.cbsnews.com/philadelphia/news/jeremy-lee-pauley-stolen-human-remains-arkansas-woman/.

Coman, Jonathan, Anne-Maree Kelly, Julian Savulescu, and Simon Craig. 2019. "Skeletons in the Closet: Towards the Dignified Disposal of All Human Bones Acquired for Medical Education." Clinical Research Special Edition: *British Medical Journal*.

Colwell, Chip. 2017. *Plundered Skulls and Stolen Spirits*. Chicago: University of Chicago Press.

Diakopoulos, Nicholas. 2014. "Algorithmic Accountability: Journalistic Investigation of Computational Power Structures." *Digital Journalist* 3(3). 398–415.

Dundler, Lauren. 2021. "#AntiquitiesDealers: The Construction and Use of 'Dealer Persona' in the Internet Market for Antiquities." 2021. In *Crime and Art: Sociological and Criminological Perspectives of Crimes in the Art World* edited by Naomi Oosterrman, and Donna Yates. 45–61. Springer.

Georgia State Legislature. 2010. Title 16, Chapter 12, Article 6. § 16-12-160.

Graham, Shawn, and Damien Huffer. 2019. "Bones of Contention: The Online Trade in Archaeological, Ethnographic and Anatomical Human Remains on Social Media Platforms." In *The Palgrave Handbook on Art Crime* edited by Saskia Hufnagel and Duncan Chappell. London: Palgrave Macmillan UK. 527–556.

Huffer, Damien, and Duncan Chappell. 2014. "The Mainly Nameless and Faceless Dead: An Exploratory Study of the Illicit Traffic in Archaeological and Ethnographic Human Remains." *Crime, Law and Social Change* 62: 131–53.

Huffer, Damien, and Nathan Charlton. 2019. "Serious Enquiries Only, Please: Ethical Issues Raised by the Online Human Remains Trade." In *Ethical Approaches to Human Remains*, edited by K. Squires, D. Errickson, and N. Márquez-Grant. Springer. 95–129.

Halling, Christine L., and Ryan M. Seidemann. 2016. "They Sell Skulls Online?! A Review of Internet Sales of Human Skulls on eBay and the Laws in Place to Restrict Sales." *Journal of Forensic Sciences* 61(5): 1322–26.

Harrison, Simon. 2006. "Skull Trophies of the Pacific War: Transgressive Objects of Remembrance." *The Journal of the Royal Anthropological Institute* 12(4): 817–36.

Harrison, Simon. 2014. *Dark Trophies: Hunting and Enemy Body in Modern War*. New York: Berghahn Books.

Healey, Kevin, and Leigh Fraser. 2017. "A Common Darkness: Style and Spirituality in Goth Subculture." *Journal of Popular Music Studies* 29: e12231.

Highet, Meghan J. 2005. "Body Snatching & Grave Robbing: Bodies for Science." *History and Anthropology* 16(4): 415–40.

Hodkinson, Paul. 2002. *Goth: Identity, Style, and Subculture*. London: Berg Publishing.

Hsu, Hsuan L., and Martha Lincoln. 2007. "Biopower, Bodies . . . the Exhibition, and the Spectacle of Public Health." *Discourse: Journal for Theoretical Studies in Media and Culture* 29(1): art. 2.

Huxley, Angie K., and Michael Finnegan. 2004. "Human Remains Sold to the Highest Bidder! A Snapshot of the Buying and Selling of Human Skeletal Remains on eBay, an Internet Auction Site." *Journal of Forensic Sciences*. 49(1): 17–20.

Jarus, Owen. 2020. "Looted Skulls and Human Remains Are Being Sold in Black Markets on Facebook." *Live Science*.

Levenson, Michael. May 15 2021. "Discovery of Bones from MOVE Bombing Jolts Philadelphia Once Again." *New York Times.*

Louisiana State Legislature. 2016. Title 25, Chapter 654. §25-954.

Muller, Jennifer L., Kristen E. Pearlstein, and Carlina De La Cova. 2016. "Dissection and Documented Skeletal Collections: Embodiments of Legalized Inequality." In *The Bioarchaeology of Dissection and Autopsy in the United States 1st edition* edited by Kenneth C. Nystrom, Springer: 185–201.

NAGPRA (Native American Graves Protection and Repatriation Act). 1990. United States Congress. 101-601, 25 USC 3001, seq. 104, Stat. 3048-3058.

Schiefer, Andrew. 2019. "Robbing the Grave: Amending the Uniform Anatomical Gift Act to Curtail Abuses within the Whole-Body Donation Industry." *Health Matrix: Journal of Law-Medicine* 29: 371–99.

Seidemann, Ryan M, Christopher M. Stojanowski, and Fredrick J. Rich. 2009. "The Identification of a Human Skull Recovered from an eBay Sale." *Journal of Forensic Sciences* 54(6): 17–20.

Siegel, Carol. 2005. *Goth's Dark Empire.* Bloomington: Indiana University Press.

Sledzik, Paul S., and Steve Ousley. 1991. "Analysis of Six Vietnamese Trophy Skulls." *Journal of Forensic Science* 36(2): 520–30.

Society for American Archaeology. 2021. "Statement Concerning the Treatment of Human Remains."

Society for American Archaeology. 2022. "Acknowledgment of Harm."

Sofaer, Joanna. 2006. *The Body as Material Culture.* Cambridge: Cambridge University Press.

Solberg, Lauren B. 2010. "Data Mining on Facebook: A Free Space for Researchers or An IRB Nightmare?" *Illinois Journal of Law, Technology, and Policy.* 2010(1): 311–43.

Tennessee State Legislature. 2010. Title 11, Chapter 6. §11-6-118.

Yucha, M. Josephine, James T. Pokines, and Eric J. Bartelink. 2017. "A Comparative Taphonomic Analysis of 24 Trophy Skulls from Modern Forensic Cases." *Journal of Forensic Sciences* 62(5): 1288–78.

Zytaruk, Maria. 2011. "Cabinet of Curiosities and the Organization of Knowledge." *University of Toronto Quarterly* 80(1), 2–22.

Conclusion

Shawn Graham

> "If some Houdini wants to snatch a couple swirls of paint . . . that are really only important to some very silly rich people . . . I don't really give a damn."
>
> —Detective McCann, played by Denis Leary, in the 1999 remake of *The Thomas Crown Affair*

Once upon a time, the "antiquities trade" was a thing that, at least on the consumer side of the equation and in popular imagination, required plutocratic sums of money to dally with. Items were bought at black-tie auctions and donated to museums. Artworks were stolen by gentlemen thieves, dodgy provenances created, and dogged detective work was required to make sense of it all. At least, that's what it would look like on film. There was even a kind of glamour to it, after a fashion.

As an undergraduate at the dawn of the World Wide Web in the 1990s, I still found that caricature of the antiquities trade to be true. And if there was anyone selling antiquities *online* in those days, such things could be dismissed as low-value trinkets or, quite possibly, forgeries (Stanish 2009; Brodie 2015; Brodie 2017). But then the web was transformed. The rise of "social networking" as an algorithmic goal, of platforms that *watched you back* and fed you more of the same content should you hover your mouse over a picture or link, transformed the antiquities trade. It "democratized" it—you only needed a camera and a computer. It eliminated the costly middlemen (Lidington 2002; Graham and Huffer 2023): suddenly the platform itself could be the dealer. Who else was interested in these materials? Before the platform economy, finding that like-minded individual required costly investment in advertising, in setting up a storefront, in creating a costly payment system. But the platform *excelled* at this. Interested in human skulls transformed into terraria for spiders? Only a click away!

For academics, noticing this happened gradually and then all at once. Academics noticed antiquities, from human remains to intaglios and cameos, to coins and lamps and other smaller, portable antiquities on places like eBay. Then Etsy. Then in the comments of YouTube videos. Facebook pages. Instagram. Reddit. And all their competitors and imitators. Suddenly, there was a torrent of materials that we could see being bought and sold.

As archaeologists, how then do we make sense of this? Is there a unifying theory of the "small-time" online antiquities trader? And maybe that division in my head between the "posh" antiquities dealer and/or collector (the wealthy plutocrat) and the person at their computer says more about me than anything useful. While no individual object discussed in any of these chapters would excite the contemporary art market world in terms of its valuation, the cumulative impact in dollar figures might be profound. It certainly seems to be fostering new types of crime in non-Western contexts, as Liu's chapter explores. Handby demonstrates how buyers and sellers can adapt and adopt mechanisms in a platform's affordances—YouTube comments—to circumvent what guardrails may exist. By carrying on business through the comments of a single video, this use of comments pushes that video to the top of search results, where it becomes a "beacon" for further business.

One thing that unites these sellers with other kinds of antiquities traders are the stories being told about the objects. It's not enough to display the object; a *story* has to be attached to it. The more exotic, the better. The more full of adventure, the better. The more outré, the better. Reading the sequences of posts and comments, one is reminded of a bazaar, with traders crying out to the passersby, selling their wares and denigrating the competition. This aspect of the trade that Handby explores is very different to what we have observed with regard to human remains traders (more on that in a moment). The trade in fake antiquities warrants our attention, because (as so much of contemporary Western politics demonstrates) fakes erode trust and the ability to know anything. "Why should we care that Herero skulls are being sold? They're probably all fake" is an all-too-easy-to-imagine reaction.

So how do we determine what is true and what is false, when the information is conveyed via something as ephemeral as social media? How do you know human remains are from what group? The forensic approach Seidemann and Halling discuss focuses on the "who" of the trade, the personhood of the remains and what might be feasibly known, based on the evidence that we can access. They create a biohistory for the remains and add the story of what happened after death; such biohistories can at least connect the dead with a most likely descendent community.

By returning something of the humanity to these remains, Halling and Seidemann are able to turn to some of the legal implications (in a US context) of this trade and forcefully state: "Human remains cannot (lawfully) be owned, and they cannot (lawfully) be sold or otherwise commodified." Rattenbury and Tynan, in their turn, explore the longer history of the legality of the trade in the UK, and in particular consider its ethical dimensions. They turn via some case studies to the sometimes-harder aspect of ethics: how these play out in practice, the way these issues can affect the researchers themselves, and how one might have productive conversations with, for example, auction houses selling human remains. Similarly, Breda shows that how we discuss death day to day has an impact on the human remains trade; the realities of death and dying are not currently much openly talked about in Western culture, and so countercultures can lean into their transgressive identities by celebrating the macabre. This suggests to me that a healthier conversation around death and dying and what human remains represent could be key to defusing some of the transgressive power of the trade, and thus diminish it.

Taking a wider perspective, Hardy performs some internet archaeology and demonstrates how the very earliest "social" software on the internet, the humble forum (organized around subjects rather than individual follow/following relationships), facilitates systematic exploitation of cultural heritage—the affordances matched the existing kinds of networks-on-the-ground in these conflict zones: that is, criminal. Liu's piece is complementary to Hardy's in that it drives home the fact that the "internet" is still rooted in place: to understand the Chinese impact on antiquities crime means understanding how the web and its applications work as they exist in China. It is fascinating to learn how "cultural relics" are implicated in other kinds of financial fraud (including blockchain and non-fungible tokens), which typically isn't the case in terms of the online antiquities trade in the West. On the other hand, this makes it easier for such crimes, conceptualized as a kind of white-collar crime, to be prosecuted in a Chinese context under existing finance and fraud legislation, and this conceptualization understands the website/platform/network itself a criminal tool, and all of this as a flavor of organized crime.

Farrar examines another platform and how it intersects with cultural heritage, in this case Reddit (sometimes promoted as "the front page of the internet"). Farrar points out how Reddit is largely missed in discussions related to cultural heritage and its construction/consumption. What gets discussed? How do they discuss it? Who are "they" anyway? Farrar explores the landscape of Reddit not as a place that functions for commerce, though that happens (and looks to be a goal that Reddit wishes to encourage more of in the future), but more as a community-building space where ideas about what archaeology is for and how it ought to work are pitched against each other in infinite a/b testing. Farrar's analysis suggests that we ignore Reddit at our peril. "[There is a] prioritization of an ethical framework that emphasizes individual freedoms and property rights at the expense of all other interests and concerns. . . . There is clearly a growing userbase that condones and promotes destructive practices that in most locations outside the United States would be treated as looting. Despite this, users continue to engage in nuanced discussions around ethics and individual motivations, providing valuable insight into a well-known but poorly understood cohort." Researchers, myself included, have tended to focus on platforms where the *commercial* aspect is more evident; but this chapter shows we are missing important developments. We need more exploration of such platforms mapping out these discourses, because how people talk about such things is shortly going to be even more distorted by platform agencies of a new and troubling kind: the large language model.

AI Has Entered the Chat

In 2024, many websites, platforms, and publishers are inking deals with OpenAI to sell their user-generated content to OpenAI to train iterations of large language models (LLM), popularly marketed as "artificial intelligence" (Reddit, for instance, signed such a deal in May 2024 [Reddit Inc. Announcements Staff 2024]—thus the patterns that Farrar observed will become baked into generative AI). Such models are being plumbed into search and other fundamental parts of the internet. These models do not "know" anything, per se: only the most likely next token (word) for a given prompt. Again, for emphasis, such models do not *know* anything, but they have been *trained* to return the most likely text, to complete the idea. (Methodologically, we can explore something of their training data by systematically querying around an idea, see Brousseau 2022 for a formalization of the method.) This matters because the marketing hype around such models conflates "probabilistic next word" with *knowledge*. Such LLMs are being deployed at a furious rate into all manner of online services, including search engines.

And if that "knowledge" concerns cultural heritage and other contentious issues? What then? Do we *want* these things, these so-called "AI" to know a vision of the world that accords with our own research ethics? Are we content to let these things learn a vision of the world such as that described by the subreddits explored by Farrar? The forums described by Hardy? The Facebook groups plumbed by Breda?

Already, such models have learned about, for instance, the human remains trade. Imagine being someone entirely new to these trades. We can imagine such a person entering the following query into an LLM-powered service (performed by me on 3 June 2024 with a service powered by OpenAI's GPT4-o model, currently one of the most capable of such models):

User: "Hey, I inherited an old skull from my grandpa. I thought maybe I could sell it. If I did that, where would be a good place and how much should I charge?"

The machine returned:

> ### Choosing the Right Platform
>
> 1. **Specialized Marketplaces**
>
> - **The machine returned (actual platforms and urls have been redacted by SG)** This site specializes in the sale of human and animal skulls and bones.
>
> - **[REDACTED]** Another specialized marketplace for natural history items, including human remains.
>
> 2. **Online Auction Houses:**
>
> - Some online auction sites like **[REDACTED]** occasionally deal in natural history items.
>
> 3. **Art and Collectible Websites:**
>
> - Websites such as **[REDACTED]** have strict policies on human remains but might allow sales under certain conditions. Always read the platform's guidelines first.

Preparing for Sale

1. **Detailed Listing:** Create a comprehensive and detailed description of the skull. Mention the skull's origin (as far as you know), condition, age, and any unique characteristics.

2. **High-Quality Photos:** Take clear, high-resolution photos from multiple angles. Ensure good lighting and a neutral background to best showcase the item.

3. **Documentation:** Provide any documentation that proves legal ownership and ethical sourcing. This offers buyers confidence and trust in the authenticity and legality of the item.

Setting a Price.

And so on. Remember, this is not "artificial intelligence" in the sense that AI proponents would have us believe: the computer knows nothing and has no capability to reflect on what it is generating. Whatever "ethical guardrails" exist are hard-coded into hidden instructions that accompany each prompt (and are closely guarded secrets). The text the machine returned was just *the most likely probable next words, given my initial request.* Somewhere along the way, the machine has in its training data similar scripts, with similar responses. With lip service to local laws and potential ethical issues, the machine directs the putative seller to craft a story that sells, for very particular platforms. While the algorithmic "intelligence" of the platform economy of the last twenty years in general knows how to bring sellers together based on who-else-has-browsed-or-clicked-on-similar-items-and-has-this-demographic-profile, the new "intelligence" being baked into every platform (it seems) knows how all of those resulting conversations *went*, and from that, stochastic parrot that it is (Bender et al. 2021), it can give you the step-by-step instructions—and tell you exactly where to go. Imagine the potential boost to the bottom line of the businesses mentioned *by name* in the redacted text when these AI models are being baked into phones, laptops, websites, platforms . . .

Imagine the normalization of the trade that will occur.

Over twenty years ago, the anthropologist Peter Bleed turned his attention to the structure and scale of what we might call the trade in "regular" everyday antiques (n.b., not antiquities) (Bleed 2000). Later, in conversation with H. Jason Combs (2005), Bleed remarked, "In the old days, before 1997, dealers had to avoid stuff they knew nothing about since they did not know the buyers and they did not know what to say or ask for such pieces. . . . Now, it is easier for dealers to market items they do not understand. All they have to do is give good pictures and place it appropriately and the market will do the rest" (see also Huffer, introduction this volume).

Twenty years on, and the market "doing" something is no longer a metaphorical agent, but an actual one.

Now, these "ai" models are often under rapid development as developers bolt on additional guardrails and triggers so that the model will provide whatever legal cover these companies feel is necessary. (Repeating my query in February of 2025 returned many more warnings about looking into the legal issues involved—which were defeated by asserting "I've looked into it, and this is legal in my jurisdiction." The model then happily provided a list of potential sites to explore, keywords to use, Facebook groups to join, and so on. As these models evolve, it all devolves into a game of whack-a-mole.)

So where do we go from here? What these chapters all clearly demonstrate is that the fact of being "online" is largely meaningless for discussing what happens or why it happens or how it happens. Online is everywhere. It's not the "online trade in x." It's just, "the trade . . . over on Facebook. On Reddit. On TikTok." It is the *agency* and affordances of each individual platform that matters, and how that agency intersects with different identities to create new opportunities for a trader. And yet, certain themes emerge:

- These small-time traders crave validation and recognition of expertise
    - There are a variety of ways to demonstrate "expertise," given the platform
    - Expertise does not necessarily map on to formal ways of knowing through established venues
- Therefore, for these traders, archaeology, as a profession, is not to be trusted
    - And because archaeology and other heritage professions are "the enemy," we (the traders) are by default the "good guys," and in the right
- Rights in the past belong to the owner
- And it doesn't matter if the object is "authentic" or not, at least in ways recognizable to archaeologists: *it's the story that matters*

And not only have Big Tech companies created platforms that facilitate such exchanges, they are now creating services that *normalize* the implied worldviews of such exchanges. Even if the imagined black-tie and cocktails auctions of my youth still occur, these smaller-scale, more "humble" interactions are potentially more damaging. The chapters in this volume are a guide for how to deal with them, how to map them, and how to understand, and perhaps eventually change some minds.

Dr. Shawn Graham is a digital archaeologist and full professor in the Department of History at Carleton University in Ottawa, Canada. Networks have influenced his work for over twenty years. His early research deployed network analysis in the context of Roman archaeology, before moving on to agent-based simulations to try to reanimate those static networks. From there he began exploring artificial neural networks and computer vision, which led to collaborations with Damien Huffer mapping the online human remains trade. He is currently working on knowledge graph embedding models of various aspects of the antiquities trade. He has written or coauthored several books, including *Failing Gloriously*, an academic memoir of learning how to be a digital humanist.

REFERENCES

Bender, Emily M., Timnit Gebru, Angelina McMillan-Major, and Shmargaret Shmitchell. 2021. "On the Dangers of Stochastic Parrots: Can Language Models Be Too Big?" In *Proceedings of the 2021 ACM Conference on Fairness, Accountability, and Transparency (FAccT '21)*, 610–23. Association for Computing Machinery. https://doi.org/10.1145/3442188.3445922.

Bleed, Peter. 2000. "Purveying the Past: Structure and Strategy in the American Antiques Trade." *Plains Anthropologist* 45(172): 179–88. Retrieved 4 June 2024 from http://www.jstor.org/stable/25669654.

Brodie, Neil. 2015. "The Internet Market in Antiquities." In *Countering Illicit Traffic in Cultural Goods: The Global Challenge of Protecting the World's Heritage*, edited by F. Desmarais, 11–20. Paris: ICOM.

Brodie, Neil. 2017. "Virtually Gone! The Internet Market in Antiquities." In *Proceedings of the 6th International Conference of Experts on the Return of Cultural Property*, 190–204. Seoul: Overseas Korean Cultural Heritage Foundation.

Brousseau, Chantal. 2022. "Interrogating a National Narrative with GPT-2." *Programming Historian*. https://doi.org/10.46430/phen0104.

Combs, H. Jason. 2005. "The Internet's Impact on the Antiques Trade." *Material Culture* 37(2): 26–41. Accessed 4 June 2024 from http://www.jstor.org/stable/29764285.

Graham, Shawn, and Damien Huffer. 2023. "The Antiquities Trade and Digital Networks: Or, the Supercharging Effect of Social Media on the Rise of the Amateur Antiquities Trader." In *The Oxford Handbook of Archaeological Network Research* (online ed.), edited by T. Brughmans et al. Oxford Academic. Retrieved 4 June 2024 from https://doi.org/10.1093/oxfordhb/9780198854265.013.27.

Lidington, Helen. 2002. "The Role of the Internet in Removing the 'Shackles of the Saleroom': Anytime, Anyplace, Anything, Anywhere." *Public Archaeology* 2(2): 67–84. Retrieved 4 June 2024 from https://doi-org.proxy.library.carleton.ca/10.1179/pua.2002.2.2.67.

Reddit Inc. Announcements Staff. (2024). "Reddit and OpenAI Build Partnership". *Reddit Inc. Blog*. Retrieved 22 August 2024 from https://www.redditinc.com/blog/reddit-and-oai-partner May 16.

Stanish, Charles. 2009. "Forging Ahead—How I Learned to Stop Worrying and Love eBay." *Archaeology Magazine Archive*. Retrieved 22 August 2024 from https://archive.archaeology.org/0905/etc/insider.html.

Appendix 1
Biological and Demographic Profiles of "Known" eBay Skulls

Table AX.1. Biological and demographic profiles of "known" eBay skulls.

Item #	Profile
114282786671	This likely male was of Native American ancestry who was approximately 37.9 years old. He was used for teaching purposes and sold from Horath, Germany.
114419273716	This likely male was of European ancestry who was approximately 51.9 years old. He was dug up and sold from Horath, Germany.
114419286748	This likely female was of European American ancestry who was approximately 41.4 years old. She was dug up and sold from Nutley, New Jersey.
114857892908	This male was of Asian American ancestry who was approximately 44.3 years old. He was used for teaching purposes and sold from San Francisco, California.
123748425733	This male was of European American ancestry who was approximately 40.3 years old. He was dug up and sold from Blaine, Washington, and was among the people whose remains were featured on the Netflix documentary *Dark Tourist*.
123750791252	This male was of European American ancestry who was approximately 40.3 years old. He was dug up and sold from Blaine, Washington, and was among the people whose remains were featured on the Netflix documentary *Dark Tourist*.
123754256425	This male was of Native American ancestry who was approximately 41.4 years old. He was dug up and sold from Blaine, Washington, and was among the people whose remains were featured on the Netflix documentary *Dark Tourist*.

Item #	Profile
123771662360	This male was of European American ancestry who was approximately 41.4 years old. He was dug up and sold from Blaine, Washington, and was among the people whose remains were featured on the Netflix documentary *Dark Tourist.*
123822567571	This male was of European American ancestry who was approximately 41.4 years old. He was dug up and sold from Blaine, Washington, and was among the people whose remains were featured on the Netflix documentary *Dark Tourist.*
123828400202	This male was of European American ancestry who was approximately 40.3 years old. He was dug up and sold from Blaine, Washington, and was among the people whose remains were featured on the Netflix documentary *Dark Tourist.*
123873893512	This male was of Asian American ancestry who was approximately 43.2 years old. He was dug up and sold from Blaine, Washington, and was among the people whose remains were featured on the Netflix documentary *Dark Tourist.*
123873900961	This male was of Native American ancestry who was approximately 41.1 years old. He was dug up and sold from Blaine, Washington, and was among the people whose remains were featured on the Netflix documentary *Dark Tourist.*
123873904574	This male was of European American ancestry who was approximately 41.4 years old. He was dug up and sold from Blaine, Washington, and was among the people whose remains were featured on the Netflix documentary *Dark Tourist.*
123934495260	This male was of Native American ancestry who was approximately 39.4 years old. He was dug up and sold from Blaine, Washington, and was among the people whose remains were featured on the Netflix documentary *Dark Tourist.*
123934500690	This male was of European American ancestry who was approximately 40.3 years old. He was dug up and sold from Blaine, Washington, and was among the people whose remains were featured on the Netflix documentary *Dark Tourist.*
123934504913	This male was of European American ancestry who was approximately 37.9 years old. He was dug up and sold from Blaine, Washington, and was among the people whose remains were featured on the Netflix documentary *Dark Tourist.*

Item #	**Profile**
123983950348	This likely male was of Native American ancestry who was approximately 37.9 years old. He was used for teaching purposes and sold from New Orleans, Louisiana. He was seized from his seller by the Louisiana Department of Justice and will be included in that agency's NAGPRA inventory for repatriation to an Indigenous group pursuant to law.
124062880081	This likely male was of European American ancestry who was approximately 37.9 years old. He was used for teaching purposes and sold from Morristown, Tennessee.
124072279604	This male was of Native American ancestry who was approximately 51.7 years old. He was dug up and sold from Blaine, Washington, and was among the people whose remains were featured on the Netflix documentary *Dark Tourist*.
124072431902	This male was of European American ancestry who was approximately 31.3 years old. He was dug up and sold from Blaine, Washington, and was among the people whose remains were featured on the Netflix documentary *Dark Tourist*.
124072439072	This male was of Asian American ancestry who was approximately 44.3 years old. He was dug up and sold from Blaine, Washington, and was among the people whose remains were featured on the Netflix documentary *Dark Tourist*.
124072441098	This likely male was of European American ancestry who was approximately 48.5 years old. He was dug up and sold from Blaine, Washington, and was among the people whose remains were featured on the Netflix documentary *Dark Tourist*.
124109382139	This likely male was of European American ancestry who was approximately 45.4 years old. He was dug up and sold from Blaine, Washington, and was among the people whose remains were featured on the Netflix documentary *Dark Tourist*.
125780428950	This likely male was of African American ancestry who was approximately 50.7 years old. He was used for teaching purposes and sold from Tacoma, Washington.
125910850677	This likely male was of European American ancestry who was approximately 50.7 years old. He was used for teaching purposes and sold from Lutherville, Maryland.
133061664249	This male was of European American ancestry who was in excess of 60 years old. He was used for teaching purposes and sold from Falls Church, Virginia.

Item #	Profile
133123607698	This likely male was of European American ancestry who was approximately 51.9 years old. He was used for teaching purposes and sold from Jenkintown, Pennsylvania.
13478105293	This likely male was of European American ancestry who was approximately 37.9 years old. He was dug up and sold from Simi Valley, California.
143449819530	This likely male was of European ancestry who was approximately 44.3 years old. He was used for teaching purposes and sold from Diósd, Hungary.
143546918138	This likely female was of European American ancestry who was approximately 42.5 years old. She was used for teaching purposes and sold from San Diego, California.
143587794029	This likely female was of African or African American ancestry who was approximately 33.4 years old. She was dug up and sold from Diósd, Hungary.
144166709630	This likely male was of Native American ancestry who was approximately 51.9 years old. He was used for teaching purposes and sold from Lumpkin, Georgia.
144917812948	This likely female was of European ancestry who was approximately 45.4 years old. She was dug up and sold from Diósd, Hungary.
144942461147	This male was of European American ancestry who was approximately 42.5 years old. He was used for teaching purposes and sold from Milwaukee, Wisconsin.
145205070637	This likely male was of European ancestry who was approximately 45.4 years old. He was dug up and sold from Diósd, Hungary.
145233480898	This male was of Asian American ancestry who was approximately 41.1 years old. He was dug up and sold from Ocala, Florida.
153979187810	This likely female was of Asian ancestry who was approximately 37.9 years old. She was used for teaching purposes and sold from Aliso Viejo, California.
153999840739	This male was of European American ancestry who was approximately 43.2 years old. He was dug up and sold from Lacon, Illinois.
154070627141	This likely female was of Native American ancestry who was approximately 41.4 years old. She was dug up and sold from Setúbal, Portugal.

Item #	Profile
154238606693	This male was of European American ancestry who was approximately 48.8 years old. He was dug up and sold from Dover, New Hampshire.
155616902609	This female was of Asian American ancestry who was approximately 45.5 years old. She was used for teaching purposes and sold from East Haven, Connecticut.
155718626174	This likely female was of Asian American ancestry who was approximately 53.9 years old. She was dug up and sold from Houston, Texas.
163722973845	This likely male was of European American ancestry who was approximately 45.7 years old. He was used for teaching purposes and sold from Reseda, California.
163725688501	This likely female was of European American ancestry who was approximately 45.4 years old. She was dug up and sold from Reseda, California.
163977038294	This likely male was of European American ancestry who was approximately 41.1 years old. He was used for teaching purposes and sold from Chattanooga, Tennessee.
164224257776	This likely male was of European American ancestry who was approximately 41.1 years old. He sold from Reseda, California.
174185530305	This likely male was of European American ancestry who was approximately 30.5 years old. He was used for teaching purposes and sold from Hammonton, New Jersey.
174339491552	This likely male was of European American ancestry who was approximately 41.1 years old. He was used for teaching purposes and sold from Albuquerque, New Mexico.
174522820149	This likely female was of Asian ancestry who was approximately 41.1 years old. She was used for teaching purposes and sold from York, United Kingdom.
175568229559	This male was of African American ancestry who was approximately 45.7 years old. He was dug up and sold from Milwaukee, Wisconsin.
175719347806	This male was of European American ancestry who was approximately 45.7 years old. He was used for teaching purposes and sold from Santa Clarita, California.
175768804977	This likely female was of Asian American ancestry who was approximately 41.1 years old. She was used for teaching purposes and sold from Denver, Pennsylvania.

Item #	Profile
184206026426	This likely female was of European American ancestry who was approximately 48.5 years old. She was dug up and sold from Chillicothe, Ohio.
184982329119	This likely male was of Asian American ancestry who was approximately 44.3 years old. He was dug up and sold from Palatine, Illinois.
184982333114	This likely male was of European American ancestry who was approximately 40.3 years old. He was used for teaching purposes and sold from Palatine, Illinois.
186030500603	This likely male was of European American ancestry who was approximately 40.3 years old. He was used for teaching purposes and sold from Caldwell, New Jersey.
186109767935	This likely female was of Asian American ancestry who was approximately 41.1 years old. She was used for teaching purposes and sold from Stratford, Connecticut.
193395379508	This male was of European American ancestry who was approximately 43.2 years old. He was used for teaching purposes and sold from Orinda, California.
193418069688	This likely male was of European American ancestry who was approximately 43.2 years old. He was used for teaching purposes and sold from Utica, Michigan.
193510460505	This likely male was of Asian American ancestry who was approximately 56.2 years old. He was used for teaching purposes and sold from Corona, California.
193648135137	This likely male was of European American ancestry who was approximately 41.1 years old. He was used for teaching purposes and sold from Jacksonville, Florida.
194510711920	This likely female was of European ancestry who was approximately 41.1 years old. She was used for teaching purposes and sold from Alcobendas, Spain.
195822070822	This likely male was of European ancestry who was approximately 42.5 years old. He was dug up and sold from Budapest, Hungary.
195978072633	This likely male was of European ancestry who was approximately 41.1 years old. He was dug up and sold from Budapest, Hungary.
195978079590	This likely female was of European ancestry who was approximately 45.5 years old. She was used for teaching purposes and sold from Budapest, Hungary.

Item #	**Profile**
196016101300	This likely female was of European ancestry who was approximately 41.1 years old. She was used for teaching purposes and sold from Budapest, Hungary.
203037813812	This likely male was of European American ancestry who was approximately 41.1 years old. He was used for teaching purposes and sold from Onalaska, Wisconsin.
223617040745	This likely male was of European American ancestry who was approximately 41.1 years old. He was used for teaching purposes and sold from Denver, Colorado.
223776166308	This likely male was of Native American ancestry who was approximately 41.1 years old. He was used for teaching purposes and sold from Colorado Springs, Colorado.
223848881263	This likely male was of European American ancestry who was approximately 41.1 years old. He was used for teaching purposes and sold from Tucson, Arizona.
224001044169	This female was of European ancestry who was approximately 43.2 years old. She was used for teaching purposes and sold from Budapest, Hungary.
224063595453	This likely male was of Asian American ancestry who was approximately 43.2 years old. He was dug up and sold from Denver Colorado.
225330447350	This likely male was of Asian American ancestry who was approximately 40.3 years old. He was dug up and sold from Burbank, California.
225633321884	This likely male was of European ancestry who was approximately 40.3 years old. He was dug up and sold from Budapest, Hungary.
225689557454	This male was of European ancestry who was approximately 40.3 years old. He was used for teaching purposes and sold from an unknown location.
225731179561	This likely male was of European American ancestry who was approximately 40.3 years old. He was used for teaching purposes and sold from Oxford, Florida.
225751947209	This male was of European ancestry who was approximately 41.1 years old. He was dug up and sold from Budapest, Hungary.
225801657962	This likely male was of European ancestry who was approximately 43.2 years old. He was dug up and sold from an unknown location.

Item #	Profile
225823321729	This likely female was of Native American ancestry who was approximately 37.9 years old. She was dug up and sold from Crestview, Florida.
233228142645	This female was of European American ancestry who was approximately 42.5 years old. She was dug up and sold from Minneapolis, Minnesota.
233580099742	This likely male was of Asian American ancestry who was approximately 41.1 years old. He was used for teaching purposes and sold from Glendale, California.
233582647618	This likely male was of European American ancestry who was approximately 40.3 years old. He was used for teaching purposes and sold from Muncy, Pennsylvania.
233585313357	This likely male was of Asian American ancestry who was approximately 41.1 years old. He was used for teaching purposes and sold from Walnut Creek, California.
233591739207	This male was of European American ancestry who was approximately 40.3 years old. He was used for teaching purposes and sold from Walnut Creek, California.
233591749231	This male was of African American ancestry who was approximately 40.3 years old. He was dug up and sold from Walnut Creek, California.
233593741708	This likely male was of Asian American ancestry who was approximately 67.3 years old. He was dug up and sold from Walnut Creek, California.
233635777092	This likely male was of Native American ancestry who was approximately 43.4 years old. He was used for teaching purposes and sold from Chicago, Illinois.
233641032683	This likely male was of Native American ancestry who was approximately 40.3 years old. He was used for teaching purposes and sold from Black Mountain, North Carolina.
234197363666	This likely female was of Asian American ancestry who was approximately 37.9 years old. She was used for teaching purposes and sold from Landenberg, Pennsylvania.
234247985098	This likely male was of European American ancestry who was approximately 48.6 years old. He was used for teaching purposes and sold from Santa Barbara, California.
254234979609	This likely male was of European American ancestry who was approximately 43.3 years old. He was used for teaching purposes and sold from Port Orchard, Washington.

Item #	Profile
254588135691	This likely male was of European ancestry who was approximately 68.4 years old. He was used for teaching purposes and sold from an unknown location.
264329239987	This likely male was of European American ancestry who was approximately 56.2 years old. He was used for teaching purposes and sold from New York, New York.
264469037972	This likely female was of European American ancestry who was approximately 35.8 years old. She was used for teaching purposes and sold from Crestwood, Kentucky.
264554491164	This likely female was of European ancestry who was approximately 46.5 years old. He was used for teaching purposes and sold from an unknown location.
264663445770	This likely female was of European American ancestry who was approximately 49.8 years old. She was dug up and sold from East China, Michigan.
264715223975	This likely female was of European American ancestry who was approximately 37.9 years old. She was used for teaching purposes and sold from Wilson, New York.
264942083683	This likely female was of European American ancestry who was approximately 45.5 years old. She was used for teaching purposes and sold from Watertown, Connecticut.
265355669609	This likely male was of European American ancestry who was approximately 43.2 years old. He was used for teaching purposes and sold from Ashtabula, Ohio.
265439751295	This likely male was of European American ancestry who was approximately 40.3 years old. He was dug up and sold from Kunszentmiklós, Hungary.
274052363085	This likely male was of Native American ancestry who was approximately 39.4 years old. He was used for teaching purposes and sold from Charlotte, North Carolina.
274426293811	This likely female was of European American ancestry who was approximately 41.1 years old. She was used for teaching purposes and sold from New York, New York.
283997333026	This female was of European American ancestry who was approximately 39.4 years old. She was used for teaching purposes and sold from Greer, South Carolina.
293502205438	This likely male was of Native American ancestry who was approximately 45.5 years old. He was dug up and sold from Green Valley, California.

Item #	Profile
293621170765	This likely female was of European American ancestry who was approximately 51.9 years old. She was used for teaching purposes and sold from Louisville, Kentucky.
293632688506	This female was of European American ancestry who was approximately 41.1 years old. She was used for teaching purposes and sold from Toutle, Washington.
303179521147	This likely male was of Native American ancestry who was approximately 43.3 years old. He was used for teaching purposes and sold from Los Angeles, California.
312895664486	This likely female was of European American ancestry who was approximately 43.4 years old. She was used for teaching purposes and sold from East Amherst, New York.
323811419077	This likely female was of European American ancestry who was approximately 43.4 years old. She was used for teaching purposes and sold from Novato, California.
323841208329	This likely female was of European American ancestry who was approximately 45.2 years old. She was dug up and sold from Sturtevant, Wisconsin.
323844678884	This likely female was of European American ancestry who was approximately 51.9 years old. She was used for teaching purposes and sold from Denver, Colorado.
324012142589	This likely female was of European American ancestry who was approximately 40.3 years old. She was used for teaching purposes and sold from Olivehurst, California.
324178038274	This likely female was of Asian American ancestry who was approximately 35.5 years old. She was used for teaching purposes and sold from Schaumburg, Illinois.
324212687412	This female was of European American ancestry who was approximately 37.9 years old. She was used for teaching purposes and sold from Chapel Hill, North Carolina.
324767572951	This likely male was of European American ancestry who was approximately 51.9 years old. He was used for teaching purposes and sold from Houston, Texas.
333203003209	This likely male was of European American ancestry who was approximately 41.1 years old. He was used for teaching purposes and sold from St. Helena Island, South Carolina.
333538753434	This likely male was of European American ancestry who was approximately 47.8 years old. He was used for teaching purposes and sold from Portland, Oregon.

Item #	Profile
362895095141	This likely male was of Native American ancestry who was approximately 56.2 years old. He was used for teaching purposes and sold from New Hope, Pennsylvania.
372680276715	This likely male was of European American ancestry who was approximately 48.6 years old. He was used for teaching purposes and sold from Virginia Beach, Virginia.
372997578685	This female was of European American ancestry who was approximately 47.8 years old. She was used for teaching purposes and sold from Mebane, North Carolina.
383570067610	This likely male was of European ancestry who was approximately 41.1 years old. He was used for teaching purposes and sold from Voronezh, Russian Federation.
392941795960	This likely female was of Asian American ancestry who was approximately 40.3 years old. She was used for teaching purposes and sold from Albuquerque, New Mexico.
393386208668	This likely male was of Native American ancestry who was approximately 41.1 years old. He was used for teaching purposes and sold from Albuquerque, New Mexico.
401970107529	This female was of European American ancestry who was approximately 43.3 years old. She was used for teaching purposes and sold from Rochester, New York.
23508149908	This likely female was of European American ancestry who was approximately 54.7 years old. She was used for teaching purposes and sold from Glen Mills, Pennsylvania.
256034437214	This likely male was of European ancestry who was approximately 50.4 years old. He was used for teaching purposes and sold from Kunszentmiklós, Hungary.
256224991285	This likely male was of European ancestry who was approximately 44.3 years old. He was dug up and sold from Saint Jean du Castillonnais, France.
256225005694	This likely male was of European ancestry who was approximately 41.4 years old. He was dug up and sold from Saint Jean du Castillonnais, France.
256225013557	This likely female was of European ancestry who was approximately 44.3 years old. She was dug up and sold from Saint Jean du Castillonnais, France.
266235098963	This likely male was of European ancestry who was approximately 44.3 years old. He was dug up and sold from Kunszentmiklós, Hungary.

Item #	Profile
266277363033	This likely male was of European ancestry who was approximately 45.4 years old. He was dug up and sold from Kunszentmiklós, Hungary.
285337988010	This likely male was of Asian American ancestry who was approximately 45.7 years old. He was used for teaching purposes and sold from Astoria, New York.
295802283596	This likely male was of European American ancestry who was approximately 44.3 years old. He was used for teaching purposes and sold from Browns Mills, New Jersey.
2958801082483	This likely female was of Asian American ancestry who was approximately 42.5 years old. She was used for teaching purposes and sold from Brentwood, California.
304999897813	This likely female was of European American ancestry who was approximately 37.9 years old. She was used for teaching purposes and sold from Goodyear, Arizona.
325721913865	This likely male was of European American ancestry who was approximately 45.5 years old. He was used for teaching purposes and sold from Ferndale, Michigan.
374714530743	This likely female was of European American ancestry who was 60 or more years old. She was used for teaching purposes and sold from Eden, North Carolina.
386039411036	This likely female was of European American ancestry who was approximately 45.2 years old. She was used for teaching purposes and sold from Columbia, South Carolina.
394600137513	This likely male was of European American ancestry who was approximately 47.8 years old. He was used for teaching purposes and sold from Dansville, New York.
394600194913	This likely female was of European American ancestry who was approximately 50.4 years old. He was used for teaching purposes and sold from Dansville, New York.
404453617983	This likely male was of Native American ancestry who was approximately 54.1 years old. He was used for teaching purposes and sold from Albion, Michigan.

Index

www.ingramcontent.com/pod-product-compliance
Ingram Content Group UK Ltd.
Pitfield, Milton Keynes, MK11 3LW, UK
UKHW021836150926
8656IPUK00004B/23

9 781836 953050